The Agony of Argentine Capitalism

The Agony
of Argentine Capitalism

From Menem to
the Kirchners

PAUL H. LEWIS

PRAEGER
An Imprint of ABC-CLIO, LLC

A B C ⬛ C L I O

Santa Barbara, California • Denver, Colorado • Oxford, England

Library of Congress Cataloging-in-Publication Data

Lewis, Paul H.
  The agony of Argentine capitalism : from Menem to the Kirchners / Paul H. Lewis.
    p. cm.
  Includes bibliographical references and index.
  ISBN 978-0-313-37877-5 (hard copy : alk. paper) — ISBN 978-0-313-37879-9 (hard copy pbk : alk. paper) — ISBN 978-0-313-37878-2 (ebook)
  1. Argentina—Economic policy—20th century. 2. Argentina—Economic policy—21st century. 3. Argentina—Economic conditions—1983- 4. Capitalism—Argentina—History. I. Title.
  HC175.L44 2009
  330.982—dc22   2009016116

13 12 11 10 09 1 2 3 4 5

This book is also available on the World Wide Web as an eBook.
Visit www.abc-clio.com for details.

ABC-CLIO, LLC
130 Cremona Drive, P.O. Box 1911
Santa Barbara, California 93116-1911

This book is printed on acid-free paper

Manufactured in the United States of America

FOR ANNE

Contents

Preface

The Agony of Argentine Capitalism is the third book of a trilogy that explores the reasons for Argentina's puzzling "reversal of development."[1] The first book, *The Crisis of Argentine Capitalism*,[2] began by describing Argentina at the opening of the twentieth century as a prosperous society, confident of its future. In the previous fifty years, the country's liberal elites had unified the country under a federal system and established a constitutional government based on a separation of powers between the executive, legislative, and judicial branches. Furthermore, they had modernized agriculture and turned Argentina into an important commercial nation that provided the world with much of its meat, corn, wheat, and linseed. Buenos Aires was one of the world's busiest ports, a booming metropolis, and a destination for millions of immigrants from Europe and elsewhere.

The Crisis of Argentine Capitalism described the crucial importance of those immigrants to the growth of industry and the diversification of agriculture. From the late nineteenth century to the early twentieth century, immigrant entrepreneurs with names like Rigolleau, Noel, Di Tella, Bagley, Braun, Bemberg, Peuser, Roberts, Tornquist, Bunge, Born, and Fraser led a successful industrial revolution. Moreover, the liberal elites proved to be highly permeable to these new elements, as a membership list of the prestigious Jockey Club showed. Parallel to the rise of manufacturing was the spread of commerce wherever the railway lines branched out from Buenos Aires to every corner of the nation. Like the industrialists, the great majority of the merchants were immigrants. With industry and commerce came urbanization and a growing middle class. In 1912 the electoral laws were changed to permit universal manhood suffrage. Four years later, the country's middle class reform party, the *Unión Cívica Radical,* elected its charismatic leader, Hipólito Yrigoyen, to the presidency. The Radicals governed through the World War I years and the 1920s, enjoying a golden period of continued industrial growth and commercial prosperity.

Up to this point, Argentina was a success story: a country poised on the verge of becoming a modern nation of the first rank. Then progress began to unravel. The great economic crash of 1929 overwhelmed the Radicals and led to Yrigoyen's overthrow by a military coup in September 1930. Many writers have located the cause of Argentina's decline there, arguing that the coup not only destroyed the country's democratic development but undermined the whole rule of law as well. The so-called Concordancia that replaced the Radicals in power was an alliance of reactionary military officers and cynical politicians who had abandoned their belief in popular government. *The Crisis of Argentine Capitalism* argued, however, that the more fundamental cause of Argentina's decline was the government that followed the next big military coup, in June 1943. That coup was brought about by a modernizing military faction that wanted to intensify the drive for industrialization. Unfortunately, its officers were impressed by the examples of Nazi Germany, Fascist Italy, and Imperial Japan, where alliances between military and industrial elites had created seemingly unbeatable world powers. Colonel Juan Domingo Perón, a military intellectual who had served as an attaché in Mussolini's Italy, soon came to head this new Argentine regime.

Although Perón openly admired fascism, his version of it was different. Instead of a regressive distribution of wealth in favor of economic elites, he adopted a perverse variation on Keynesianism, in which popular consumption would be the driving stimulus for industrialization. Having captured the trade unions, he favored the redistribution of wealth among the workers, through high wages, many fringe benefits, price controls, and social spending. Also, unlike other fascist rulers, Perón was not concerned with building up large business combines. Instead, he encouraged a large number of small industrialists who, protected against foreign competition and heavily subsidized by the state, would add to the regime's mass base. In other respects, however, Perón adopted the fascist model of a state-directed, self-sufficient economy in which a corporatist form of organization would penetrate, control, and coordinate all significant social groups: business, labor, farmers, the professions, culture, women, and youth. Everyone would be required to join one or more of these organizations, called "syndicates" (*sindicatos*).

The Crisis of Argentine Capitalism described the problems created by this system, which eventually brought about its downfall and Perón's forced exile. It also made clear that Perón left behind a mass of well-organized labor unions and small businessmen who were capable of preventing any return to the economic liberalism that had preceded him. This populist alliance successfully destabilized every subsequent government, whether civilian or military. In the process, Argentina became politically polarized and economically debilitated by chronic "stagflation" (stagnant production and persistent inflation), up through the 1980s.

Guerrillas and Generals: The "Dirty War" in Argentina,[3] the second book in this trilogy, dealt with the tragic explosion of violence that swept Argentina in the 1970s. The book overlapped chronologically with *Crisis* in tracing the guerrillas' origins to the underground resistance movement that sprang up after Perón's overthrow. It also explored in more depth the social pathologies of post-Perón Argentina, stemming from stagflation and political instability, and showed how these led to the emergence of terrorist groups. *Guerrillas and Generals* described the structure, ideology, and tactics of those organizations, of whom the two most important were the leftwing Peronist "Montoneros" and the Trotskyite/Maoist "People's Revolutionary Army." The apparent inability of civilian politicians to suppress terrorism led to the coup of March 1976 and the military's Process of National Reorganization (the *Proceso*), whose aims were to destroy the guerrillas and overcome the stagflation that had undermined Argentina's institutions. Justifying its extreme measures by an ideology called the National Security Doctrine, the military launched a counterinsurgency program based on "dirty war" tactics that included torture and murder. *Guerrillas and Generals* also described how factions jockeying for power inside the regime eventually caused it to self-destruct. The book's denouement covered the Alfonsín government's trials of the Proceso leaders, the revolts by military rebels to prevent the extension of punishment to lower-level officials, and, finally, the pardons granted by Menem.

The Agony of Argentine Capitalism returns to the subject of Argentina's political economy and describes the failed attempt, under President Carlos Menem, to end the decades-long stagflation by a free trade, free enterprise experiment. Ironically, the final crisis that brought the experiment to an end came not under Menem, but under his successor, President Fernando De la Rua. So dramatic was the crash that at the book's end we see the disappearance of nearly all of the Argentine companies that led the initial drive for industrialization, as well as most of those that came on the scene later. The collapse of Argentina's capitalist class was so devastating that today there is little support for free enterprise and free trade. The political pendulum has swung back to a populism more reminiscent of traditional Peronism under the governments of Cristina and Néstor Kirchner. Like Perón, the Kirchners seek to extend state control to all aspects of the economy and to redistribute income derived from the most efficient sector, agriculture. History is repeating itself in Argentina, but this time the damage is being done to a much weaker society.

Argentina's "reversal of development" should be an intellectual challenge for those of us who live in First World capitalist countries. Near the end of *The Crisis of Argentine Capitalism,* I quoted the famous economist Paul Samuelson as saying: "The shadow on the wall for all of us, I fear, is not the totalitarian revolution of a Lenin or a Mao. It is not a relapse into the *laissez-faire* of a Queen Victoria or President Coolidge. Argentina, I dare to suggest, is the pattern no modern man may face without crossing himself and saying, 'There but for the grace of God...'"[4] Argentina was, like North America and Western Europe, rich in natural resources. It had the advantage of an educated, skilled working class, a modern agriculture, and a creative business elite. Nevertheless, those natural advantages were negated by irresponsible politicians. Therein lies a cautionary tale.

Abbreviations

AAA	Argentine Anti-Communist Alliance
ABRA	Association of Banks of the Argentine Republic; represents branches of foreign banks in Argentina
ADEBA	Association of Argentine Banks
AEA	Association of Argentine Entrepreneurs
AFJP	*Administradora de Fondos de Jubilaciones y Pensiones;* private pension fund system
AMIA	Jewish community center in Buenos Aires
ANSES	National Social Security Administration
APDT	Argentine Private Development Trust Company
ARI	Alternative for a Republic of Equals; Radical Party splinter
ATE	Association of State Workers
B&B	Bunge and Born conglomerate
BOLSA	Buenos Aires Stock Exchange
CAC	Argentine Chamber of Commerce
CARBAP	The CRA's branch for Buenos Aires and La Pampa provinces
CATAC	*Confederación Argentina del Transportes Automotor de Cargas;* truck haulers federation

CC	*Confederación de Comercio;* Confederation of Commerce, subgroup of CGE
CEI	Citicorp Equity Investments
CGE	*Confederación General Económica;* General Economic Confederation, Peronist umbrella organization for farmers, industrialists, and merchants
CGT	*Confederación General de Trabajadores;* General Confederation of Workers
CI	Confederation of Industry; subgroup of CGE
CONINAGRO	Confederation of Agricultural Cooperatives; *Confederación Intercooperativa Agropecuaria*
COPAL	*Coordinadora de la Producción Alimentica;* federation of food processing industries and main component of MIA
CP	Confederation of Production, agricultural subgroup of CGE
CRA	*Confederación Rural Argentina,* Argentine Rural Confederation, represents small and medium-sized ranchers and farmers
CTA	Confederation of Argentine Workers, unofficial, leftist labor federation
CTERA	Teachers union
DEP	Directorate of Public Enterprises
DGI	Internal Revenue Service
ELMA	*Empresas Líneas Marítimas Argentinas;* state-owned merchant fleet
ENCOTel	*Empresa Nacional de Correos y Telégrafos;* state postal and telegraph service
ENTel	*Empresa Nacional de Telecomunicaciones;* state telephone company
ERP	*Ejército Revolucionario del Pueblo;* 1970s guerrilla organization
FAA	*Federación Agraria Argentina;* Argentine Agrarian Federation, represents tenant farmers
FAP	*Fuerzas Armadas Peronistas;* 1970s guerrilla organization

FAR	*Fuerzas Armadas Revolucionarias;* 1970s guerrilla organization
FIEL	Foundation for Research on Free Markets, private, pro-business foundation
FREPASO	*Frente para un País en Solidaridad;* Front for a Country in Solidarity, a center-left political coalition
FpV	*Frente para la Victoria;* Cristina and Néstor Kirchner's Peronist faction in Congress
IMF	International Monetary Fund
IMPSA	*Industrias Metalúrgicas Pescarmona;* holding company for the Pescarmona Group
INDEC	*Instituto Nacional de Estadística y Censos;* statistics and census bureau
LIBOR	London Interbank Offered Rate; rate at which banks borrow money from other banks, quoted daily from London
MERCOSUR	South American free trade zone, originally composed of Argentina, Brazil, Paraguay, and Uruguay
MIA	*Movimiento Industrial Argentina;* UIA free trade faction
MIN	*Movimiento Industrial Nacional;* UIA faction for protectionism
NCO	Non-commissioned military officer
OAS	Organization of American States
ONCCA	*Oficina Nacional de Control Agropecuaria;* government regulatory agency for agriculture
PAMI	Social Security Medical Aid Fund
PCR	Revolutionary Communist Party
PdVSA	Venezuelan state oil company
PJ	*Partido Justicialista;* Peronist or Justicialist Party
PYMEs	Small and medium-sized business firms
SEGBA	*Servicios Eléctricos del Gran Buenos Aires;* state electrical company
SIDE	State Intelligence Service

SOCMA	*Sociedad Macri;* holding company for the Macri conglomerate
SOMISA	State steel company
SRA	*Sociedad Rural Argentina;* Argentine Rural Society, represents large ranchers
UBs	*Unidades de Base;* "base units," neighborhood sectors for political organizing
UCeDe	Union of the Democratic Center
UCR	*Unión Civica Radical;* Radical Party
UIA	*Unión Industrial Argentina* Argentine Industrial Union, federation of large industrialists
UOM	Metalworkers union
UPCN	Union of Civil Personnel of the Nation, civil servants union
UTPBA	Journalists union of Buenos Aires
VAT	Value added tax
YCF	*Yacimientos Carboníferos Fiscales;* state coal company
YPF	*Yacimientos Petrolíferos Fiscales;* state oil company

Chapter One

The Rise to Power

"Argentina a year or two after the centenary of her Republic presents a study in development that the history of few nations can rival," wrote William Henry Koebel, a British writer of many books about Latin America. The year was 1912. The previous quarter of a century had seen a modernizing, liberal elite come to power in Argentina, consolidating the country politically and opening it up to trade and investment. An era of rapid progress followed that made Koebel confident in the country's future, for he thought it was neither superficial nor accidental. "In considering the present prosperity of Argentina it is necessary to remember that success has been brought about not by undue speculation of the 'wild cat' order, but has been wrung from the land by means of unsparing labor."[1]

The effects of modernization were spreading outward in every direction from Buenos Aires, Argentina's capital and chief port. Koebel noted that great improvements in the production of cattle and grains followed the extension of the railways to every corner of the country, drawing to the port this bountiful increase. Buenos Aires itself, with 1.25 million inhabitants, "its boulevards and palatial public buildings, its plazas and parks, its motor cars, tramways, 'tube', and the whirl of its general traffic...causes the newcomer to open his eyes in wonder." The long line of docks was filled with ships from all parts of the world. While some were loading up meat, corn, wheat, and linseed to carry to Europe, others were bringing in new settlers to populate Argentina's empty spaces and its towns. The great influx of immigrants, some bringing their capital, others just their labor, were important to Argentina's rapid economic and demographic growth. "The conglomeration of races that is building itself firmly about the nucleus of the old Spanish families is truly amazing," Koebel wrote. "British, French, Italians, Germans, Austrians, Russians, Danes—these are only some of the nationalities involved. But, once in Argentina, it is the fashion to be Argentine. Surely no higher compliment can be paid to a country than this desire for adoption."

The immigrants came to find opportunities that were lacking back home. Land could still be bought cheaply on the fringes of the pampa, and there were many business opportunities in Buenos Aires and the booming towns of the interior. Labor was much in demand. Even a modest workman, if he saved his wages, could hope to start his own business someday. "There are probably few countries in the world that have offered so favorable a field for the operations of the capitalist as Argentina," Koebel concluded. And, unlike many Old World societies, there was freedom: "One of the great merits attaching to the Argentine rule is the absolute freedom which its government extends to all. Liberty is no catchword here....Indeed, it is a little difficult to disassociate freedom from the open, generous, sun-swept soil of the Republic." True, labor conditions in the country's more remote areas might be less civilized, and in the cities strikes might occur, but in the latter case "the points at issue are seldom grave in a land where the demand for labor exceeds the supply." While a few European immigrants may have turned out to be Anarchists, "the sting of anarchy surely cannot fail to atrophy in the free atmosphere of Argentina." Moreover, the Argentine police were quite efficient in dealing with it. Not that they were overbearing: "Excellently policed, endowed with a generous constitution, and with a government that has proved itself sympathetic toward enterprise, Argentina is fully as much a land of law and order as is England, France, or Germany."

We may shake our heads at such effusiveness, knowing as we now do how the rule of law was soon to break down in Europe and how grim working conditions in Argentina really were during that period. Still, there was enough truth to this picture of Argentina in 1912 as a land of opportunity to attract a sixteen-year-old Saúl Menem from Yabrud, in present-day Syria, and make him want to stay.

Saúl Menem spent the next few years roaming throughout Argentina with his older brother, Manuel, who had preceded him. They worked at various jobs, finally becoming peddlers on muleback in the distant northwest province of La Rioja. This was, and continues to be, one of Argentina's poorest regions. Its western half is formed by the Andes Mountains, whose high, bare ridges run north and south, with isolated valleys in between. The eastern half is a vast semi-arid plain with monotonous scenery. There is little sign of life other than an occasional *rancho* or a cluster of rude shacks forming a hamlet. Domingo F. Sarmiento, in his classic *Life in the Argentine Republic in the Days of the Tyrants,* described the plains as "desolate," except for the occasional oasis where reservoirs allow enough irrigation to grow oranges, figs, and grapes. Farming and ranching were also possible in the mountain valleys, which received adequate rainfall. Sarmiento compared the geography to that of Palestine: "a strange combination of mountain and plain, fruitfulness and aridity, parched and bristling heights, and hills covered with dark green forests." To him, the people even resembled Arabs, riding on donkeys and clothed in goatskins: "melancholy, silent, sedate, and crafty." Those living in the oases of the plains, surrounded by desert, lived an austere existence. Theirs was a patriarchal, almost feudal, society, with the poor laborer strongly attached to his master. Both were hostile to the cities.[2]

Perhaps it was La Rioja's resemblance to the Middle East that attracted the two young Syrians. The province at that time had a population of just under 80,000, half of whom lived in the capital, also called La Rioja. This was a pleasant, modest town, situated on a plateau with the Andes Mountains a short distance behind it. Nevertheless, the Menems preferred the back country and finally settled down in the village of Anillaco, in one of the mountain valleys, about 35 kilometers north of the capital. It was a remote but fertile location, with vineyards, apple orchards, and walnut trees. They had saved some money and opened up a general store. Having found his home at last, Saúl went back to Syria to marry a woman from his old hometown, Mohibe Akil, and bring her back with him to La Rioja. They were to have four children, of whom their eldest son, Carlos Saúl, born on 2 July 1930, would one day be president of Argentina. Meanwhile, Saúl Menem's business prospered. He bought land, established a vineyard, and eventually set up a wine bodega. The winery, *Saúl Menem y Hijos,* produced a rich, full-bodied *tinto* that was highly regarded throughout the province. In time the Menem family, though *turcos* (the Argentine pejorative for any Middle Easterner), became the most prosperous in Anillico.

THE YOUNG *POLITICO*

Although Saúl and Mohibe Menem remained Sunni Muslims, their four children, like many offspring of immigrants, showed their desire to assimilate as Argentines by converting to Roman Catholicism. Carlos, the future president, not only embraced Argentine Catholic nationalism but felt a strong identity with his native province. In school he learned about Facundo Quiroga, the notorious caudillo of La Rioja, who first fought the Spanish for Argentina's independence, then fought the neighboring Province of Córdoba to obtain La Rioja's independent status, next fought the Unitary Party in Buenos Aires that wanted to centralize all political power in the capital, and finally fought his former Federalist ally, Juan Manuel Rosas, who, according to generally accepted legend, arranged for Quiroga's murder. Young Carlos was fascinated by the "Tiger of the Llanos,"as Quiroga was often called. He obtained a copy of Sarmiento's work, whose Spanish title was *Facundo* because it held up Quiroga as the quintessential "barbaric" caudillo whose disappearance was necessary for civilization to triumph. Although Carlos read the book many times, dog-earing various pages and underlining certain passages, he came to regard Facundo Quiroga as a model to follow rather than an example to avoid. The passages he underlined were to help him capture the style of his hero. As a teenager, he began wearing his hair long, with mutton-chop sideburns, as Facundo had, and he continued to do so for much of his adult life. He also liked to wear the mountaineers' poncho and ride on horseback through the mountains and valleys of La Rioja where Facundo was known to have lived, in order to capture his spirit.[3]

Carlos Menem went to primary school in Anillaco, but when he reached high school age, his family—increasingly prosperous—sent him to a *colegio nacional* in the city of La Rioja. Such *colegios* have strict admissions standards, so his acceptance is an indication of his quick intelligence. When not in school, Carlos worked at many different jobs in the family's business: clerk at the general store, truck driver, traveling merchant. All of the Menem children would go to university. Carlos entered the University of Córdoba's Law School in 1952, graduating two and a half years later.

Carlos Menem was active in student politics, joining a conservative movement for provincial rights. He also became captain of the school's basketball team. When it won the national championship in 1953, the players were invited to Buenos Aires to be congratulated by President Juan Perón and the First Lady, Evita Perón. This was a pivotal event in the young man's life. Like many others, he was dazzled by this charismatic couple and subsequently joined his university's Peronist student organization. On graduating, in 1955, Menem returned to La Rioja and entered the law firm of an old family friend. When a military coup overthrew Perón a few months later, Menem turned his attention to defending local Peronist leaders who had been purged and jailed. Among those were former Governor Juan Melis and some of his cabinet ministers. No other lawyer in La Rioja dared to take their cases, but Menem did—and got them freed.[4]

In June 1956 a group of army officers joined with some trade union leaders in a revolt aimed at returning Perón to power. Menem and other young La Rioja Peronistas demonstrated in favor of the revolt and were arrested as troublemakers. They were released after three days, however, so this did little to dampen Menem's political enthusiasm. He had been lucky, though: in Buenos Aires the revolt's leaders were summarily executed on orders from General Pedro Aramburu, the junta's chief. The following year, Menem helped to found La Rioja's branch of the *Juventud Peronista* (Peronist Youth) and at the same became the attorney for the provincial branch of the General Confederation of Workers (*Confederación General de Trabajadores,* or CGT). He also took on a lot of *pro bono* work for poor people in the province. When democracy was restored in 1958, he was the neo-Peronist *Unión Popular's* candidate for the National Senate, but was forced to withdraw because the Constitution set the minimum age at thirty, and he was only twenty-eight. After the elections, Menem took a train to Buenos Aires, where he met with John William Cooke, whom Perón had appointed to head his underground, and returned to La Rioja as Cooke's contact man.[5] In 1962 Menem ran as a Peronist for a seat in the national Chamber of Deputies, but a military coup that overthrew the democratic government of Arturo Frondizi cancelled the results. When elections were again scheduled in 1963, Menem stood as candidate for governor of La Rioja, with support from a coalition of Peronists and other populists. This time he had to withdraw from the race when Peron sent out orders from Madrid, his place of exile, for his followers to boycott the elections.

With his career seemingly at a standstill, Menem took a trip to Syria in 1964 with his parents to visit their old hometown, Yabrud. Although Saúl and Mohibe had allowed their children to adopt Catholicism, certain Muslim practices still prevailed in the family. One of these was the practice of arranged marriages, and for Mohibe it was essential for Carlos to marry a Muslim girl from Syria. Her son was becoming something of a "ladies' man" and lately had been getting rather serious about a *riojana* named Ana María Luján. Mohibe quickly intervened to break up the romance and whisk Carlos off to meet the bride that she had picked for him, Zulema Yoma. The Yomas came from Yabrud and, in the old days, had been neighbors of the Menems. Like the Menems, they had settled for awhile in La Rioja and still had several businesses there, run by their relatives; but in 1959 Zulema's father had gone back to live in Damascus. The Yomas were Alawites, an offshoot of the Shia branch of Islam, but this didn't seem to bother the Menems, especially since the Yomas were well connected in the new Syrian regime, which recruited its top leaders from the Alawite sect. Zulema's brothers and sisters were active in the Ba'athist Party, and two of them worked in the Spanish Embassy. Zulema herself had a degree in decorative arts and was a student at Damascus' School of Fine Arts.[6]

Carlos and Zulema were betrothed during this visit, but the wedding would not take place for another two years. After the arrangements were settled, Carlos started on his return trip to Argentina, with a planned side trip to Spain. He hoped to pay his respects to Perón, who was living in a heavily guarded estate outside of Madrid. Although Menem was president of La Rioja's Peronist Party and of its Peronist Youth, he was turned away by Perón's suspicious bodyguards when he showed up at the mansion. Fortunately, he had the address of a fellow Syrian, Jorge Antonio, who at that time was Perón's chief financial backer. Antonio knew Carlos' parents and welcomed him to his luxury apartment on the Avenida Castellana. A few days later, after running a background check, Antonio took Carlos to join a small group of Peronist Youth leaders who were scheduled to meet Perón.

Perón was a gracious host and sufficiently impressed by Carlos Menem that he asked Jorge Antonio to keep him in Madrid for another couple of weeks so that they could talk again. "Don't lose sight of him, Jorge," Perón told him. "That kid has class." When they met again, Perón assured Menem that he would soon make his triumphal return to power in Argentina. Indeed, on 2 December, just ten days after Menem arrived back in Argentina, Perón made an unsuccessful bid to fly back to Buenos Aires. He had secretly boarded a flight chartered by Peronist trade union leaders, but when his plane made a refueling stop in Rio de Janeiro, Brazilian authorities arrested him on orders from the Argentine government and sent him back to Spain.[7]

Argentine politics had reached a stalemate. The armed forces had proscribed the Peronist Party and attempted to purge the trade unions that constituted its mass base, but most military officers preferred some sort of civilian rule. Unfortunately for them, the only party capable of offering a serious alternative to Peronism was the *Unión Cívica Radical,* or Radical Party, and the Radicals were split over whether democracy required legalizing the Peronists. One faction, led by Arturo Frondizi, was willing to cooperate with Perón. In 1962 Frondizi allowed the Peronists to run in congressional and gubernatorial elections, but their impressive victories were quickly followed by a military coup. Elections were held again in 1963, under close military supervision and with the Peronists again excluded from running. This time the Radicals won behind the candidacy of Arturo Illia, an elderly doctor from Córdoba. Throughout his administration, the General Confederation of Workers (CGT)—dominated by Peronist trade unions—refused to recognize his legitimacy. The workers disrupted the economy with strikes, street riots, and factory seizures. As political temperatures rose, Illia finally decided to allow the Peronists to participate in the 1965 congressional elections. History repeated itself: the Peronists won big, Illia's days were numbered, and the military now decided that civilian rule had to be postponed until the society could be thoroughly purged of Peronism's poison. Their choice for dictator was a tough cavalry general named Juan Carlos Onganía, who took over when Illia was ousted in June 1966.

Onganía abolished all political parties, censored the press, suppressed strikes, and invaded the University of Buenos Aires campus to crack down on student demonstrators. To halt inflation and restore economic growth, he imposed a wage freeze and sought to create a business-friendly climate. The Peronists were uncertain about how to respond. The trade unions, their mass base, split. The moderates, led by the Metallurgical Workers' Union chief, Augusto Vandor, signaled to the government a willingness to cooperate. For them, Perón was a spent force, and they had better make the best deal they could with Onganía. Raimundo Óngaro, head of the Printers' Union, spoke for the intransigent Peronists who vowed to continue the struggle to bring their exiled *Líder* back to power. He began building a loose underground coalition of Marxist "combative" unions, liberation theology priests, and Peronist Youth groups increasingly inclined toward "direct action." As for Menem, at first he had protested Onganía's takeover by organizing a Peronist demonstration in La Rioja on 17 October 1966, "Peronist Loyalty Day." The protesters placed a wreath at the statue of Argentina's great liberator, General José de San Martín, to show their patriotism, but when they began shouting *vivas* for Perón, the police attacked with clubs. Menem suffered a cracked collar bone. After that incident, he pretended to resign himself to the prosaic life of a provincial lawyer and opened up his own law office with his younger brother, Eduardo. However, he continued to represent the provincial CGT and even got in touch with Óngaro.

Onganía's tough approach to governing paid off, in the short run. Throughout 1967, 1968, and the first quarter of 1969, inflation dropped from an annual rate of over 22 percent to under 4 percent, while the GNP's growth more than tripled, from only 2 percent to almost 7 percent. Businessmen showed their confidence in the regime by increasing their gross domestic investment by over 30 percent, most of which was spent on importing new machinery and equipment. Feeling triumphant, Onganía's men in the Interior Ministry began working on a new constitution that would replace Argentina's liberal democratic institutions with corporatist-type economic chambers. Then in May 1969 the regime was rocked by riots that started in the cities of Corrientes and Rosario and finally climaxed in a spectacular popular upheaval that lasted for days in the city of Córdoba. Nothing like the *cordobazo* had ever been seen before in Argentina. The scale of violence shattered Onganía's confidence, causing him to shuffle his cabinet. There was no more talk of changing the Constitution, but economic policy became more conciliatory toward the workers. Peronists were in no mood to be conciliated, however. Vandor, now sensing that the regime was fatally stricken, hurried to Spain to be reconciled with Perón. In La Rioja Menem made a public speech praising the *cordobazo* rioters for rising up against tyranny, and went into hiding afterwards—but not for long. Onganía's days were numbered.

Ever since Perón's overthrow, there had been an underground movement using terrorist tactics to keep Argentina in turmoil. Labor union militants and the *matones* (killers) they used as bodyguards were among the original recruits, but gradually they involved more and more gunmen from the Peronist Youth. These young recruits were often devout Catholics and nationalists, but had become revolutionaries under the influence of liberation theology. They were *national* socialists, not Marxists, and competed with the Communists for the allegiance of the workers, students, and intellectuals. They played a leading part in the *cordobazo,* and in the months following that event, they delivered a series of blows to the Onganía government that finally brought it down. This was the armed movement that would later be known as the Montoneros, after the patriot militia that had fought Spain for Argentina's independence.

The Montoneros were only one of several terrorist groups that emerged after the *cordobazo*. On 30 June 1969, just a month after the *cordobazo,* gunmen broke into Vandor's office at CGT headquarters and killed him. To raise money for arms and explosives, terrorist groups resorted to kidnappings of businessmen for ransom. Kidnappings also were good for publicity. In March 1970 the Paraguayan consul in Corrientes was kidnapped; and on 29 May came the shocking news that ex-President Aramburu had been kidnapped from his Buenos Aires apartment. Aramburu had been prominent among military liberals who recently called for Onganía to schedule elections and restore civilian rule, so many people suspected Onganía's hardline supporters of foul play. Their fears were heightened a few days later when the Montoneros announced they had tried Aramburu for killing the Peronists captured during the June 1956 uprising and had executed him. No one had ever heard of the Montoneros, so it was widely assumed that this was a ruse to throw off suspicion against the government. On 6 June tanks surrounded the Casa Rosada, Argentina's presidential palace, and forced Onganía to resign.

Military liberals and hardliners then hammered out a compromise by which a little-known general, Roberto Levingston, would succeed Onganía. Meanwhile, terrorist violence escalated. A group calling itself the Revolutionary Armed

Forces (FAR) firebombed a chain of Minimax convenience stores owned by the Rockefeller family. Another group, calling itself the Peronist Armed Forces (FAP), was robbing banks to build up a war chest and was working with "combative" Peronist unions to set up factory cells. Trotskyites fielded a guerrilla organization, the People's Revolutionary Army (ERP), which also sought to infiltrate the industrial unions. Trained in revolutionary Cuba, it differed from the other terrorist groups by setting up a rural guerrilla *foco* in the mountains of Tucumán. In July FAR took over the small town of Garín, in Buenos Aires Province, robbing the bank and seizing weapons from the police station. A few weeks earlier, the Montoneros showed they were no phantom organization by seizing the mountain resort town of La Calera, in Córdoba Province, and carrying off money and arms. Some of the Montoneros were captured by soldiers, however, and forced to reveal the names of their accomplices. More gun battles and arrests followed, providing police with information that led them to a farmhouse in Buenos Aires Province, where they discovered Aramburu's body. Terrorists struck back throughout 1970 with isolated attacks on remote police stations and assassinations of labor union officials such as José Alonso, Vandor's successor as the CGT's general secretary, and Rogelio Coria, former head of the Construction Workers' Union, who were accused of collaborating with the military.

Both the number of people involved in guerrilla organizations and the scale of violence rose sharply throughout 1971. Estimates as to the exact number of terrorist attacks vary, but all point to a significant increase in 1971, as compared to 1970 and 1969. Those included bank robberies, kidnappings, armed assaults on military and police installations, bombings, and assassinations.[8] What surprised the military especially was the widespread support the guerrillas received in public opinion polls and also at the funerals of slain Montoneros. When, in March 1971, a second *cordobazo* resulted in General Levingston's replacement as president by the army's chief, General Agustín Lanusse, a more liberal officer, it was clear that the military were about to retreat to the barracks. It also was clear that only by incorporating Peronism into the legal political system would it be possible to restore peace to Argentina.

Lanusse wanted to hand over power to a broad front of democratic parties, even including those Peronists who would agree to repudiate Perón, but he met with no success. Finally, on 14 November 1972, Perón forced the issue by landing at Buenos Aires' Ezeiza Airport with a group of his followers. Carlos Menem, who only a few days before had given the keynote speech at the Peronist Youth convention, was one of the entourage. Enthusiastic crowds cheered Perón's return, and even opposition party leaders came to pay him homage. Defeated, Lanusse agreed to let the Peronists present candidates in a general election scheduled for 11 March 1973; but he salvaged his pride by decreeing that Perón could not run. Perón, aware now that he held all the trump cards and that his return to power was only a matter of time, agreed to the conditions and named a stand-in for the presidential race: Héctor Cámpora, an old loyalist who once had served him back in the 1950s as president of the Chamber of Deputies. The Peronists, aware that their hour was about to arrive, campaigned on the slogan: *Cámpora al Gobierno, Perón al Poder* ("Cámpora in the Government, Perón in Power").

GOVERNOR MENEM

Carlos Menem's colorful populist style, his speechmaking talent, his proven courage, and his many personal sacrifices for Peronism secured him the party's nomination for Governor of La Rioja in the upcoming elections. He would run against the entrenched conservative regime of Guillermo Domingo Irribarren, the military-appointed governor. Menem could count on his followers in the Peronist Youth; on the local CGT leader, Julio Corzo, a "combative" trade unionist of the extreme left; and on the province's Catholic hierarchy, under the leadership of Msgr. Enrique Angelelli, a prominent figure in the Movement of Third World Priests. First, however, Menem had to improve relations with his wife, Zulema Yoma de Menem, whom he had married in Syria back in 1966.

Theirs was a stormy, loveless marriage. They had two children: Carlos Saúl Facundo, born in 1968, and Zulema Eva, born in 1970. Their names indicate Menem's devotion to both Peronism and the caudillo Quiroga; unfortunately, he was not equally devoted to his wife. Forced to marry her against his will, he spent much of his time with other women. That brought on violent scenes at home. At one point Zulema even went back to Syria, taking her infant son with her. She came back to La Rioja, however, under pressure from her family, all of whom had now settled in the town of Nonogasta, a short distance from Anillaco. Like the Menems, they had branched out into many different businesses and had become one of the province's most prosperous families. Although Menem and Zulema continued to quarrel, the Yomas saw him as a politician with a future and decided to back him. Under pressure again from her family, Zulema remained with him and contented herself with dreams of living in the governor's palace.

Menem ran a rousing, populist campaign, attacking Governor Irribarren and the provincial "oligarchy." He didn't even spare his half-brother Amado, who headed the Menem vineyards, nor his younger brother, Eduardo, who served as an undersecretary in Irribarren's government. It was all for show, however. Eduardo secretly helped Carlos evade the governor's ban on Peronist meetings, and Amado contributed liberally to the campaign. The Montoneros, who controlled the Peronist Youth, canvassed assiduously for him among the poor. On 11 March 1973, Menem was swept into office with 67 percent of the vote as part of the political tidal wave that also brought Cámpora to the Casa Rosada. At thirty-eight, he was Argentina's youngest governor.

Ironically, victory exposed the ideological divisions that lay just under the surface of Peronism. The Montoneros expected to transform Argentina into a socialist state *(patria socialista)* along the lines of Fidel Castro's Cuba. Cámpora's two sons were Montoneros, and from their positions as chief of the president's staff and presidential private secretary, they were able to influence his cabinet choices and policies. Within a few days after the inauguration, executive decrees released all captured guerrillas from prison and abolished all anti-terrorist laws. Most of the Peronist trade unions in the CGT were outraged by this, since many of their leaders had been murdered by leftist guerrillas. Moreover, they knew very well what the fate of independent trade unions would be in a communist state. What they wanted was a *patria sindicalista*—a capitalist economy in which the workers would get a bigger slice of the economic pie. Perón sided with them. He had been willing to use the Montoneros as a battering ram against the military dictatorship, but now their usefulness was over. It was time to re-establish the old Peronist corporative order, with the unions as its "backbone" *(columna vertebral)*. As always, he insisted on complete obedience to his commands ("verticality").

On 20 June Perón, his wife María Estela (best known by her nickname, Isabel), his private secretary José López Rega, and an entourage that included Cámpora—now out of favor—boarded a private flight for Buenos Aires. In Buenos Aires the Peronist trade unions had planned a huge demonstration to greet their returning Leader on the highway from Ezeiza Airport and had brought in thousands of people from all over the country for the event. They also stationed *pistoleros* at various points to ensure that no one would disrupt things. Meanwhile, the Montoneros, supported by the governor of Buenos Aires Province, were assembling armed guerrillas with the intention of taking over the demonstration and asserting their supremacy within the party. While Perón's plane was on the way, a ferocious gun battle broke out between the two factions and raged for hours around the speakers' platforms that had been erected upon an overpass. Eventually the Montoneros were driven off, but not before Perón was forced to land at an Air Force base and taken to his home under heavy guard. He was furious. Over the next few days, he was visited by CGT leaders, opposition party politicians, and top military officers, all of whom warned him that guerrillas had infiltrated Cámpora's government and were preparing to launch more *cordobazo*-type insurrections. After that, Perón forced Cámpora's resignation. A caretaker government was hastily set up under Raúl Lastiri, López Rega's son-in-law. New presidential elections were scheduled for September in which Perón would be a candidate, with Isabel as his running mate. He won in a landslide.

The swiftness of their fall from grace dumbfounded the Montoneros. They soon learned that Perón had no intention of creating a *patria socialista*. Moreover, they discovered that José López Rega exerted a powerful countervailing influence over Perón. He had made himself an indispensable go-between in carrying out Perón's schemes, and as the head of a spiritualist lodge that practiced a form of voodoo, he had the superstitious Isabel completely in his power. Once Perón was back in the Casa Rosada, he made López Rega his Social Welfare minister, with a huge budget to spend as he chose. The "Sorcerer" used it to buy weapons and create a private army of right-wing terrorists that came to be known as the Argentine Anti-Communist Alliance (AAA). Now the Montoneros understood what the non-Peronist guerrillas had told them all along: that Perón was really a bourgeois "bonapartist" and not a true revolutionary. When Perón suddenly died at the beginning of July 1974, at the age of seventy-eight, Isabel succeeded him as president, and José López Rega became her *éminence grise.*

As governor of La Rioja, Menem also moved to the right, removing the leftists from his cabinet and replacing them with moderate Peronists. He watered down a land reform plan that he once had supported and also began distancing himself from CGT radicals like Julio Corzo. He still cultivated the image of an old-fashioned caudillo, with his bushy sideburns, a brown gaucho shawl draped over his shoulders, and Indian *bombo* drums beating incessantly at his political rallies. But after Perón died, he closed down Corzo's newspaper, *El Independiente,* in order to appease Isabel and López Rega, and even began envisioning himself as Isabel's running mate in the next elections. Throughout 1975 he traveled around the country to speak at Peronist meetings, ostensibly to promote her re-election but also to promote himself as vice president. As a reborn Peronist of the right, he now denounced both "Marxists" and "Yanquis," and praised the military's ongoing campaign in neighboring Tucumán Province against ERP's guerrillas.[9]

Meanwhile the economy deteriorated. Aggressive labor unions, xenophobic restrictions on foreign investment, and continued terrorist violence all contributed to the downward spiral. By contrast, the guerrilla organizations grew in size and strength as a series of mergers resulted in two large groups. The Montoneros still claimed to be Peronists but had gone underground and resumed their attacks on the police and military after Isabel succeeded Perón. ERP had always identified more with Fidel Castro and now was trying to launch a Cuban-style rural guerrilla war. Both organizations raised large sums of money by kidnapping wealthy businessmen and landowners for ransom, both had large arsenals of arms and explosives, and both had extensive networks of front organizations that reached into every social group: students, workers, doctors, lawyers, politicians, journalists, educators, civil servants, the military, and even bankers who were willing to launder their money.

Isabel's government drifted, too weak to keep the unions under control, too infiltrated by Montoneros and their sympathizers to stop terrorism, and too mired in corruption scandals to earn the public's respect. Repeated warnings by the armed forces failed to bring about reform, so on 24 March 1976, Isabel and all her cabinet ministers, all Peronist provincial governors and their ministers, the Peronist congressmen, CGT leaders, and officials in other Peronist organizations were swept up in a military coup and placed under arrest. The new military junta, headed by the army's chief, General Jorge Videla, announced a Process of National Reorganization ("the *Proceso*") that would restore order, prosperity, and civic virtue. Menem was arrested at the Governor's Palace, taken to Buenos Aires, and placed in the brig of a navy ship anchored in the harbor. Three months later he was transferred to a military prison at Mar del Plata, a resort on the Atlantic.

Located near Bahía Blanca, Argentina's largest naval base, Mar del Plata was under the control of Admiral Emilio Massera, the Navy chief and second most powerful man in the Junta. Massera was a born conspirator who had his eye on the presidency. His aim was to supplant Videla, call for elections, and win the presidency openly as the hero who restored democracy. Massera had a newspaper, *Convicción,* which employed political prisoners to turn out his propaganda. He needed Peronist support, however, and so took an interest in Menem because of the latter's supposed contacts with the Montoneros. Menem was allowed "conditional liberty," meaning that he was free to walk about but had to stay within the town's limits. Zulema was allowed to join him there. It's not certain how much help Menem gave, but a large number of opportunistic Peronists who worked closely with Massera would later appear in Menem's government after he became president.[10]

Menem's fortunes sank a bit in 1980, after Massera was eased out of the Junta, because he was moved to Tandil, under the army's jurisdiction. Zulema was still with him, but eventually she discovered that he was seeing other women. After a violent quarrel, she left him and took an apartment in Buenos Aires. Soon afterward Menem was heard to criticize the Proceso's interior minister and was sent to a steamy jungle village near the Paraguayan border. There he stayed until his final release, after which he also moved to Buenos Aires and joined the law firm of Hugo Grimberg, an old friend from a wealthy Jewish family who had once served on La Rioja's Supreme Court. Grimberg's luxurious offices now became a meeting place where his friends and law partners would gather around Menem as a man whom they perceived to have a political future.

Meanwhile, the Proceso gradually imploded. Its "dirty war" tactics—such as mass arrests and torture—succeeded in smashing the guerrillas, but it failed to reform the economy or end corruption. Many military officers wanted the state to either own or closely regulate all economic activities useful for national defense, and therefore blocked any attempts to introduce free market reforms or privatize state industries. Some officers also were greedy and used their power to extort money and property from wealthy citizens. Terror tactics, initially aimed at the guerrillas, gradually blanketed the entire society. As public support withered, in April 1982 the Proceso tried to win it back by invading the Falkland Islands, which the British had seized from Argentina in 1833. The British government sent a task force to the Falklands that forced the Argentines to surrender. A humiliated Argentine military was forced to call elections in October of the following year. Raúl Alfonsín, leader of the Buenos Aires branch of the Radical Party, won the presidency.

GOVERNOR AGAIN: THE MENEM MODEL

As soon as elections were scheduled, Menem announced his intention of running for governor. With the help of the Yoma family, he and Zulema were reconciled again. After an energetic campaign, Menem won re-election with 54 percent of the vote.

Although he governed a poor, peripheral province, Menem quickly established his reputation as a dynamic leader. His methods, however, were unorthodox and almost certainly unsustainable in the long run. There would be no unemployment in La Rioja under Governor Menem, because the provincial government would be the employer of last resort. From 1983 to 1989, the public payroll expanded from 12,000 employees to over 40,000—out of a total population of 200,000 and an economically active population of only 67,370. It hardly mattered that many of those were only political hacks who seldom showed up at work except on payday. Menem answered his critics by saying that the number of teachers had increased by 40 percent and the number of sanitation workers by 68 percent. He also ben-efitted from the results of an Industrial Promotion Law put into effect in 1979 by the Proceso to help poor provinces like La Rioja. At that time there had been about 2,000 people working in traditional industries such as construction, lumber, wine, or the processing of fruit and vegetables; but by 1987 there were 6,000 new industrial jobs in textiles, metallurgy, chemicals, leather goods, plastics, electron-ics, clothing, and machine shops. An industrial park arose on the east side of the capital—and indeed the city's entire aspect underwent modernization, and new shops, houses, and apartment buildings sprouted up.[11]

In 1987 the Alfonsín administration cancelled the Industrial Promotion Law, sending La Rioja's economy into temporary chaos and touching off strikes by public employees and threatening the closure of factories, with massive unem-ployment to follow. At that moment Menem's Economics Minister, Antonio Erman González, a former treasurer for the Yoma enterprises, hit upon a scheme to overcome the crisis. The provincial government would issue bonds to the amount of 10 billion pesos with which it would pay off the strikers and all the businessmen who supplied goods and services to the public sector. Although this was strictly illegal, since the Constitution gives the federal government the sole authority to print money, Menem went ahead and decreed that the provincial bonds, or scrip, should be accepted as legal tender by shops, factories and banks. The bills bore a picture of Facundo Quiroga, who was made to look a great deal like Governor Menem. This ingenious scheme allowed Menem to mop up unem-ployment by adding more people to the public payroll. Their pay was low, their tasks were ill-defined, the wages were not paid in real money, and the jobs were insecure, but the recipients found their situation preferable to being unemployed, so they rallied around Menem.

Meanwhile, the provincial government spent heavily and borrowed heavily to keep the local economy going. Since Menem never filled the positions on the provincial Tribunal of Accounts, there was no agency to monitor the budget; on the other hand, he did appoint all the members of the Supreme Court, which was headed by his close friend, Raúl Granillo Ocampo, with whom he had many busi-ness connections—some of them of a questionable sort. Most lower court judges were Menem appointees too, and the Peronists controlled the provincial legisla-ture. Thus, Menem governed with a free hand, and he made sure that his family, friends, and in-laws got favorable treatment from the Banco de La Rioja. The Governor's Palace was constantly the scene of lavish parties, with sports stars, television personalities, and political influentials flown in by the governor's private airplane. In every provincial capital and other large cities throughout

Argentina, there were Casas de La Rioja, ostensibly to promote the province's products, but really to promote Menem's career on the national scene.[12]

THE RENOVATIONIST

Menem's election as governor was one of the few victories the Peronists could celebrate in 1983. Their presidential candidate, Italo Luder, lost badly to the Radicals' Raúl Alfonsín. Worse, the Radicals won an absolute majority in the lower house of Congress, the Chamber of Deputies. In the upper house, the Senate, provincial parties held the balance of power. The Peronists did manage to win 12 of the 22 provincial governorships, but the Radicals won in the four biggest provinces: Buenos Aires, Córdoba, Santa Fe, and Mendoza. All in all, it was a shocking setback for the Peronists, who were unused to defeat.

The Peronists had been too involved in the violence leading up to the Proceso. Thus, when Luder's running mate, Herminio Iglesias, made menacing remarks about the Radicals' candidates, it reminded many middle-class Argentines of the Dirty War. Iglesias, head of the Metallurgical Workers' Union in the industrial suburb of Avellaneda, was a throwback to the times when labor leaders stayed in power by using thugs to silence their rivals. By contrast, Alfonsín was a human rights lawyer who had opposed military rule and now embodied the widespread desire to establish democracy on a permanent basis. Unless Peronism changed its image to match the country's mood, it would suffer many more defeats. One man who understood this was Antonio Cafiero, an economist who had served as Perón's Minister of Commerce in the 1950s and as Isabel Perón's Economics Minister in 1975. A leading figure in the Buenos Aires Province party organization, he had lost out to Herminio Iglesias for the vice presidential nomination in 1983. Now he sought to oust Iglesias and the old, corrupt trade union bosses from the party leadership by organizing a "Renovationist" faction that would appeal more to the middle class. Menem, who also saw his best chance for the presidency arising from new leadership and a new style, joined him.

In December 1984 the Peronists held a party congress at the Odeon Theatre in Buenos Aires. Cafiero, Menem, and other Renovationists tried to attend but were attacked by thugs and *pistoleros* hired by Lorenzo Miguel, the CGT leader. Miguel then imposed Herminio Iglesias as the party's general secretary. Undeterred, the Renovationists held a separate convention in February 1985, which was attended by most of the Peronist provincial governors. The party was now split in two: an "Orthodox" wing with most trade unionists on one side, and a younger, more middle-class "Renovationist" wing on the other. Both presented lists of candidates for the November 1985 midterm elections. With the Peronist vote thus divided, the Radicals swept to another victory; however, the Renovationists could also claim a "victory" of sorts, since their candidates got three times as many votes as the Orthodox slate. With that sort of momentum, the Renovationists swept the party's primaries a year later. Cafiero ousted Iglesias as president of the Peronist Party in Buenos Aires Province. In September 1987 he won the governorship of Buenos Aires, which was soon followed by his election as the party's national president. Menem was elected vice president.[13]

Menem already had begun to prepare to battle Cafiero to represent the party as its presidential nominee in 1989. He busily traveled about the country in a small private airplane, promoting his image as a responsible, moderate Peronist by calling upon his party to cooperate with Alfonsín in a spirit of bipartisanship. That did not go down well with the CGT, but it did win support from most Peronist governors, who usually were in poor peripheral provinces and were dependent upon federal revenue-sharing. Even the unions gradually came around, for Cafiero—despite his long service to the party—seemed ignorant of the complex network of precinct captains, local union bosses, and provincial machines that constituted the Peronist apparatus. To win support, it was necessary to "press the flesh" at *asados* (barbecues), meet with neighborhood committees, distribute favors judiciously, and make promises of future support that would require winning office to fulfill. As a natural-born caudillo, Menem was good at that, but Cafiero was diffident with people. He made a serious mistake by passing over Eduardo Duhalde, the party boss of Lomas de Zamora, a big industrial suburb, for his vice gubernatorial running mate in 1987; then he compounded that by picking Italo Luder instead of Duhalde to head the provincial party's congressional list. From then on, Duhalde, with his large personal following, was in Menem's camp, which weakened Cafiero's grip on the Buenos Aires provincial party organization. Cafiero's view of the Renovationist mission was to transform Peronism into something similar to the European Social Democratic parties. To democratize it, he instituted direct primaries, to be held for the first time in July 1988. Ironically, those primaries would result in his downfall as Peronism's leader.

When Menem picked Duhalde to be his running mate, he opened the way for a reconciliation with the right-wing trade union leaders, all of whom were opposed to Cafiero's reforms. Duhalde once had complained that none of the Renovationists ever went into the slums to meet the people who were Peronism's mass base, but Menem was different. A true populist who still wore his Facundo Quiroga sideburns, Menem acquired an old garbage truck that he dubbed his *Menemovil,* covered it with flags and microphones, and he and Duhalde, dressed in ponchos, drove slowly through all the working-class suburbs of Greater Buenos Aires, waving and throwing kisses to the multitudes who poured into the streets to cheer them. Every so often Menem would stop and give a short speech promising a big wage increase (*salariazo*) when he became president. The crowds became hysterical, holding up their children to be kissed—and blessed. At one stop, in Lanús, a man handed Menem a huge loaf of bread. After kissing it, Menem began breaking it into pieces and distributing it among the cheering onlookers. As the time for voting drew near, Cafiero tried to fight back by reminding the public of Menem's former ties to the Montoneros, but it did him little good: Menem won with over 53 percent of the vote.[14]

The 1989 presidential campaign followed the same pattern as Menem's previous races, but on a grander scale. A hotel owner in Mar del Plata donated a new

Menemovil, a big touring bus that contained a conference room, bar, television, and telex. With it, Menem and Duahlde began a nationwide barnstorming tour which, as usual, drew huge cheering crowds. Another reconciliation was arranged with Zulema, this time with a Catholic marriage ceremony—their original wedding having been in Syria under Muslim rites. Since the Argentine Constitution emphasized that the president must be a Catholic, Menem wanted to shore up his religious credentials. It was a tenuous reconciliation, but it held out the prospect of Zulema becoming Argentina's First Lady.

Indeed, those prospects were excellent because by 1989 Alfonsín's government was mired in one of the worst economic crises in the country's history. He had inherited a bad situation from the Proceso: an inflation rate of around 350 percent, a foreign debt of about $46 billion (up from $8.1 billion at the time of the 1976 coup), and a GDP that was shrinking at a yearly rate of 4.3 percent. By 1989 inflation had risen to just below 5,000 percent, the foreign debt stood at $63 billion, and the GDP was shrinking by 6 percent. There was a serious shortage of investment capital. Foreign investors shunned Argentina, and domestic capitalists were sending their money out of the country. Although the government announced various "stabilization programs" between 1985 and 1988, none of them attacked the structural causes of hyper-inflation and stagnant growth: inefficient state companies whose large annual losses led to chronic budget deficits; wage, price, interest, rent, export, and currency exchange controls that caused economic distortions; and excessive government expenditures on padded payrolls, subsidies, and make-work projects to disguise unemployment that also contributed to fiscal deficits. Instead, the Alfonsín administration preferred to try to pay its way by issuing bonds with various names—BAGON, BARRA, TACAM, and TIDOL—which carried increasingly higher interest rates as the economy worsened and which drove up the government's debts. Those bonds also competed with the private sector for investment capital, and did so at an advantage, for not only were their promised returns higher but private banks were often forced to buy them. Roberto Lavagna, the Secretary of Industry and Commerce, criticized this "festival of bonds" just before he resigned his office in July 1987, predicting that the country's financial system would collapse when it finally became evident that the government was unable to pay off its mounting debt.[15]

Hyper-inflation brought with it economic paralysis, social disruption, and political irrationality. Since prices changed daily—even hourly—production halted and stores closed because no one knew what prices to charge. Consumption dropped too, because wages couldn't keep up. With inflation running close to 200 percent a month, on payday workers would rush to the stores to spend their wages before they became worthless; by the end of the month they might be reduced to bartering. Many workers were laid off. A survey of Argentina's 300 largest companies found that 45 percent of their workforce was suspended and another 18 percent had been permanently dismissed. Some companies preferred to just reduce the number of hours their employees worked, but then wages had to be reduced too. People on fixed incomes, such as pensioners, were utterly impoverished. Naturally, social tensions rose. There were strikes, a rise in crime, and a deterioration in family life as people lived under constant tension.[16] There were wide swings in public opinion, with some people longing for another military takeover. For the most part, however, there was a deep revulsion against Radical Party rule that all but guaranteed a Menem victory. Alfonsín was constitutionally unable to succeed himself, so Eduardo Angeloz, the governor of Córdoba, had the unenviable job of trying to salvage the Radicals' fortunes.

La Rioja's surface glitter contrasted greatly with the gloom that was overtaking the rest of Argentina. And Menem had charisma, especially among the poorer sectors of the population. With his populist style, and looking like a traditional caudillo, he ran as an outsider, a critic of the "system" and its ruling class. Unlike Alfonsín, Angeloz, or Cafiero, whose speeches were carefully constructed models of logic, Menem's approach as he stood before the *Menemmovil* in the impoverished *villas de miseria* was instinctive, emotional, and self-confident. His platform was simple: a *salariazo* for the workers and a big stimulus to the economy *(shock productivo)* to bring back jobs. His motto made a direct appeal to them: *Síganme, que no los defraudaré* ("Follow me: I won't betray you"). Menem crisscrossed the country, drinking *yerba mate* with the common people, kissing their babies, dancing *sambas* with the local girls, meeting with neighborhood and village party leaders at barbecues—twenty hours a day, with five or six or seven stops a day, during which he personally attended to all the details of the campaign. Then, on 14 May 1989, he buried Angeloz at the polls and led the Peronists to an absolute majority in the Senate. The Peronists had 112 seats out of 254 in the Chamber of Deputies, but could count on sufficient support from minor parties for a working majority. They also controlled a majority of provincial governorships and legislatures. Although the official transfer of power was scheduled for 10 December, an embattled and exhausted Alfonsín, beset by food riots in various cities around the country, turned over the presidency to him on 9 July.

Chapter Two

The Crisis of Argentine Capitalism

For Argentina's political pundits, President Menem's first government was a surprising mixture of appointees. As expected, he filled his presidential office with close personal friends: Alberto Kohan (presidential private secretary), Raúl Granillo Ocampo (legal and technical secretary), Amira Yoma (appointments secretary), Gustavo Beliz (press secretary, speech writer), Humberto Toledo (presidential spokesman), and Juan B. Yofre (head of the State Intelligence Service—SIDE). Eduardo Bauzá, with whom he had some shady business dealings, became the interior minister, and Antonio Erman González, who inspired La Rioja's massive use of scrip to pay its bills, was to be vice president of the Central Bank. Julio Corzo (health and social action minister) was a labor leader from La Rioja.

Many cabinet appointments went to men identified with Peronism's conservative wing. Jorge Triaca (labor minister) was head of the Plastics Workers Union and known as a collaborationist. He had been imprisoned with Menem on the naval ship *33 Orientales* after Isabel Perón was overthrown and had been a big supporter during the presidential campaign. Antonio Salonia (education and justice minister) was an educator with good contacts among the private schools, especially those run by the Catholic Church. The Defense Ministry went to Italo Luder, a centrist, but Humberto Toledo, his undersecretary, had strong contacts with the right wing army faction known as the *carapintadas*. Those were men who had risen in revolt to stop attempts by the federal courts to prosecute lower-level military officers after Alfonsín had put the Proceso's junta leaders on trial for human rights violations. Alfonsín had given in to the *carapintadas* by issuing them an amnesty, but they still were agitating because the new military chiefs were forcing them into retirement. Roberto Dromi (public works minister) was identified with the Proceso too, having been appointed by the Junta as intendant of Mendoza. Still another cabinet minister, Domingo Cavallo (foreign affairs), had served the Proceso, first as undersecretary of technology and later as president of the Central Bank. Cavallo, a Harvard-trained economist, was also a member of the Mediterranean Foundation, a Córdoba-based free market society, which further raised eyebrows among those who expected Menem to head a radical populist government. Another eyebrow-raising appointment was that Alvaro Alsogaray, head of a conservative pro-business party called the Union of the Democratic Center (U.CeDe), as Menem's special advisor on the foreign debt. Equally surprising was Menem's choice of Javier González Fraga, another pro-business economist, as Central Bank president. But the real shock came when Menem announced his choice for the Economics Ministry: Miguel Mor Roig, an engineer and high-level executive with the huge Bunge & Born conglomerate. And when, a few days later, Mor Roig died suddenly of a heart attack, Menem picked another B&B executive, Néstor Rapanelli, to replace him.

Most Argentines did not know that during his campaign Menem had received large sums of money from representatives of Bunge & Born. Other large contributors were Pérez Companc, the country's largest oil company; the Loma Negra cement company; SOCMA, a holding company for construction firms, waste disposal services, and the Sevel automotive works; Technit, another holding company that owned engineering, manufacturing, and construction firms; Bridas, another large local oil firm, which was associated with British Petroleum; and Aluar, Argentina's chief aluminum company. Secret contacts between Menem and big local capitalists had begun immediately after he secured his party's presidential nomination. In return for their support, he promised that he would select his future Economics Minister from their group and that he would consult them when formulating the government's economic strategy. Those promises were repeated at several subsequent meetings.[1]

THE ROOTS OF STAGFLATION

Local industrialists had never been so important politically as they would become during Menem's first few years in office. Argentina's prosperity had traditionally depended on its exports of meat and grains, produced mainly on large estates called *estancias*. The owners of those properties, known as *estancieros,* tended to believe in the classical liberal economic doctrine of "comparative advantage," under which countries would specialize in those goods that they could produce competitively and trade them for other goods, which they could produce only at high cost. For orthodox liberal economists, that meant that Argentina would concentrate on temperate climate agricultural products and depend on other countries for its industrial goods. To be sure, there were certain agro-industries that, because they used local raw materials, could be competitive too; but Argentina's shortage of iron ore and coal—the traditional ingredients for making steel—meant that it had to import most of its manufactured goods. Those industrial establishments that did exist in the cities were mainly owned and managed by immigrants and were aimed at supplying working-class people who could not afford the better-quality foreign imports. Those establishments also tended to be small in scale, poorly capitalized, and inefficient. They could expect no help from the government in the form of protective tariffs, tax incentives, or any kind of subsidy. Most banks turned them down for loans, forcing them to keep going by reinvesting their own meager profits. Now and then a crisis that disrupted world trade—such as World War I or a recession—would force Argentina to rely on its local industries, and then they would expand, but those crises were usually followed by a restoration of global commerce and the collapse of many local companies.

The prolonged disruption of world trade during the Great Depression and World War II forced a change of attitude, convincing many Argentines that they could no longer depend on foreigners to supply their industrial goods. The Army's officer corps, especially, came to see such dependence as a threat to national security. This view was most cogently expressed by Juan Perón, a nationalistic colonel who had once been an attaché in Mussolini's Fascist Italy. After he came to power in 1946, he set about making Argentina self-sufficient by subordinating industry, agriculture, trade, finance, and labor to state economic planning. His system, which he called "the organized community," was very similar to Mussolini's "Corporate State." Because the military considered oil and gas, iron and steel, electric power, railroads, airlines, telephones, and the merchant fleet essential for national economic independence, they were converted into state companies. However, their goods and services were provided at below-market rates in order to lower business costs for private industry and to gain popularity among the general public. Their management usually consisted of political appointees, while their workforce was almost always larger than necessary, in order to keep down unemployment. Inefficient management and featherbedding workers naturally resulted in low productivity, shoddy goods and services, and chronic deficits that had to be covered by printing money.

Outside of these "core" economic activities, Perón encouraged privately owned import-substituting industries, which would supply domestic needs. He would increase the domestic market by giving workers greater buying power through price and rent controls, high wages, and generous fringe benefits. Perón courted popularity by creating strong labor unions whose power was combined in a single nationwide confederation, the CGT. To compensate industrialists for price controls and high wages, Perón provided easy credit, high protective tariffs, and a variety of subsidies. Private companies, buffered against competition, discovered that they didn't have to be efficient. Profits depended more on having the right political connections than on productivity. The workers, whose job security was practically sacrosanct, had no incentive to produce either. Naturally, this system of low productivity and high demand generated inflation, only temporarily disguised by price controls. By 1950 economic and social tensions began to mount, as did criticism from Perón's opponents. His attempts to crush all criticism only alienated former supporters in the Army and the Catholic Church, who perceived a trend toward totalitarianism. In September 1955 a military revolt drove him from office.[2]

Even so, most of Perón's system survived him. Most of the labor unions were still loyal to him and hoped for his triumphant return from exile. Their organizational strength, combined in the CGT, made it impossible for anti-Peronists to govern. The military, too, was still wedded to the idea of state control of the "core" industries, many of which were run by their officers. Civilian politicians, such as those in the Radical Party, also saw the state enterprises and government regulatory agencies as sources of political patronage. Moreover, they recognized the mass voting power of the labor unions and often tried to court them. Even many industrialists preferred the old autarchic economic system that protected them, subsidized them, and provided them with captive markets. Often their companies were small in scale, by modern standards, and operated with old machinery or hand labor. Free trade threatened such "hothouse capitalists" with real competition. Thus there was a substantial coalition that supported economic nationalism and rejected globalism as a conspiracy by the United States and international finance to dominate Argentina.

Nevertheless, there were structural "bottlenecks" in this closed system that made it unstable. Economic self-sufficiency was impossible because Argentina did not possess all the resources needed to keep the economy going. Import-substituting industrialization, originally seen as a way to replace foreign consumer goods (such as textiles, clothing, cosmetics, basic pharmaceuticals, or household appliances), usually had not required a lot of start-up capital or sophisticated technology. As time went on, however, machines and their parts would break down and have to be replaced. Companies would be tempted to start new production lines to keep up with modern consumer trends, which would require new and different technology. As import substitution led to the growth of more consumer goods industries, Argentine economic planners discovered that the country now was more dependent on foreign imports than ever before, except that now those imports were of capital goods, such as heavy machinery and equipment, or of intermediate goods such as steel and industrial chemicals. Those were expensive to buy, and to produce them in Argentina would require large investments of capital. There were only a few possible ways to meet those costs: earning foreign exchange through exports, inviting in foreign direct investment, or borrowing from foreign lenders. Borrowing and direct foreign investment might compromise Argentina's economic independence, and thus were risky options. As for exporting, Argentina's industrial goods simply were not competitive on the world market. Going back to exporting meat and grains would earn foreign exchange, but it also would mean dealing with the traditional rural elites, Perón's sworn enemies.

Perón tried to overcome this dilemma by forcing agriculturalists to sell their goods at below world market prices to a state monopoly that would then export them at a profit, thus generating the capital with which to further industrialize.

The scheme was a failure because farmers and ranchers refused to produce under those conditions. The long-term effects were even worse because Argentine agriculture, deprived of investment capital, fell behind its traditional competitors such as the United States, Australia, and Canada, and so in the post-Perón period it was unable to recapture its lost markets. Devaluation might have helped, but that would also raise the cost of capital goods. Unable either to cast off Perón's legacy or eliminate its inherent contradictions, Argentine governments after 1955 zigzagged erratically between orthodox liberal policies aimed at modernizing the economy, and populist economic policies that courted popularity and protected embedded interests.

Populist economics sought greater social equality through the redistribution of income. That meant high wages and generous spending by government on pensions, health care, and housing. Such measures also aimed at encouraging industry and generating full employment by increasing mass purchasing power. When, inevitably, they also generated inflation, the government would impose price controls. Another control mechanism was to manipulate foreign exchange rates, creating a dual system that overvalued the peso to make it cheaper to import machinery while simultaneously undervaluing it to encourage agricultural exports. Despite these machinations, heavy government spending led to chronic budget deficits because of insufficient revenues. The government's income was derived mainly from indirect taxes, such as sales taxes, tariffs on imports, and taxes on agricultural exports (euphemistically called "retentions"). Price controls and "retentions" aggravated the problem by discouraging production and exports. Deficits were then covered by printing more pesos, which fueled inflation. Stagnant production meant that supply was always less than demand, while stagnant exports produced chronic balance of trade deficits. Thus, Argentina suffered from both stagnation and inflation, a condition that came to be known as "stagflation." Borrowing from abroad could serve as a stopgap, but sooner or later there would be a balance of payments crisis in which Argentina would teeter on the verge of default and bankruptcy.[3]

Such crises frequently led to violent changes of government. The new authorities, usually military officers with civilian orthodox economists as allies, would emphasize the virtues of order, discipline, self-restraint, efficiency, balanced budgets, investor confidence, and the need for foreign capital. Translated into policy, these meant currency devaluations to boost exports, wage freezes, strict controls on printing money and extending bank credit, and attempts to make Argentina seem attractive to foreign investors. The downside results inevitably were declining real wages, rising unemployment, and a snowballing number of bankruptcies by Argentine companies that were too poorly capitalized and inefficient to survive without considerable help from the government. The chief beneficiaries were the big agricultural exporters and foreign companies who bought up failing local manufacturers at bargain prices. Soon the populists would be accusing the conservative government leaders of being part of a sinister web of international finance. The political pendulum would then swing again, bringing to power a more interventionist government determined to control all key economic factors so as to ensure "national economic sovereignty."

Between Perón's downfall in September 1955 and Menem's taking office in July 1989 these sudden, violent swings in political fortunes produced 17 presidents in 34 years, for an average of only two years in office, although the Constitution called for a six-year term. Nine presidents were military men, and only eight were civilians. Of those eight civilians, only five were elected, and one, Isabel Perón, succeeded her deceased husband constitutionally as vice president. Five of the military presidents and four civilians were forcibly removed from office. Cabinet ministers concerned with directing economic policy came and went with even greater frequency. The post of Economics Minister was initiated by President Frondizi in 1958, but before that the Lonardi and Aramburu military governments assigned economic decision making to either treasury or finance ministers. All in all, there were 38 of these economic "czars" during those 34 years. The average minister in charge of the economy served less than a year. Most served for only a few months, and a couple of them were in office for only a few days![4]

By the mid-1970s it was clear that this situation could not continue. Although the state was everywhere with its intricate web of incentives, rules, and restrictions, it had become a battlefield in which the major pressure groups—the military, labor, *estancieros,* and industrialists—fought each other for larger shares of a shrinking economic pie. The March 1976 coup that replaced Isabel Perón with the Proceso aimed not only at uprooting leftist terrorism but also at removing the economic conditions that encouraged extremism. General Jorge Videla's economics minister, José Martínez de Hoz, sought to reduce the size of the state by privatizing most of its companies. Downsizing the state and opening the economy to freer trade would also break the power of entrenched business and labor interests. His attempts failed, partly because there was little public support for them. Economic liberalism was viewed as an elitist doctrine that favored only *estanciero* interests. The military also refused to sell off any of its enterprises and vetoed any suggestion that it discipline its own "defense" spending.[5]

The Proceso's ineffectual attempts at reform were followed by a return to the closed economy. Alfonsín not only refused to pay on Argentina's foreign debt but also increased tariffs and issued a long list of goods that could not be imported. Economic policymaking resembled Perón's old corporatist system in which labor, business, and government leaders would work out a plan covering wages, credit, public expenditure, prices, and production goals. All the participants would then pledge themselves to abide by it.[6] Government spending also remained high, at around 56 percent of the GNP (not taking into account the growing "underground economy"). About 40 percent of all spending went to the funding of state enterprises and their deficits; about one-fourth was allocated to the social security system, whose obligations were becoming more pressing as the population was ageing; some 17 percent went to the Federal Government bureaucracy; and another 18 percent was claimed by the provinces and the Federal District (the city of Buenos Aires) under the Constitution's requirement for revenue-sharing.[7]

By 1987 the state-owned companies, excluding those run by the military, were costing the Treasury over $3 billion a year. Although Fabricaciones Militares published no figures about its expenditures, losses, workforce, or output, its estimated deficit in 1980 was around $560 million. There is no reason to believe that this military conglomerate had gotten more efficient over the next seven years; to the contrary, its losses would almost certainly have been greater. Still, Congress specifically exempted the thirteen largest state enterprises and Fabricaciones Militares from any privatization schemes. That might still have been justified if the companies had really been contributing to a healthy economy, but in fact their services were deteriorating. YPF (*Yacimientos Petrolíferos Fiscales*), the state oil company, produced less every year, so that by 1987 Argentina was forced to import oil and petroleum byproducts. YPF's finances were so precarious that it had not paid its employees in months. The state railroad company lost about $1.2 million a day throughout 1986. Meanwhile, more than half of its railway network was described by inspectors as being either in "bad" or "unusable" condition. Over 60 percent of the *Empresa Nacional de Telecomunicaciones* (ENTel) telephone network was either "obsolete" or "not working." The Government Accounting Office refused to approve ENTel's budgetary reports because it viewed them as fictitious. The state coal company, YCF (*Yacimientos Carboníferos Fiscales*), may have been more honest in its reporting, but it still never managed to balance its books. The National Grain Board simply refused to send any statements to the Government Accounting Office. *Aerolíneas Argentinas* consistently lost money and piled up debts. ELMA (*Empresas Líneas Marítimas Argentinas*), the merchant fleet, was kept afloat by the lobbying pressure of the powerful Seamen's Union and Dockworkers' Union. They also forced the company to hire many more workers than necessary and blocked the introduction container shipping. SEGBA (*Servicios Eléctricos del Gran Buenos Aires,* the electricity company supplying Buenos Aires), Gas del Estado, Agua y Energía, and ENCOtel (*Empresa Nacional de Correos y Telégrafos,* the state postal and telegraph company) were all heavily featherbedded, inefficient drains on the Treasury.[8] In response to rising public criticism, Alfonsín created a Directorate of Public Enterprises (DEP) to oversee the state companies. Enrique Olivera, an economist and manager at the Banco Francés, became DEP's president, but soon quit when he saw all his initiatives being blocked by either the Ministry of Economy or the Ministry of Public Works.[9]

Unable to close the public sector's budgetary deficits through privatization or greater efficiency, Alfonsín sought to bring in more revenue through high export taxes, even though they discouraged the earning of foreign exchange. That was necessary because most other taxes were evaded. Treasury Secretary Mario Brodersohn noted in 1986 that 40 percent of the names on the official tax register had false addresses. The Internal Revenue Service (DGI) estimated that only 13 percent of all registered Argentine citizens actually paid all the taxes they owed and that tax evasion cost the Treasury about $20 billion a year. Argentina had a virile underground economy that some estimates placed at between a third and a half of the GDP. Many small companies evaded the controls of an under-staffed bureaucracy and sold almost all their products on the black market. The underground economy also dealt in foreign currencies, furnished employees who worked for cash outside the labor and social security laws, and provided loans to trusted clients at above the legal interest rate. Around 40 percent of the country's industrial labor force was believed to be unregistered, but for very small firms it was close to 100 percent. Those workers were paid about half of what union labor got, but they paid no taxes on their wages nor any social security contributions.[10]

The underground economy also facilitated illegal transfers of money out of the country. Businesses that had overseas branches could convert pesos into dollars and put those dollars into foreign bank accounts quite easily by under-invoicing their exports and over-invoicing their imports. Another trick was "back-to-back lending." Whenever the government overvalued the peso, a clever Argentine entrepreneur would open an account in a foreign bank. Using his deposit as a guarantee, he would then get that bank to grant him a line of credit, in dollars. With those dollars he would buy pesos on the black market at below the official rate, which he would then take to the Central Bank and exchange them for artificially low-priced dollars. Then he would pay off his loan at the foreign bank and pocket a tidy profit. Other Argentines with fewer opportunities for such sophisticated methods of capital flight would simply try to smuggle goods or dollars out of the country. The total amount of capital leaving Argentina illegally every year was impossible to gauge with precision, but estimates varied from $2 billion to almost $9 billion. In addition, another $5 billion was thought to be hidden, in dollars, in safety deposit boxes or in people's homes.[11]

Not only was money flowing out of Argentina illegally, but foreign companies were gradually downsizing their investments as well. A shrinking economy and widespread tax evasion left Alfonsín with few choices for bringing inflation under control and stimulating production. One option was to promise that the government would hold the line on printing more pesos if business and labor would accept price and wage controls. That was the essence of the June 1985 Austral Plan, so called because Alfonsín issued a new currency, called the *austral,* to symbolize the government's strong commitment to the plan. The public's reaction was enthusiastic. The president's poll ratings, which had been sagging badly, shot up. So did the price of shares on the Bolsa. Conversely, inflation came down, from just over 25 percent to less than 5 percent. In the November congressional elections, voters rewarded the Radicals with a gain of one seat in the Chamber of Deputies, while their Peronist rivals lost eight.

It gradually became evident, however, that the Alfonsín government was not really holding the line on spending; all it was doing was delaying its payments to suppliers and holding up paychecks to teachers, policemen, and civil servants. Once the ruse became evident, there was no way for the government to impose wage and price controls. Inflation once again began its relentless upward climb.

The government tried to win back public confidence by introducing new stabilization plans: first the *australito,* later the Plan Primavera, but without success. In the September 1987 congressional elections, with inflation running over 100 percent, the Radicals lost their majority in the Chamber, while the Peronists regained lost ground.[12]

Desperate for money, the Alfonsín government issued a great number of bonds paying returns considerably higher than those for savings accounts or stock dividends. Each issue had a name, each was payable in a certain currency, and each carried a different interest rate. The earlier bonds, like BAGON, TIDOL, TACAM, and BARRA, were payable in *australes;* but as it became clear that the government's debts to bondholders amounted to more *australes* than were available at the Central Bank, a new dollar-denominated bond called BONEX was issued. Holders of earlier bonds could trade them in for BONEX bonds at an exchange rate of 135 *australes* to the dollar—a good bargain, since the dollar was then trading on the black market at 300 to one. That sort of manipulation was necessary because the government simply lacked credibility. It could force local banks to buy its bonds, and it did; but to attract individual investors, it had to offer very high rates of interest. At a time when U.S. Treasury bonds were paying 8.7 percent and dollar-denominated Uruguayan treasury bonds were paying between 8 and 11 percent, the Argentine BONEX (Series 80) was paying 33.9 percent, and *austral*-denominated bonds like BAGON and TIDOL were paying 50.5 percent and 176 percent, respectively. Roberto Lavagna, a Peronist who served briefly as secretary of industry and commerce, criticized this "festival of bonds" for competing with the private sector for investment capital, thus preventing Argentina's economic recuperation. He predicted that the country's financial system would collapse when it finally became clear that the government would not be able to pay off its massive debts.[13]

By 1989 both the internal and the foreign debts were regarded as being unpayable. Fearing a collapse of the banking system, Argentines were shifting their accounts to the local branches of foreign banks, which they considered to be safer. Capital flight was accelerating, while foreign and domestic investment were sharply cut back. Private investment at the beginning of Alfonsín's administration was over 14 percent of the GNP, but now it was down to 8 percent. The World Bank would extend no more loans until serious reforms were undertaken. In London, Argentine government bonds were selling on the secondary market at 22 percent of their face value: less than those of Brazil, Chile, Colombia, Ecuador, Mexico, or Venezuela. But the worst aspect of the growing crisis was hyper-inflation, which had reached 3,000 percent at the beginning of the year and would top out at 4,923 percent (or about 200 percent a month) by the time Alfonsín resigned in July.[14]

Hyper-inflation provided Carlos Menem with a blank check to institute reforms because it so disrupted daily life in Argentina, including all financial and economic arrangements. Production halted for lack of investment, and also because no one knew what prices to charge. If a merchant stayed open, he had to guess what to charge for his goods, and usually he would add a little extra "just in case." In super-markets, price changes were announced frequently over a loudspeaker, so that a loaf of bread or a bottle of milk might cost more by the time a customer reached the checkout. Many shops simply shut their doors. By the same token, wages eroded before they could be spent, and workers faced layoffs as factories and stores closed. Pensioners fared even worse. By the time their monthly checks arrived, they were almost worthless. For the same reason, no one put away money in the bank. It was impossible to make any long-term plans. Public services deteriorated, absenteeism left offices short of staff, repairs were neglected, crime was on the rise. Workers everywhere were on strike, with labor violence often spilling out into the streets and disrupting traffic. Family life deteriorated as members lived under constant tension. Fathers and mothers were out of work, while school closings meant that children were running around the neighborhood unsupervised. Alfonsín's decision to resign early and turn over the presidency to Menem came in the wake of huge riots in the industrial suburbs of Buenos Aires and cities in the interior such as Córdoba, Rosario, and Mendoza. Mobs broke into shuttered grocery stores and other commercial shops and looted them. When the police tried to stop them, they were met with flaming barricades of automobile tires soaked in gasoline—and sometimes with sniper fire. Looters frequently set fire to the buildings as they left.[15]

THE BUSINESS ELITES

As the situation worsened, even those businessmen who traditionally depended on political influence and state patronage began to view the old system as having reached its end. The last few years had seen the collapse of some of Argentina's most important firms. La Celulosa, Argentina's largest paper company, had sold out to Citigroup's investment arm. Other notable bankruptcies were the Cerro Negro construction materials company; Bonafide, a producer of coffee and desserts; and Noel, an old, established manufacturer of candies. Some of Argentina's biggest conglomerates, such as Bunge & Born, the Bridas oil company, and Garovaglio & Zorraquín, had survived so far, but were weakened. If the crisis went on much longer, many more leading companies would be heading for bankruptcy. Businessmen who might have hung on to the Radicals out of fear of Menem's caudillo style, now backed him with their fingers crossed.

Argentine capitalists were fragmented into many competing interests, which is why they traditionally exerted less political influence than might be expected. Industrialists, farmers, merchants, and financiers might agree on the need to protect private property and rein in trade union power, but beyond that they would find it difficult to cooperate. Various umbrella organizations were created over the years, but each one eventually failed. Agriculturalists and merchants tended to be free trade liberals, but many industrialists favored some degree of protectionism—although the ones who processed local natural resources, such as the food and beverage industries, were also free-traders. These agro-businesses accounted for over 70 percent of Argentina's industrial exports.[16]

Each of these groups was further divided into organizations representing distinct and often antagonistic interests. The *Sociedad Rural Argentina* (SRA) represented the largest *estancieros;* medium-sized farmers and ranchers were in the *Confederación Rural Argentina* (CRA); small producers and tenant farmers joined the *Federación Agraria Argentina* (FAA); and the *Confederación Intercooperativa Agropecuaria* (CONINAGRO) represented the agrarian cooperatives. Industrialists also were divided. Most of them belonged to the Unión Industrial Argentina (UIA) but were split into two contending factions: the Movimiento Industrial Argentina (MIA) and the Movimiento Industrial Nacional (MIN). MIA grouped together the more free enterprise and export-oriented industrialists, among whom the food processing companies and the oil and mineral exporting companies were the most influential. MIN tended to represent both small industrialists from the country's interior provinces or larger companies with close ties to the state as suppliers and contractors. The metallurgical, construction, and textile industries were the most influential components of this faction, which tended to be more oriented toward the domestic market and to favor protectionism. The two factions were not homogeneous or rigidly opposed to each other, however. Depending on the issue, members of one faction would vote with the other side.

There also was a holdover from the Peronist corporativist period called the *Confederación General Económica* (CGE) that had temporarily succeeded in forcing all segments of the business class to come together in a single organization. Its agricultural section was called the *Confederación de Producción* (CP), and before it was dissolved by the Proceso, it attracted some small farmers. The CGE also had a *Confederación de Industria* (CI) and a section for small merchants, called the *Confederación de Comercio* (CC). The big merchants, however, belonged to the Argentine Chamber of Commerce (CAC). The financial sector's peak organization for domestic bankers was the Association of Argentine Banks (ADEBA), while the big foreign banks had their Association of Banks of the Argentine Republic (ABRA). The Bolsa de Comercio were the brokers on the Buenos Aires stock exchange.

Within these broad categories of agriculture, industry, and commerce, there were other divisions: ranchers versus farmers, manufacturing versus mining or construction, wholesalers versus retailers, large companies versus small, foreign companies versus domestic. Even within these sub-categories, interests diverged according to what was being produced. Each field had its own chamber to lobby for it.[17]

Argentine companies were further weakened by the fact that most of them were family-owned, more like European firms than like those of the United States, where corporations have largely replaced family enterprises at the top levels of the economy. The corporation is a more advanced form of business institution because it is more efficient at raising large sums of capital by issuing stock that attracts numerous investors. It is also more flexible at coordinating the components of large, complex organizations. By keeping ownership and management separate, it is able (at least theoretically) to recruit its executives from a wider talent pool. By contrast, most Argentine companies were family-owned, often run by the founder himself or an heir. Most didn't offer shares on the Bolsa, and if they did, they usually made certain that the family controlled a majority. Such closely held corporations were mainly legal devices to protect the family against ruinous lawsuits. Some were organized as conglomerates, with a holding company supervising several subsidiaries. Even so, family members managed all of the conglomerate's holdings. Often a conglomerate acquired its own bank, using depositors' money to provide loans to its subsidiaries.

The Pérez Companc Group was a typical Argentine conglomerate. Its founder, Carlos Alberto Pérez Companc, bought decommissioned U.S. Navy vessels after World War II and began transporting cargo between Buenos Aires and Patagonia. Over the years he branched out into maritime insurance, oilfield maintenance, and eventually oil drilling. By the 1990s the conglomerate was headed by Jorge Gregorio ("Goyo") Pérez Companc, an adopted son, and its total holdings spread over thirty-three companies, including Argentina's largest private bank, the Banco Río de La Plata. Its interests encompassed oil, gas, electric power, insurance, shipping, telephones, construction, hotels, shopping centers, and large estancias. It also had a charitable foundation, which the tax authorities accused of using tax-free money to give interest-free loans to the conglomerate's various companies.[18]

Perhaps even more characteristic is the empire built by Francisco Macri, a quintessential "self-made man." He arrived in Buenos Aires from Italy in 1949, worked as a bricklayer while studying engineering at night, and finally started a small construction company. His reputation grew because he was careful to finish his jobs on time and avoid cost overruns. His Italian background eventually helped him become a subcontractor for Fiat, and that, in turn, led to government contracts. Although construction was Macri's core business, he branched out into manufacturing car radios, garbage collection, street repairs, telephone maintenance, oil and gas, and electronics. He also acquired a large block of shares in the Banco de Italia y Río de la Plata and became its president. Then Fiat loaned him the money to take over its automobile plant in Córdoba, which he renamed Sevel, to give his company a more national image. By the 1990s this former bricklayer owned a billion-dollar conglomerate headed by a holding company called SOCMA (Sociedad Macri, S.A.).

Other Argentine conglomerates fit this same general pattern. Technit, the largest conglomerate of all, was founded by Agostino Rocca, an Italian steel executive who had run Finsider, Mussolini's steel monopoly. Forced to flee Italy after the war, he came to Argentina in 1945 and began an engineering works with the help of Italian capital and encouragement from Perón. The original company, called Dalmine, produced steel pipelines for the state oil company, YPF, then branched out into heavy mechanical equipment and steel girders. In 1962 Rocca launched a steel mill, Propulsora, and set up Technit as a holding company over his expanding empire. After his death in 1978, his son Roberto took over.

In a similar fashion, Amalia Lacroze de Fortabat took over the Loma Negra cement company after her husband died in 1976. Alfredo Fortabat had started

Loma Negra after discovering large calcium deposits on some of his estancias back in the 1940s. He was an early supporter of Perón, which paid off handsomely in government contracts. Amalia proved to be an even better executive, however, greatly increasing Loma Negra's operations and profitability until it became not just Argentina's largest producer of construction materials but also a holding company for a vast array of investments.

Bridas, second only to Pérez Companc among Argentine oil companies, was started in the 1960s by Alejandro Bulgheroni, a businessman from Mendoza whose grandparents had immigrated from Italy in the previous century. He invested in some oilfield equipment being sold at a bargain by Amoco, one of several foreign oil companies whose contracts had been annulled by the government in 1964. At first, Bridas operated as a junior partner with YPF or with private local companies like Pérez Companc or Astra, but in 1976 it joined with a French company to land a contract for operating a major oil platform. After that, Bulgheroni won other drilling contracts and quickly became a millionaire. Unfortunately, that attracted the attention of the Montoneros, who, using Bulgheroni's beloved nephew as bait, kidnapped him. Although he was ransomed, the experience left him psychologically damaged, so that his son Carlos had to assume control of the firm. Under Carlos' leadership the company continued to expand, joining with the Army's industrial complex, Fabricaciones Militares, to enter the petrochemicals field. It also bought control of the Banco del Interior y Buenos Aires (BIBA) and branched out into the paper, fishing, and electronics industries.

No survey of Argentina's leading conglomerates at the beginning of the 1990s would be complete without mentioning the Soldati Group, Benito Roggio & Sons, and the Pescarmona Group. The Soldati family is Italian-Swiss in origin and arrived in Argentina in the early twentieth century. Its business ventures began with a drug company, after which it set up a firm to provide coal for the Italo-Argentine Electric Company. In 1927 Pío Soldati formed the Sociedad Comercial del Plata (SCP), to furnish business loans to other members of the Swiss-Argentine community. The family also became major shareholders in the Italo-Argentine Electric Company. Like the Bulgheronis, the Soldatis' growing fortunes attracted the Montoneros' attention, leading to the kidnapping of Santiago Soldati, the eldest son of the Soldati Group's chief, Francisco. Santiago was ransomed, but the Montoneros struck again in November 1979, gunning down Francisco Soldati just after he sold his electric company to the state for a handsome price. The fact that the Economics Minister who arranged the deal, José Martínez de Hoz, was also a member of Italo-Argentine's board excited nationalist feelings, and it is probable that Francisco was murdered in reprisal. Santiago succeeded him at the head of the conglomerate, which then owned about sixty different companies, spread over many different fields.

As with many other Argentine companies, the Benito Roggio & Sons Group traces its origins to Italy. The early founder of the first construction firm, Benito Roggio, was, like Francisco Macri, a bricklayer. He started building modest houses in Córdoba and sent his son, Héctor Marcelo to the university to study architecture. Like many other entrepreneurs, the Roggios courted Perón and thus acquired a contract to build Argentina's first automobile plant, for Kaiser Industries, in Córdoba. In the 1960s the Group took over a local bank, the Banco de Suquía. Always sensitive to the need to nurture political contacts, the Roggios expanded even more under the Proceso, earning almost a billion dollars in public works contracts. The Roggios have been fierce rivals of Francisco Macri in competing for government construction work. In 1986 the City of Córdoba terminated Macri's garbage collection contract and turned over the concession to one of the Roggios' enterprises. Then the Roggios extended the "garbage wars" by picking up contracts from many of the suburbs that ring the City of Buenos Aires, confining Macri's territory to the central city. To add further injury, they beat out Macri to win a contract to extend and manage the City of Buenos Aires' subway lines. Those fights eventually split the Argentine Construction Chamber, with the Macri family pulling out to form a rival Argentine Construction Union.

The Pescarmona Group is also an Italo-Argentine family-run conglomerate whose origins date back to a foundry set up in Mendoza in 1907 to cast replacement parts for machinery used by the wine industry. During the next three decades, the company diversified into producing turbines. Luis Pescarmona, who took over in 1947, successfully lobbied the Perón government for military contracts. Other contracts—from Coca Cola and Otis Elevators—followed, so the rapidly expanding business was placed under a holding company, IMPSA (Industrias Metalúrgicas Pescarmona, S.A). Luis' son, Enrique, became general manager of IMPSA in 1972, after obtaining degrees in engineering and business administration. Under him, IMPSA built a thoroughly modern factory to produce turbines and reactors for the government's nuclear power program—and later for its mega-hydroelectric power plant at Yaciretá, on the Paraguayan border. IMPSA's turbines gained so much favorable comment that Pescarmona was able to begin exporting them.

These examples of Argentine conglomerates display certain common characteristics. All are family-owned and family-operated. Their chief executive officer is either the founder himself or his heir, and all of the CEOs, with the exception of Ms. Lacroze de Fortabat, are either immigrants or their descendants. Each conglomerate started as a single firm but eventually branched out into many different fields: mining, construction, transportation, manufacturing, farming, and, in some cases, finance. All of them cultivated politicians in order to land important state contracts; thus, all of them were part of what Argentines call *la patria contratista:* the cozy relationship between government and business so characteristic of rent-seeking "hot-house capitalism."

The Bunge & Born conglomerate was different. It was a vast agro-industrial empire whose roots extended back to the early nineteenth century when two Dutch immigrant brothers, Karl August and Hugo Bunge, opened up an import-export business that traded between Argentina, Antwerp, the Belgian Congo, and the Dutch colonies in Asia. They also started a bank to finance their trade. In 1884 Ernesto Bunge, Karl August's grandson, formed a partnership with his Belgian immigrant brother-in-law, Jorge Born, to set up a major grain-exporting company, Bunge & Born ("B&B"). Soon afterward they started a flour-milling company called Molinos Río de La Plata, as well as a bank, the Banco Tarapacá, to extend loans to grain farmers. Meanwhile, two of their close friends from Antwerp, Alfredo Hirsch and Jorge Oster, arrived in Argentina and added their capital to the firm. By 1910 B&B had extended its operations into Brazil, Canada, and the United States and had become one of the world's major suppliers of agricultural products, thanks largely to an ingenious telegraph network that gave it a big advantage in the grain trade. That attracted more capital from Europe, which enabled B&B to set up more banks around the world and also expand its interests in Argentina to include grain elevators, warehouses, food processing plants, and companies turning out agricultural byproducts: paints and varnishes made from linseed and cottonseed oils (Alba), cotton textiles (Grafa), sulfuric acid and simple chemicals (Sulfacid and Compañía Química), and pharmaceuticals (Química Hoescht). Molinos Río de La Plata also branched out into vegetable oils, margarine, mayonnaise, rice, and yerba mate. Another new company, Centenera produced bags and containers to hold grain, flour, and edible oils.[19]

Despite this growth and diversification, B&B remained family-owned and managed. A majority of the conglomerate's shares remain in the hands of four families and their in-laws: the Bunges, with regard to B&B's European headquarters in Antwerp; and the Bunges, Borns, Hirschs, and Osters with regard to the South American headquarters in Buenos Aires. Representatives of these families participate directly in the running of their firms and make all the final decisions. They also insist upon a code of company behavior that is at great variance with that of the typical Argentine firm. The rules were laid down, more or less formally, by B&B's dynamic president Mario Hirsch, who greatly expanded its manufacturing operations before his death in 1987. B&B would not engage in direct lobbying (although it would occasionally do favors for some politicians). It also would not sign any contracts with the state, and it would promptly pay all of its taxes. To avoid any situations that might lead to scandal, managers were not to get romantically involved with female employees or even to use the familiar form of address in the office. Also, Hirsch was concerned about keeping B&B's operations secret. No one was to talk about the company to outsiders or employees, and none of the shareholders was permitted to engage in any other businesses on the side.[20]

Jorge Born III, who succeeded Mario Hirsch as B&B's president, violated several of those rules. It was not his fault, of course, that the Montoneros kidnapped him and his brother Juan, in September 1974. Juan was released after two months because of his poor health, but Jorge was held for nine months, until the B&B directors raised $60 million to pay his ransom. It was a record ransom for the modern age, but B&B suffered no great disruption because the financial burden was spread so widely among its different families. It was a different matter, however, when during the Alfonsín period Jorge hired one of his former kidnappers, Rodolfo Galimberti, to be his bodyguard. Later, he and Galimberti became partners in a television consulting firm called Hard Communications. Argentines thought this was carrying Stockholm syndrome too far. But the worst transgression, so far as B&B's families were concerned, was Jorge's decision to involve the company deeply in politics by contributing heavily ($700,000 or $1 million, according to different sources) to Menem's campaign and placing company executives in the cabinet to fashion economic policy.[21]

Nevertheless, Jorge Born saw himself as the leader of Argentina's industrialists, who were facing a serious challenge by the international financial elites: the U.S. Treasury, the International Monetary Fund, the World Bank, and the Paris Club. These were Argentina's chief creditors, and they wanted the new government to start paying on its huge foreign debt. The government would have to raise taxes, and the IMF was insisting that it install a value-added tax (VAT) that would be hard to evade because it would record all sales and purchases abroad. Argentina's creditors were also using the debt as a lever to pry open its protected economy and open the way to free trade and foreign investment. Born convinced other leading Argentine industrialists of the danger and got them to contribute heavily to Menem's campaign as well. By controlling the Economics Ministry, Born expected to preserve as much of the old system as possible.

The "strategic alliance" between Menem and Argentina's big conglomerates ran contrary to the pro-labor tradition of Peronism and to Menem's own previous policies. This anomaly would lead to many quarrels in cabinet meetings between the politicians and the economists, but Menem had seen Alfonsín being overwhelmed by hyper-inflation and the social upheavals it created. He knew that he had to act quickly and boldly before his own popularity evaporated, and so he gave top priority to fundamental economic reform, regardless of the costs.

Chapter Three

Trials and Errors

Carlos Menem was the quintessential pragmatist. As he worked his way up through the ranks of Peronism, he had made his arrangements with trade unionists, provincial elites, Montoneros, military officers in the Proceso, "Renovationists," and "Orthodox Peronists" as circumstances seemed to dictate. When running for president, he spoke as a populist but secretly courted the *alta burguesía*. Argentine "Big Business" viewed him cautiously, but after he made his cabinet appointments, traditional Peronists were shocked. Throughout his ten years in the presidency, Menem had to tread carefully among the factions in his cabinet, whose mutual hatreds seethed just below the surface. Still, he had a powerful trump card in his hand: he had a mandate to end hyperinflation and economic stagnation. The unprecedented economic crisis forced both the Peronists and the Radicals in Congress to grant him extraordinary powers. Two laws, in particular, concentrated enormous power in the presidency: the State Reform Law and the Economic Emergency Law.

The State Reform Law, passed in August 1989, gave the president the power to intervene in any executive agency or state company and either dissolve it or privatize it. The Economic Emergency Law of September 1989 allowed the president to downsize the civil service by removing public employees' right to tenure, suspended all subsidies to private businesses, and granted to foreign investors equal access to local financing and markets. With his control of Congress, Menem quickly added more powers to his arsenal. The Constitution permits a president to issue executive decrees that have the force of law, but these are supposed to have the approval of Congress. Menem pushed further, citing past occasions when presidents issued decrees "of necessity and urgency" during extraordinary crises, such as internal revolts. From the time that the Constitution was adopted in 1853 to Menem's arrival at the Casa Rosada, such emergency decrees had been issued only 35 times; over the next five years, however, Menem resorted to them on 336 occasions. Most of them had to do with controversial changes in tax and labor laws that Menem feared might be blocked in Congress, even by his own party.[1]

Menem was not willing to take any chances, either, that the courts might find his actions unconstitutional. He offered the five sitting justices of the Supreme Court ambassadorships and other prestigious posts to induce them to resign. When none of them would, he threatened to have them impeached. Then, finding that he lacked the necessary two-thirds majority in Congress for impeachment, he got Congress to increase the number of justices from five to nine. Actually, he got to appoint six new justices, because Chief Justice José Severo Caballero resigned after Congress passed the reform. All six were friends of Menem.[2]

Menem's top economic priority was to privatize the state enterprise sector. Given his image as a populist, he had to act boldly in order to gain credibility. Thus, he pushed hard to sell off state companies without too much regard for procedures. His main concerns were to (a) reduce the foreign debt by offering shares to Argentina's creditors, (b) permanently reduce the fiscal deficit by getting rid of loss-producing enterprises, and (c) use cash proceeds from sales to other investors to meet current government expenses. Because of his sense of urgency, he did not bother to haggle with prospective buyers over terms. Under ideal conditions he might have gotten higher prices, and he might have divided the state monopolies into competing private companies for greater efficiency. Instead, he opted for speed. Over the next eight years, he liquidated almost all of the state's economic empire, including the military's portion.[3]

ENTel and Aerolíneas Argentinas were the first to be offered for sale. Not surprisingly, the employees of those companies resisted privatization by using the usual bureaucratic ploys: ignoring directives, pigeonholing papers, and using procedural rules to slow down action. They had been threatened before but always managed to outlast would-be reformers. This time, however, they met a determined government that simply replaced the old management with interventors, backed by committees of technical experts who closed down unprofitable divisions, dismissed redundant employees, and used the police to suppress strikes.

ENTel's sell-off was typical of Menem's approach. First, he named María Julia Alsogaray, the daughter of his foreign debt negotiator, as interventor, with plenary powers to find buyers. The company was to be divided into two monopolies, one for northern Argentina and one for the south. To attract buyers, he raised telephone rates, installed new equipment, and had the federal government assume all of ENTel's debts. When the telephone workers went on strike, he sent in soldiers to man the plants and threatened to fire anyone who failed to return to work—with no indemnities or severance pay. On the other hand, he promised to set aside 10 percent of the shares for the workers. The union gave in. The original sales gave Manufacturer's Hannover, Bell Atlantic, and Pérez Companc most of the northern monopoly; Telefónica de España, CEI-Citicorp (Citibank's local investment arm), the Soldati Group, and Technit formed a consortium to control the southern monopoly. The northern deal fell through, however, when Manufac-turer's Hannover failed to come up with the financing. It and Bell Atlantic were then replaced by Italy's STET and France's TELECOM (both state companies), along with the J.P. Morgan Bank. Only about 10 percent of ENTel's shares were paid for in cash; 40 percent were paid for in three-year notes with three years of grace; about half was purchased through debt-swaps that cancelled around $5.5 billion of Argentina's foreign debt. Overall, ENTel's sales brought about $1.3 billion to the Federal Treasury, and also saved the Treasury at least as much as the $1.46 billion it had paid out to cover the company's deficits in 1989.[4]

PLAN B&B

Businessmen were pragmatists too, which made them unreliable political allies. They followed Jorge Born into the "strategic alliance" with Menem because they had no choice: with Argentina teetering on anarchy, Menem was their only hope. Gilberto Montagna, the UIA's president summed up their feel-ings: "Gentlemen, we're going up in an airplane. If anyone wants to join us, let him. But we have no parachutes. The Unión Industrial Argentina is going to be on board."[5]

Surveys of businessmen's attitudes taken over many years showed that direc-tors of Argentina's largest companies gave lip service to free markets, economic deregulation, privatization of state enterprises, and government fiscal responsibil-ity; however, they consistently blocked any attempts at those kinds of reforms. That was true especially of companies that did business with the state or which aimed at local consumer goods markets. The most resistant to change were the small and medium-sized firms (known in Argentina by the acronym, PYMEs–*pequeño y mediano establecimientos*), who dominated the business scene numerically and provided more than half of all recorded jobs and sales. They had reason to resist, because even under modest free market reforms, such as that undertaken by the Proceso, they tended to get squeezed out very quickly by the big conglomerates. But even big business's willingness to countenance reform was circumstantial, depending upon how it thought change might affect a particular industry or company. Only a small percentage of businessmen favored opening the country to free trade.[6]

Menem split the business elites by giving the big conglomerates incentives to buy into the privatized enterprises and to participate in economic policymaking. As the state companies were sold off, Argentine big business got to own shares in them at attractive prices. Pérez Companc got 25 percent of Telecom and over 14 percent of Telefónica. Another 8 percent of Telefónica went to Technit and 5 percent to the Soldati Group. Four small Argentine companies picked up a total of 12 percent of Aerolíneas, making them junior partners with Spain's Iberia Airlines. Later, when the oil industry was privatized, Menem divided it into many individual companies: oilfields, pipelines, petrochemical plants, oil tankers, and retail outlets. In many cases Argentine companies like Pérez Companc, Bridas,

Astra, Soldati, Technit, and Ipako (Garovaglio y Zorraquín) obtained majority control, either alone or with other Argentine firms. The same was true when Gas del Estado was broken up and privatized piecemeal, and also when the electric power industry was sold off. Thus, after the first wave of purchases about 25 percent of the telephone industry, 31 percent of the electric power industry, 38 percent of the gas industry, and 56 percent of the oil industry were in private Argentine hands. When the state steel factories were sold, Technit bought up over 90 percent of the shares.[7] Even though in most cases the Argentine companies had to borrow heavily to take advantage of their opportunities, a modern domestic capitalist elite seemed to be emerging.

Nevertheless, traditional habits were hard to throw off. Nestor Rapanelli, the Economics Minister, reflected the desire of Jorge Born and other leading Argentine businessmen to retain as much of the old system of state subsidies and protectionism as possible. Plan B&B, as devised by Born and Rapanelli, was certainly no sharp break with the past. While recognizing that chronic fiscal deficits were a main cause of inflation, Rapanelli sought to close them by increasing the "retentions" (taxes) on exports and cancelling export subsidies. Exporters were compensated, he claimed, by his devaluation of the *austral* by 150 percent, fixing it at 650 to the dollar. Exporters were not impressed, however, because the dollar was being quoted on the black market at 800 to 1; moreover, by the time "retentions" were deducted, an exporter who turned in his dollars at the Central Bank would receive only 455 *australes*. Meanwhile, Rapanelli also raised the rates for public services such as gas, oil, electricity, water, railways, and subways. The average increase was about 350 percent. To attack inflation, the economics minister met with the heads of Argentina's 350 largest companies and got them to agree on "voluntary" price controls.

Nevertheless, hyper-inflation remained a problem because government spending was still not under control. The federal government continued to bail out the remaining deficit-ridden state companies and also was required by law to share its revenues with the provinces. Another financial drain was the wage bill for the excessive number of employees at all levels of government. To meet these burdens, Rapanelli had to print more money. Between Menem's taking office in July and mid-November, the money supply grew by over 300 percent.

Rapanelli's attempts to balance spending by raising taxes was largely foiled by the big business conglomerates. Bunge & Born, Technit, Pérez Companc, Pescarmona, and others had contacts within the Economics Ministry that provided them with insider information about pending tax increases or exchange rates, enabling them to adjust their prices in advance or make a quick profit on the currency market. Business elites were especially adept at currency speculating. During the latter half of 1989 they were busily trying to bring off a financial coup by buying up dollars on the black market to drive down the value of the *austral*. The *austral's* legal exchange rate was set at 650 to the dollar, and so far it was holding up at that price because of the public's optimism about Menem's determination to stabilize the economy; but eventually speculators would undermine it. Then the government would have to devalue the currency, and the speculators would reap a windfall by purchasing cheap *australes* with appreciated dollars.[8]

Rapanelli was harried from all sides. In August a big Argentine private steel company, Acindar, closed down its huge mill in Villa Constitución, claiming that its ability to export steel was being destroyed by retentions, cuts in export subsidies, and higher electricity rates (the mill indeed used more electricity than the entire neighboring city of Rosario, Argentina's second-largest). It also complained about a new VAT tax Rapanelli had imposed, under pressure from the International Monetary Fund. That step already had cost him his friendship with his former employer, Jorge Born, who attacked him publicly in a four-page manifesto whose contents were widely circulated by the press. The VAT would not produce a fiscal surplus, Born argued, but would discourage investment. Instead of trying to pursue a balanced budget, as the IMF and foreign bankers urged, the government should be encouraging economic growth by lowering taxes. Now Acindar tightened the screws on the government by laying off 5,000 employees.[9]

In addition to those problems, Rapanelli found himself caught in a crossfire between the government's economic liberals, who felt that Plan B&B did not go far enough toward freeing Argentina's markets, and traditional Peronist populists who worried that even modest reforms were eroding the party's mass support. The chief liberals were Domingo Cavallo, the outspoken Foreign Minister, who insisted on privatizing the remaining state enterprises and opening the economy to free trade; Alvaro Alsogaray, the foreign debt negotiator whose daughter, María Julia had negotiated the privatization of ENTel; Javier González Fraga, the Central Bank president; and Rodolfo Frigeri, the Treasury Secretary. González Fraga warned that the economic situation was still fragile. Although the cost of living had come down somewhat, in August and September the *austral* was still declining on the black market as the money supply grew. And although the Central Bank's reserves were higher than before, that was mainly because of the issuance of more government bonds, which only increased the level of indebtedness. There was still a huge fiscal deficit, which would never improve unless there were many more privatizations. Opposing these liberals were Vice President Eduardo Duhalde; Interior Minister Eduardo Bauzá; and the leader of the Peronist bloc in the Chamber of Deputies, José Luis Manzano. These populists called for the "peronization" of the economy—i.e., a return to the corporate state.[10]

The populists won the first battle when González Fraga and Frigeri resigned in October. González Fraga had been forced out by Rapanelli after presenting him with a set of strongly-worded recommendations: free the exchange rate and let the *austral* float; open the country to free trade; privatize more companies; and issue a new charter for the Central Bank that insulated it from political pressures to finance state companies' deficits. Almost immediately after González Fraga's departure, the *austral* plunged to 1,000 to the dollar. Sensing the danger, Menem called a meeting of the top leadership of the UIA, CGT, and the two major political parties to get them to agree to a "social compact" that would freeze prices and wages. Meanwhile, Rapanelli quickly devalued the currency to the black market rate, but there was no holding the line. The next day, 11 December, saw another round of panic buying of dollars that drove the *austral* down to 1,300. A desperate Rapanelli then announced another increase in export taxes (retentions), big hikes in utility rates, and a two-year moratorium on the government's redemption of its bonds that were about to fall due. That effectively dried up the market for future Argentine government bonds. Retail prices jumped by an average of 50 percent, and goods began disappearing from store shelves. Strikes broke out all over the country, the *austral* fell to 1,540, and depositors began withdrawing *australes* from their bank accounts to buy dollars on the black market.

On 14 December Menem met with Jorge Born and told him that Rapanelli would have to go. The next day Rapanelli resigned, but left behind a memo advising Menem to keep Cavallo and Bauzá from interfering with economic policy-making. The former, he said, was scheming to become economics minister himself and would try to sabotage anyone else who held that office; the latter was simply an economic illiterate.

Not long afterward, Jorge Born himself would become a casualty of Plan B&B's failure. Backing a Peronist like Menem, getting Bunge & Born involved in the new government, and his bizarre relationship to Galimberti had stirred up resentment among many of the conglomerate's shareholders, including Born's own brother, Juan. More importantly, he had angered Elena Hirsch, the widow of Born's predecessor, who was a major shareholder and one of Argentina's richest women. Ms. Hirsch had close friendships with other shareholders in Paris and Antwerp, as well as a wide circle of family and friends in Argentina. That, and the fact that the conglomerate's many companies were doing poorly, enabled her to arrange an extraordinary shareholders' conference in June 1991 at which Born was voted out of office—the first time in Bunge & Born's history that an incumbent president was ousted. He was replaced by Ms. Hirsch's nephew, Octavio Caraballo.

THE CRONY CABINET

Disillusioned with the "business community" and its approach to economic problems, Menem now turned to his old crony, Antonio Erman González, whose loyalty to him was unquestionable: The B&B Plan's failure had shown the limitations of the national business elites, who were still dedicated to a closed economy and state protection. Instead of capitalist competition, they sought to use political influence as the way to profits. Even Menem himself was not fully converted to the idea of free markets. The Peronist side of him still believed in an active, interventionist state, but one that was led by politicians, not businessmen. While appointing González to the Economics Ministry, Menem also took Rapanelli's advice and moved Eduardo Bauzá from the Interior Ministry to the Ministry of Health and Social Action. Bauzá could still distribute patronage but would have less contact with local Peronist bosses. Dealing with them would now fall to the new interior minister, Julio Mera Figueroa, who had been Menem's campaign manager. Cavallo stayed on at Foreign Affairs and continued to criticize the economic strategy.

Indeed, the economic situation was serious. The GNP had fallen by 5.2 percent, and industrial production by 7.7 percent in 1989. Retail sales were down sharply, and a growing number of small businesses were going bankrupt. The *austral* dropped to 3,000 to the dollar in January and would plunge to 6,200 by March. Between March 1989 and March 1990, inflation rose by more than 20,000 percent, a record for the postwar world. The looting of supermarkets broke out again in the poorer *barrios* of Buenos Aires, Córdoba, and Rosario. Not surprisingly, all of this took a heavy toll on Menem's popularity. Public opinion polls showed that whereas 71 percent of those interviewed had approved of Menem in October 1989, by February 1990 only 33 percent did; conversely, negative responses to him rose from only 7.5 percent to 37 percent. More than half of the respondents expressed disapproval of the government's economic policies and said they had no faith in its ability to restore prosperity.[11]

González's first steps were to end government controls on prices, interest rates, and exchange rates. He also promised to cut public spending by early retirements, the closure of certain agencies—such as the Mortgage Bank (Banco Hipotecario)—and ending many subsidies. Despite this, he made no effort to control the money supply. The Central Bank continued to print more currency, so that in January alone the amount of *australes* in circulation went from 3.5 billion to 4.5 billion. In February the Argentine Business Council, headed by figures like Jorge Born and Francisco Soldati, called on the government to protect the Central Bank from political pressures to issue more money. The Council also recommended privatizing more agencies such as the Customs Bureau and the social security system, increasing subsidies for non-traditional (i.e., industrial) exports, decentralizing wage bargaining to the level of the individual company, and liberalizing the labor laws to permit more temporary and part-time hiring.[12]

The labor movement was divided and considerably weaker than it had been twenty years earlier. During that time Argentine industry had become more capital-intensive and employed fewer blue-collar workers. By 1990 it was estimated that one out of four workers in manufacturing were in PYMEs, and most of them were unregistered *cuentapropistas* (black market laborers). The trend toward underground employment was also helped along by the prolonged recession that persisted throughout the 1980s, creating an "industrial reserve army" that depressed wages and discouraged strikes. Thus, by the time Menem came to office, the trade union movement was split into at least three broad factions. First, there were the pro-government "collaborationists" of the so-called Group of Fifteen. Their top leader, Jorge Triaca, became Menem's labor minister and, later, his interventor in the privatization of SOMISA, the state steel company. Another "collaborationist" in the government was Luis Barrionuevo, head of the Waiters' Union, who headed the Social Security Administration. Both were corrupt and eventually would be forced out of the government by scandal. But not all "collaborationists" were as bad. Many of them trusted Menem as a fellow

Peronist and liked his willingness to appear before the workers in person to explain the need for change. Second, there were the "militants," led by Lorenzo Miguel of the Metalworkers' Union (UOM), who were neither pro- nor anti-Menem. They were unhappy with privatization and willing to strike for better terms. Menem dealt with them skillfully by granting generous severance packages, reserving 10 percent of the shares in each privatized company for the union to control, and turning over each industry's social welfare funds to the union to manage as well. There were also targeted wage increases for unions that went along with official policy, a tactic which tended to make the "militants" less militant. Finally, there were the "combative" unions, under the leadership of Saúl Ubaldini, head of the beer workers and general secretary of the CGT. Ubaldini opposed privatization, liberalizing the labor laws, and balanced budgets. He was a fearless leader but effective only as long as he could get Lorenzo Miguel's cooperation.

Miguel and Ubaldini threatened a general strike to prevent massive job losses at the recently privatized telephone companies, but ultimately backed down when they learned that Menem wouldn't bargain. Then, in February 1991, Menem used the old Peronist "Law of Professional Associations" to break a strike by railway workers protesting the privatization of the state railroads. After declaring the strike illegal he intervened the union,[13] closed down whole lines and workshops, and began firing workers en masse. New elections for the union's leaders were supervised by government interventors who made certain that the results came out "right." Miguel, a pragmatist, eventually came to terms with Menem, broke with Ubaldini, and became the CGT's general secretary. Strikes declined sharply after that.[14]

Even so, Menem was unable to get Congress to reform the labor laws. Like the UIA and the IMF, he insisted that "flexibilization" was necessary to attract more investment and make Argentine goods more competitive in global markets. "Flexibilization" meant changing workplace rules that created "closed shops," made it nearly impossible to dismiss a worker, restricted an employer's ability to assign different tasks and working hours, required employers to contribute heavily to union insurance plans, mandated an extra month's pay (*aguinaldo*) at the end of each year, and empowered the Labor Ministry to supervise collective bargaining. While Congress willingly approved almost every one of Menem's privatization plans, between 1989 and 1995 it approved only 8 out of 20 proposed labor reforms, and even those that passed were seldom applied in practice because of CGT pressure on the Labor Ministry. The most that Menem could do was to get exemptions for the PYMEs.

Unable to bring down labor costs, Menem and González sought to defeat inflation by a bold, unorthodox stroke: the Plan Bonex. The Central Bank was printing money every month to pay its debts to local commercial banks holding government IOUs. Gonzalez decided to end that inflationary practice by ordering the Central Bank to seize all short-term time deposits of Argentina's private banks, which were held in *australes,* and convert them into ten-year dollar-denominated Treasury bonds called "Bonex-89." Those bonds would then be used to pay off the government's debts to the commercial banks, and they in turn could use the bonds to pay their depositors. According to one approving observer, "this conversion scheme...had the double effect of dramatically reducing the supply of money in the economy on the one hand, and recapitalizing the Central Bank on the other," so that it "ceased to be a source of inflationary pressures."[15]

The *International Currency Review* had a more sour view of Plan Bonex, noting that

with malicious folly, the government invented a new method of trying to cure inflation without stopping its own spending orgy—a method which is unprecedented even in Argentina, for its total disregard of moral values and respect for the individual. The government's "reasoning" went more or less as follows: "Inflation is, after all, the product of too much money chasing too few goods. So let us simply therefore reduce the amount of money. And since we can't do that by stopping government waste, or by issuing any more bonds (since no-one will buy them), or by raising taxes (since no-one will pay them), let's do it by robbing people of their bank accounts."[16]

The seizure happened without warning and affected all time deposits of 1 million *australes* or more (about $500 at the black market rate). The *International Currency Review* reminded readers that: "Since short-term deposits were the only way of storing needed funds at the bank with some sort of hedge against inflation, this drastic measure directly and immediately deprived a large proportion of the population of the money needed for daily living."

Inflation leveled off, temporarily. A new spate of privatizations helped: two government-owned television stations, Channels 11 and 13; the state petrochemical companies; some oilfields of secondary importance; and some companies owned by Fabricaciones Militares. But then recession set in. The Plan Bonex had confiscated the equivalent of around $3 billion, a lot of which was needed, not just for families' daily expenses, but for companies to pay their suppliers and employees. Retail sales plummeted by an estimated 60 percent, and nearly a third of the shops in downtown Buenos Aires went out of business. Unemployment began to rise. Inside the Cabinet a rift began to open as Domingo Cavallo took up the cause of businessmen who were unable to meet their debts because of a lack of liquidity. He and Central Bank vice president Felipe Murolo urged that businessmen be allowed to pay off their bank loans with the new bonds; Antonio Erman González, Alvaro Alsogaray, and Central Bank president Rodolfo Rossi opposed that idea on the part of the bankers, who wanted cash, not bonds. Menem sided with González, so Cavallo had to back off.[17]

FAMILY SCANDALS AND MILITARY THREATS

Menem and Zulema began quarreling again soon after Menem was elected president. She had demanded to sit beside her husband in the Chamber of Deputies during his inauguration; when informed by the Chief of Protocol that the president's family had to sit in the balcony, she threatened to boycott the ceremony. Other spats followed, as he continued to see other women and she took a delight in dabbling in politics. At one point she threatened divorce, whereupon her brothers, Emir and Karim, acted as intermediaries. Using the threat of an open scandal to pressure Menem, they demanded the Foreign Affairs portfolio for Karim, a top advisory post in the Economics Ministry for Emir, and the Ministry of Social Action for Zulema. Menem compromised, but forced them to lower their demands: Karim would be secretary for "Special Affairs" in the Foreign Ministry (from which post he could continue his lucrative contacts with the Middle East); Emir would be a presidential consultant; Amira, Zulema's sister, would continue as Menem's appointments secretary; and Zulema would have to be content with being First Lady—no ministry for her.[18]

Zulema relented, under family pressure, but other blowups soon occurred. After another quarrel she refused to accompany Menem on a September 1989 visit to the United States. Her political activities soon became embarrassing too: she was a strong supporter of the *carapintada* leader, Mohammed Ali Seineldín and even invited him to dinner at the presidential mansion in Olivos. That was an uncomfortable occasion for Menem, who was trying to pick his way cautiously through the minefield of military factionalism. With the intention of pacifying civil-military relations, he had the day before issued pardons to 277 military officers who had either been convicted of human rights violations under the Proceso or had taken part in the three *carapintada* revolts under Alfonsín. Colonel Seineldín was one of the beneficiaries of those pardons. Over dinner the *carapintada* chief urged Menem to go further and extend the pardons to the Proceso's most prominent leaders—Generals Jorge Videla, Roberto Viola, Ramón Camps, Carlos Suárez Mason; Admirals Emilio Massera and Armando Lambruschini; and Brigadier Orlando Agosti. He also hoped to enlist Menem's support for a purge of the military's top echelons that would put the *carapintada* in control. Seineldín was confident of success. After all, the president was known to have worked with Massera during the Proceso and had appointed several *carapintada* sympathizers to his government. Moreover, like Seineldín himself, Menem and Zulema were both *turcos*.[19]

That Menem may have explored some sort of compromise with Seineldín seems evident from the fact that the army's chief of staff, General Isidro Cáceres, made a speech on 23 January 1990 saying that the army would act to preserve order if police forces proved insufficient. This announcement, which had Menem's prior approval, overturned the Defense Law passed under Alfonsín that strictly confined the military's role to defending the nation's frontiers. Menem then issued a decree that made it possible for the military to take part once again in preserving internal order. With that, Italo Luder, the defense minister, resigned. He had been frustrated for some time by the machinations of his undersecretary, Humberto Romero, a *carapintada* sympathizer who now succeeded him at the head of the Defense Ministry.

So far, so good for Colonel Seineldín. But in March the pro-*carapintada* General Cáceres died of a heart attack, and his replacement at the head of the army was General Martín Bonnet, who believed firmly in upholding the fundamental military principles of hierarchy, discipline, and obedience. He soon convinced Menem that the *carapintada* were inimical to all that. Unless the rebels were squelched, there would be *two* armies: one obedient to the civilian authorities and one not.

As time passed and Menem failed to act, Seineldín became more aggressive, touring the country and making speeches attacking the administration's liberal economic policies—which he pointed out were contrary to Menem's campaign pledges and to traditional Peronism. Meanwhile, Menem and Zulema had reverted to open warfare. In February she walked out of the presidential mansion and took an apartment in downtown Buenos Aires, telling the press that her husband was a womanizer (*mujeriego*) and that he had filled his government with corrupt politicians. She complained of threats against her life and hired some *carapintadas* as bodyguards. Soon she returned, however, but only to participate in a particularly violent quarrel on 3 May, after which it was Menem who left the house to bunk in with friends. This time Carlitos and Zulemita, the two spoiled children of a dysfunctional marriage, sided with their mother. But then Zulema went too far. Early one morning in June, people in downtown Buenos Aires found the buildings covered with posters accusing Menem and his Cabinet of corruption. An investigation discovered that they had been produced and distributed by the secretary for tourism, a friend of Zulema's. Immediately, Menem sent his Presidential Guard (*Casa Militar*) to Olivos with orders to expel his wife and children.[20]

Colonel Seineldín also overplayed his hand with Menem. Throughout the year the army's Qualifications Board, which decided on promotions, retirements, and disciplinary matters, had been placing lower-level *carapintadas* under barracks arrest and forcibly retiring their leaders from active service. As Seineldín's case came up for review in November, he grew desperate and sent Menem a thinly veiled threat, telling him to change his policy "before events occur that neither you nor I desire." In reality, Seineldín already had arranged with some active duty officers and NCOs to launch a revolt on 3 December. Seineldín was not to take part in the uprising, however, because General Bonnet put him under arrest for threatening the president. Bonnet and Menem were aware that the revolt was brewing, and Menem had ordered that there would be no negotiations with the *carapintada:* they had to be utterly crushed, once and for all, and quickly.

The last *carapintada* revolt was the bloodiest of all because in some units NCOs overthrew their officers and murdered them. That outraged the loyal troops, who counterattacked without mercy and forced the rebels' unconditional surrender. With order now restored, Menem removed the army's remaining grievances by pardoning the Proceso leaders who were still in prison. Their release in early January 1991 brought protests from human rights groups, but for the armed forces it represented closure on a festering issue.

CORRUPTION SCANDALS

Opinion polls show that nine out of ten Argentines believe that public officials—especially politicians, bureaucrats, judges, and labor leaders—are dishonest. Even the military's officer corps, once considered incorruptible, has been badly tarnished by revelations of widespread smuggling and extortion under the Proceso. Bank scandals, in which unlawful capital flight is facilitated or depositors' funds are misappropriated, are fairly common. But while Argentines are cynical about public officials, they also admit that lawlessness is spread throughout the entire society. Large majorities told pollsters that everyone evaded taxes, bought goods on the black market knowing that they probably were stolen, commonly violated traffic rules, or had witnessed acts of corruption but failed to denounce them. They admitted that they had paid bribes to avoid traffic fines, "greased the wheels" of the bureaucratic machinery, or avoided paying a tax. Carlos Nino, writing on Argentine corruption, observed that: "If...we analyze the way Argentines talk, we realize that to say that something is against the law is a way to start a conversation, not end one." Some authors have estimated that the state loses over $100 million a year in payouts to people making false claims for pensions and family allowances. There are about 300,000 cases a year of people who are long dead but still receive pension checks. The state loses another estimated $2.5 billion through tax evasion.[21]

Carlos Nino attributes the general corruption of Argentine society to anomie. There is an abundant literature on this theme, going back to classics from the 1960s like Juan José Sebrelli's *Buenos Aires, vida cotidiana y alienación;* Julio Mafud's *Psicología de la viveza criolla;* and Ezeqiel Martínez Estrada's *Radiografía de la Pampa (X-Ray of the Pampa).* On the other hand, Adrián Guissarri is more sympathetic to Argentina's "common man." In his view, the underground economy flourishes as self-protection against a lawless state's confiscatory powers, high taxes, invasive bureaucratic regulations, ubiquitous economic controls, restrictions on trade, and occasional property seizures. Locating the origins of the underground economy in the Peronist corporate state of the 1940s, he argues that as state power grew so did the evasive practices of civil society. While the underground economy may be illegal, it is a rational defense against a real threat, and therefore it is ethical. Nino, however, turns Guissani's argument around. For him, the plethora of economic rules and regulations that Argentine bureaucrats generate is in response to a cultural proclivity towards illegality.[22]

Whichever side we might choose in that debate, the causes of anomie and lawlessness are less important for our present study than their economic effects. In addition to lost revenue for the state, the lack of respect for the rule of law discourages investors, both foreign and domestic. Serious investors, as opposed to mere speculators, avoid countries where property rights are insecure, governments default on their financial obligations, and judges are corrupt. Max Weber argued persuasively that modern capitalism's greater dynamism, as compared to earlier forms of private enterprise, stemmed from its origins in the Calvinist ethic—an ethic that combined natural human acquisitiveness with an asceticism that encouraged capital accumulation over consumption, a belief in work as a duty and end in itself, a desire to organize work and production in the most rational manner, and a view of business as a high "calling" that demanded respect for contractual obligations. The fact that the bulk of early capitalists were drawn from the lower middle class revealed, he argued, how widely the "Protestant ethic" had permeated the societies of Northern Europe, where the capitalist revolution first took root, as opposed to places like Italy, where "the universal reign of absolute unscrupulousness in the pursuit of selfish interests in the making of money" held back bourgeois capitalist development.[23]

Argentina had long been under "the universal reign of absolute unscrupulousness," and continued to be under Menem. The president himself was hardly an example of probity as he dashed about the countryside in his new red Ferrari, a gift from a European motorcycle manufacturer seeking to enter the Argentine market. *The Economist* reported that "Argentina's gossip columns are full of news about the free-spending habits of Mr. Menem's family: how his son paid over $1 million for a house in Buenos Aires; how his daughter spent thousands of dollars on clothes in Miami." Menem's political appointees were little better. Mr. Cavallo once blurted out that he could not survive on less than $10,000 a month, which was far more than his salary. Luis Barrionuevo even bragged about the fortune he had compiled, first as union leader and then as head of Social Security. "No one ever made money in this country by working," he said.[24] A number of ministers and agency heads were forced to resign because of corruption scandals, and others were tried for corruption after Menem left office.

Squabbles inside the government over spoils began early, even while Rapanelli was in charge of economic affairs. Emir Yoma and Miguel Angel Vicco (Menem's private secretary) operated an influence-peddling network with the help of Eduardo Bauzá (Interior) and José Luis Manzano. The schemers had a falling-out over the privatization of the Bahía Blanca Petrochemical Complex, however, when it was learned that Bauzá and Manzano were getting a large sum of under-the-table money from Technit, the highest bidder. Rapanelli tried to stop the sale when he learned of this scheme, which led to demands by the culprits that Menem replace him. Bunge & Born fought back by getting the State Intelligence Service (SIDE) to present Menem with a thick dossier on the shady Bahía Blanca negotiations. When those details got out to the rest of the cabinet, Yoma and Vicco, irate because they had been excluded from the deal, got the losing bidder, Garovaglio & Zorraquín, to complain to Menem. Then Bauzá and Manzano, seeing their plans unraveling, met with Yoma and Vicco to invite them to participate. After patching up their quarrel, these *políticos* then went on to attack Rapanelli and demand the "peronization" of the economy. Rapanelli, already in a weak position because of runaway inflation, was soon forced to resign.[25]

Bauzá continued to be a source of embarrassment to the administration even after González replaced Rapanelli. In February 1990 he was accused of fraud in the purchase of some 1,300,000 laboratory coats that Argentine schoolchildren are often required to wear. As minister of Health and Education, he had agreed to pay the supplier more than three times the usual price, presumably in return for a kickback. The deal was investigated by the administrative prosecutor (*Procurador General*), who took the case to the Tribunal of Accounts, a watchdog institution set up decades earlier to guard against corruption in government. Halfway through the hearing, however, Menem issued an executive decree abolishing the Tribunal of Accounts, replacing it with an Office of Controller-General, staffed by more of Menem's friends. He also dismissed the *Procurador General*.[26]

Emir Yoma finally was forced out of the government in December 1990 when he tried to extort money from the U.S.-owned Swift Meat-packing Company. Swift wanted to build a model slaughterhouse in Rosario and had asked Yoma to facilitate a permit to import the necessary machinery. Yoma got the permit but decided to keep it in his pocket until he was paid a large sum in cash and given one of the company's airplanes, valued at $400,000. Instead of paying the bribe, Swift complained to the U.S. ambassador, Terence Todman, who then sent copies of Swift's complaint to Antonio Erman González and Domingo Cavallo, along with a cover letter saying that he had received similar complaints from seven other U.S. companies trying to do business in Argentina. Somehow, Horacio Verbitsky, the editor of the muckraking daily *Página 12,* got hold of a copy of Todman's letter and published it, causing a sensation. Menem summoned a press conference at which he denied the charges and called Verbitsky's news story a "case of journalistic delinquency." Todman responded with his own press conference in which he backed up Verbitsky and added that both he and Swift had been under intense pressure from the government to retract the charges. Then Menem had to call a second press conference to call Todman a liar and deny that any pressure tactics had been used. Todman then responded with *his* second press conference at which he affirmed all that he had alleged.

Just as Argentina and the United States seemed on the verge of a breach in diplomatic relations, Domingo Cavallo returned from a vacation in Cancun. At a cabinet meeting, he informed everyone present that he had checked out Todman and Swift's accusations and found them to be accurate to the last detail. Moreover, if steps were not taken to rectify the matter, Swift was ready to close down its extensive operations in Argentina, and he, Cavallo, would resign from the government. At that point Raúl Granillo Ocampo, Menem's legal and technical secretary and longtime close friend (but a supporter of close ties with the United States), sided with Cavallo. Menem pretended to be surprised, called Emir Yoma into the meeting and had Cavallo repeat what he had just said. Emir was quick to understand that Menem was now distancing himself from the scandal and would no longer shield him, so he confessed.[27]

GOVERNMENT SHAKEUP

December 1990 had been a stressful month for Menem, with the *carapintada* revolt and the outbreak of "Swiftgate." Also, inflation had shot up again, after having leveled off at mid-year. The *austral,* which had been quoted at 1,540 to the dollar when González first took over, seemed to stabilize at 6,000 in July. But then it hit 7,000 in December and almost 9,000 in January. That was due in part to the *carapintada* uprising, which shook the public's confidence; but it also was caused by the government's backsliding into its old habit of printing money to cover its deficits. Although its revenues were up, thanks to privatizing some $16.5 billion worth of state enterprises and doubling the number of federal tax collectors, its spending on welfare payments had risen as some 85,000 state enterprise employees and 217,000 federal, state, and local bureaucrats were stricken from the public payrolls. As unemployment climbed to about 15 percent of the potential workforce and industrial real wages declined by between 15 and 20 percent, the economy began to slip into recession, without bringing down inflation. The GDP declined by half a percentage point in 1990, but manufacturing was down by over 7 percent. In brief, it was back to "stagflation." Menem's popularity ratings sank to an alarming 29 percent as 1991 began, and that provoked a major cabinet reshuffle.[28]

After a frustrating year, Antonio Erman González surrendered the economics portfolio to Domingo Cavallo, who had sought it for so long. González moved to the Ministry of Defense, replacing the much-respected Peronist Guido Di Tella, who only a few days previously had taken the job away from the pro-*carapintada* Humberto Romero. Di Tella then took Cavallo's place as foreign affairs minister. Rodolfo Díaz was the new labor minister; and Avelino Porto, one of the founders of the new private University of Belgrano replaced Alberto Kohan at Health. (Kohan, a *menemista de la primera hora,* had already replaced the ethically challenged Eduardo Bauzá in that office a few months previously, having moved over to the cabinet after being chief administrator of the Presidential Office.) Alvaro Alsogaray, who often had clashed with Cavallo, was dropped, as were Jorge Triaca (Labor) and Roberto Dromi (Public Works), both of whom were alleged to have demanded bribes from investors bidding on the privatized companies. Triaca became the interventor of SOMISA, the giant state steel mill, where he would again be named in a bribery scandal; Dromi was made ambassador to Spain, but left behind such a stench of corruption that the Public Works Ministry was abolished.

On the surface, these changes seemed to be little more than minor tinkering: the cosmetic replacement of embarrassing ministers with some men of better reputation. Very soon, however, Argentina would be carried along on a wave of radical reform by the new economics minister, Domingo Cavallo.

Chapter Four

Free Markets and Convertibility

Domingo Cavallo was a brilliant man—and knew it. Born in 1946, the son of a broom manufacturer in the town of San Francisco, in Córdoba Province, he had a long string of university degrees after his name: bachelor's degrees in accounting and economics, and a doctorate in economics, all from the University of Córdoba; and a second doctorate in economics from Harvard. He had worked in the provincial government as undersecretary for Development and then as one of the directors of the Provincial Bank. That was during the Ongania/Lanusse era, when he was still in his twenties. Those jobs provided him with contacts in the military. Later, General Videla appointed him undersecretary of Interior, because of his provincial contacts, and then gave him a big promotion to president of the Central Bank. In the latter post he was largely responsible for having the federal government assume payment for the domestic and foreign debts of many of the biggest private companies in Argentina. That saved the heavily indebted companies and made him their hero, but it greatly raised the level of the state's public debt. After the Proceso, Cavallo joined the Mediterranean Foundation, a pro-free market "think-tank" in Córdoba, and also became a member of the Peronist Party. He was a close friend of Córdoba's governor, José Manuel de la Sota, a Peronist "revisionist," and served as a federal deputy from 1985 to 1989. Then Menem, as part of his outreach to the business world, brought him into his cabinet as foreign minister.

Cavallo performed his duties well as foreign minister, but his real ambition was to run Argentina's economy as head of the Economics Ministry. He was contemptuous of Rapanelli and González for their failed attempts to control inflation and stimulate growth, and his ego periodically prompted him to make vehement public criticisms of their strategies. Those might have cost him his job, but his high reputation in business circles gave him a certain independence in the Menem government. Finally, at the end of January 1991, a desperate Menem turned the Economics Ministry over to him.

As economics minister Cavallo has been described as "dynamic," "tenacious," "firm," "confident," and a man of "inexhaustible energy." However, the same authors also describe him as "egotistic," "unpredictable," "obstinate," and "mercurial." Those adjectives might also be applied to Carlos Menem, and the wonder is that the two men were able to work together. Nevertheless, they did, at least for a few years. Menem gave Cavallo free rein to pursue a radical new economic strategy as the last chance to save his floundering administration, reserving for himself the job of clearing away political obstacles to Cavallo's policies.[1]

Cavallo's long-term goal was to create a strong, independent Argentine capitalist class. To cure local businessmen of their dependence on the state, he intended to open the economy to global competition, eliminate artificial controls on economic behavior, and encourage domestic industry to take advantage of the privatization process. It was difficult to sell this idea to industrialists, who—despite their public rhetoric—were fearful of foreign competition. They knew, deep down, that foreign companies were technologically and organizationally superior, and also had better access to large amounts of credit. Nevertheless, the UIA pretended to go along. By muting its dissent, it hoped to leave open channels of communication with the government through which it could try to negotiate exemptions, exceptions, and compromises.[2]

THE CONVERTIBILITY PLAN

Cavallo's grand strategy, unveiled at the end of April 1991, was called "The Convertibility Plan" because of its bold central feature: the free convertibility of the *austral* and the dollar, at a rate of 10,000 to 1. Wedded to this was a new law requiring the Central Bank to keep on hand exchange reserves, in dollars or gold, equal to 100 percent of the country's money supply. The bank would be allowed to print more money *only* if its exchange reserves grew by the same amount; conversely, if its exchange reserves decreased, it would have to tighten the money supply. In short, there would be no more irresponsible printing of money to cover government deficits. At the time the plan was announced, the Central Bank's reserves totaled about $4 billion, of which $3.2 billion was set aside to cover the money supply.

The plan immediately had a favorable psychological impact, generating public confidence in the government's sincerity about controlling inflation. And, indeed, inflation came down quickly, from a rate of 5.5 percent a month in April to 2.8 percent in May, and to 1.3 percent at the end of August—the lowest it had been since 1974. The Central Bank's exchange reserves swelled as foreign capital poured in to take advantage of a new round of privatizations, along with an estimated $6 billion from overseas accounts held by Argentines. That allowed an expansion in the money supply and, together with lowered interest rates, stimulated a 6 percent increase in economic growth. Suddenly, the Buenos Aires Bolsa, where daily sales of stocks averaged $7.9 million at the beginning of August boomed to $65 million a day, just before the midterm Congressional and provincial elections of September/October. Cavallo was careful to give Menem full credit for the economic turnaround. Despite the Radicals' gloomy warnings about "hyper-presidentialism," Menem's personal poll ratings were back above 50 percent, and three-fourths of the public approved of the Convertibility Plan. Not surprisingly, the Peronists swept almost all of the midterm races.[3]

The Convertibility Plan received broad support initially from almost all interest groups. Even the labor movement, with the exception of Ubaldini's faction, was willing to give it a try. After all, falling inflation improved real wages. The *estancieros* in the Sociedad Rural were enthusiastic. The press, on the whole, wrote favorably about the plan's boldness and contrasted Menem's strong leadership with Alfonsín's indecisiveness. The UIA promised its support, but also expressed its opposition to opening the country to foreign imports. The industrialists' fears were reflected in the UIA's May 1991 internal elections, when Gilberto Monagna, the incumbent president, was narrowly defeated by Israel Mahler. Montagna, who owned the Terrabussi Biscuit Company, had represented the more pro-free trade MIA faction; Mahler, a metallurgical magnate, was supported by the more protectionist MIN. After winning, Mahler wrote Cavallo expressing the UIA's willingness to help stabilize the economy, but also made it clear that the industrialists expected more government aid in the form of tariffs, subsidies, lower taxes (including employers' Social Security contributions), and more flexible labor laws.[4]

Menem met with the UIA leaders at the beginning of September and promised them tax cuts and easy loans, but he could go only so far without undermining Cavallo. Inevitably, the Convertibility Plan would require painful sacrifices from both business and labor if it was to succeed. Avoiding deficits meant drastic cuts in spending along with increases in revenue. One obvious place to cut was in the wide range of government subsidies to business: "industrial promotion" schemes designed to encourage firms to locate in distant provinces, below-market prices for the state enterprises' goods and services, below-market interest rates for government loans, and "buy national" laws that gave local industries monopolies. All of those would be cancelled during the coming year. Privatization was another way to reduce government expenditures, and Cavallo stepped up the pace. More oilfields were sold off in 1991, and after the elections were over, still more were put up for sale. In 1992 the government's steel mills, big electrical power plants, water and sanitation companies, Gas del Estado, several railway lines, and the Buenos Aires subway system went on the block. That was followed in 1993 by the sale of the Buenos Aires commuter railways, more electrical power companies, the highway system (which was converted into toll roads), and the state oil company, Yacimientos Petrolíferos Fiscales (YPF). Also, much of the Social Security system was privatized.

In most cases, these divestitures did not provoke a great public outcry, except among the state employees who lost their jobs. The state enterprises were so inefficient and featherbedded that there was little to mourn about their sales. The railroads, for example, were overstaffed, employing some 90,000 people whose wages accounted for about three-fourths of all expenditures. The remaining money was not enough to replace or maintain their increasingly obsolete engines, run-down cars, or worn-out tracks and roadbeds. Though their official budget was around $300 million, in 1990 they ran a $900 million deficit. The state electric companies were no better. SEGBA, which supplied Greater Buenos Aires, operated with worn-out equipment and deteriorating transmission lines, partly because other state enterprises refused to pay their electricity bills and partly because electricity rates were kept very low for political reasons. Its main generator, the Atucha I nuclear power plant, was shut down for a long period in 1989 because of broken-down equipment, which resulted in power outages and brown-outs in the capital, whose residents retaliated by refusing to pay their bills. In all, SEGBA collected only 3 billion *australes* in revenues while spending almost 30 billion, much of that on its employees whose union leaders sat on the company's Board of Directors. The Social Security fund was partly privatized too, to protect the pensions, which often in the past had not been paid because the fund had been raided to cover other "urgent" government needs. Similarly, the highway system was on the verge of collapse when Menem authorized its privatization. Only 30 percent of the roads were in good repair. It cost the federal government some $150 million annually just to keep the system from collapsing altogether, and the ongoing financial crisis made it highly unlikely that the situation would improve.[5]

Even YPF's sale came to be seen as inevitable, despite the history of oil as a hot-button issue in Argentina ever since the first fields were discovered in 1907. Nationalists always had rallied around the company, despite its inefficiencies, rather than see a precious natural resource under the control of foreigners. Even Perón had been stymied by his usually tame followers in Congress when, in 1955, he tried to involve Standard Oil of California in the operation of Argentina's oil-fields. By 1992 YPF was the country's largest enterprise, employing over 50,000 people and undertaking a range of activities all the way from exploration and extraction to operating pipelines and service stations. It had yearly deficits in excess of $6 billion, mainly because its products were sold at below-market prices, and also because other state companies using its oil and gas often refused to pay their bills. Cavallo sold off YPF in stages, first breaking it up into its component parts. Purchasers were guaranteed the right to sell oil and gas on the world market as well as domestically, with no taxes on their exports or on the importation of needed equipment. If the government should later decide to limit exports, the purchasers were guaranteed the right to sell their products inside Argentina at international prices. By 1994 most of YPF had been sold off, in most cases to Argentine buyers like Pérez Companc, Bridas, Astra, and Technit.[6]

Businesses that were used to "sweetheart contracts" to supply the state were adversely affected by the privatizations. It was common for them to vastly overcharge the government for their goods and services. On the other hand, in financial crises it was common for the government to hold back on its payments to suppliers. Indeed, those had not been paid at all while Antonio Erman González was wrestling with the economy. Now, at least, they finally would collect: but only in bonds, which (ironically) they could use to purchase shares in the privatized companies.[7]

To close the government's chronic budget deficits, Cavallo adopted supply-side economics, which assumes that by lowering and simplifying taxes, the government will actually increase its revenues. On the one hand, he reduced or eliminated many taxes. The hated export taxes (retentions) were eliminated. Withholding taxes and the VAT were reduced. The tax rate schedules for individual and corporate income were simplified. On the other hand, Cavallo followed González's policy of cracking down on tax evasion. Besides adding staff, the DGI (internal revenue service) increased the number of its computers between 1990 and 1993 from only 20 to over 1,000 and installed programs allowing it to cross-check data. Its agents now began to pay unannounced visits to companies, focusing especially on the largest enterprises. If a company's books were not in order, or if there was evidence of black market commerce, the company could be closed down and its executives put in jail. Tax revenues increased dramatically by about $2 billion a month between 1990 and 1993.[8]

FOREIGN INFLUENCE

Cavallo and Menem urged the need to "insert" Argentina into the global economy. Continued success for the Convertibility Plan required, above all, a steady influx of foreign capital, either in the form of loans or, preferably, in direct investments. To lure investors, the Menem administration repealed the old law requiring foreigners to sign in with the Registry of Foreign Investors. It also eliminated the need to get government approval to invest in areas of the economy deemed to be "strategic." Foreign investors also were put on the same legal footing as domestic investors with respect to contracting loans. Restrictions on capital movements in and out of Argentina were abolished, which opened the way for speculators with their "hot money." However, the government was confident that a growing economy would result in more capital inflows than outflows.

Since the United States was the leader of the advanced capitalist nations, Menem made special efforts to cultivate it, thus turning his back on Peronism's traditional identification with the Third World. One of his first trips abroad, in September 1989, was to the United States, where he was given such a warm welcome by President George H. W. Bush that he subsequently sent two ships to the Persian Gulf War in 1990 to aid in the blockade of Iraq. Although both Radicals and Peronists in Congress criticized this action, it got a mixed reaction from the public, some of whom were pleased to see their country playing a greater role in the world stage. Also in 1990 Menem achieved a diplomatic triumph by visiting the People's Republic of China and signing a treaty to open consular relations. China opened its markets to Argentine grain exports and promised a $20 million line of credit. In that same year he restored diplomatic relations with Great

Britain, which had been broken since the 1982 Falkland Islands War. That opened the way to an agreement with the European Economic Community allowing Argentina easier access for its exports.

Diplomacy helped to improve Argentina's image abroad as a responsible global citizen. Argentina signed nuclear non-proliferation treaties, dismantled its atomic missile program, promised to end its production of chemical weapons and destroy any of those remaining in its arsenal, and participated in United Nations peace-keeping missions in Yugoslavia, Cyprus, and Somalia. Closer to home, Menem met with the presidents of Brazil, Paraguay, and Uruguay in March 1991 to cre-ate a regional free trade zone, which became known as MERCOSUR. This was a customs union, rather than a common market, because its member states were not ready to surrender their sovereignty to a supra-national body. Still, they agreed to gradually coordinate their macro-economic policies more closely and to keep reducing their tariffs on one another's goods until all tariffs were eliminated. Meanwhile, with a combined population of over 190 million, it was hoped that MERCOSUR would provide each of them with a larger market.[9]

The Menem/Cavallo strategy for growth matched perfectly the reigning eco-nomic ideology shared by the U.S. Treasury, International Monetary Fund, World Bank, and Inter-American Development Bank. Like the so-called "Washington Consensus," it included in its goals export-oriented growth, fiscal discipline, pri-vatization of government companies, tax reform, market-determined interest and exchange rates, deregulation, free trade, and the encouragement of direct foreign investment. Bolstered by income from privatization, Argentina signed agreements with private banks and the IMF to pay off about $12 billion of its foreign debt, something that Alfonsín had always refused to do. That opened the way for Argentina to participate in the Brady Plan, under which it could refinance its remaining debt by issuing long-term dollar-denominated bonds backed by the U.S. Treasury. Those could then be sold to private investors through banks, pen-sion funds, or mutual funds. The IMF and the World Bank followed up with loans and credit lines to encourage Argentina along its new path. With that sort of imprimatur, European investors began snapping up Argentine securities.

Foreign investment took many forms. Between 1989 and 1993 total foreign investment added up to around $9.35 billion. Most shares acquired in the priva-tized state companies were the result of debt-for-equity swaps, about $6.3 billion. Additional shares bought amounted to another $266 million. Of the remaining $3 billion or so, over two-thirds came through profits reinvested by foreign com-panies already located in Argentina. The final $868 million represented new investments in the private sector, with just under half ($384 million) going toward the purchase of private Argentine firms. This pattern changed somewhat in 1993 and 1994. In 1993 debt-for-equity swaps still amounted to a respectable $916 million, but additional purchases of state enterprise shares reached a record of $2.32 billion. By 1994, however, the bulk of the state sector had been privatized, so investment in that area fell to under $300 million. Nevertheless, Argentina continued to attract foreign capital. Reinvested profits remained at over $800 million in both

1993 and 1994. New investments in the private sector soared to just under $3 billion, two-thirds of which were fresh start-ups.[10]

Eduardo Basualdo warns us that some of this "foreign investment" was actually money owned by local conglomerates who channeled it back into Argentina through third parties. Pérez Companc, for example, used a dummy brokerage firm it set up in the Cayman Islands to make purchases in the oil, gas, and electric power fields. Still, the vast majority of overseas capital was truly foreign, with most investors coming from the United States, France, Italy, Spain, Great Britain, Canada, and Chile. These represented more than 60 percent of all the investments in the privatized state companies. Most foreign investors preferred to work through consortia in which many countries, including Argentina, had a share. In the early scramble to acquire the state enterprises, most of which were either monopolies or dominant in their areas, Argentine capitalists were well represented: over 30 percent of the electric power industry; about a third of the oil, gas, and petrochemicals sector; over 25 percent of the telephone industry; and over 90 percent of the steel industry. In many cases, the consortia controlling these companies selected the management from their Argentine associates, for their political contacts and lobbying skills. The foreign companies provided the new technology necessary to improve efficiency and that part of the management needed to oversee its application; foreign banks, which often were directly involved as partners, put up the operating capital and took over the financial administration.[11]

The privatization contracts usually contained clauses guaranteeing that the new owners would not overcharge their customers and would maintain high standards of service, but there was an ongoing debate about whether those were actually honored. Gerchunoff and Canovas conclude that the new owners used their monopoly positions to drive up prices and failed to produce the expected market-driven efficiencies. Occasionally the government would step in to limit sharp price increases, but would always indemnify the companies afterwards by reducing their taxes. Within the new management, the banking interests involved were more interested in getting a quick return on their investment and therefore favored the distribution of dividends over the reinvestment of profits in long-term improvements. The question also arose as to whether foreign direct investment actually added to Argentina's total accumulated capital, or whether the free repatriation of profits cancelled out any real benefits.[12]

In practice, the efficiency of the privatized companies varied greatly between industries. The telecommunications industry was a success story. Between 1990 and 1996 Telefónica spent far more than its original purchase price to expand and upgrade its services. The number of public telephones quadrupled, the telephone network was digitized, and many more private lines were installed. This went well beyond the demands of its contract, although customers still complained about the rise in the cost of a telephone call. There also were modest gains in the production of gas, petrochemicals, and electricity. Again, prices went up, but that was caused as much by rising demand in a reinvigorated economy as it was by the elimination of price controls. More troubling was the tendency for ownership to become more concentrated in these sectors as the big consortia, benefitting from the foreigners' superior technology, began to squeeze out smaller competitors. Even inside those consortia, the foreign investors began buying out the domestic participants. YPF's privatization also resulted in oligopoly, with seven companies dominating production by 1993: four Argentine, two U.S., and one French. Oil prices also rose in tandem with this process, raising suspicions of collusion. The oil companies also worked together to lobby, usually with success, against any return of government regulation of the industry as well as any investigations of price-fixing. On the other hand, the new companies were undeniably more efficient in their production methods, as well as being more profitable. The airline industry was probably the least successful example of privatization. Bad as Aerolíneas Argentinas had been with regard to service and equipment, its takeover by Iberia Airlines resulted in worse conditions. Domestic flights were cut by 23 percent, mechanical failures became more common, and safety standards deteriorated. Iberia was reported to have lost $70 million in the first year and was little inclined to invest more.[13]

As for the repatriation of profits, up through 1997 far more foreign capital entered Argentina through direct investments than was taken out in profits or royalties. Even so, Argentines were divided over whether the sell-off of the state enterprise sector was ultimately a benefit to the country or not. On taking office, Menem predicted that privatizations would reduce Argentina's foreign debt by $30 billion. Later, Antonio Erman González revised that to $10 billion. In fact, the debt was not reduced at all. From $63 billion in mid-1989, it grew to about $70 billion by the end of 1993. The government had contracted new loans; interest had accumulated on the unpaid principal of old loans; and the government had assumed the outstanding debts of the state enterprises, totaling some $20 billion, in order to facilitate their sale.[14] On the other hand, the Argentine government was spared the annual burden of covering the state enterprises' deficits, which already had reached between $5 billion and $6 billion in mid-1989, when Menem first assumed office.

LABOR'S TRAVAILS

Privatization, and the great influx of foreign capital in all parts of industry, accelerated the shift from labor-intensive to capital-intensive industry that had been going on since the 1960s. By the beginning of the 1990s, there were fewer workers in manufacturing than there had been twenty years earlier. In private industry, unions had fought a losing battle against the challenges of technology. Industrial unions also suffered from the fact that, in the larger companies, the real growth in factory jobs was in the administrative and technical areas. White-collar workers in industry were less likely to belong to unions or to join blue-collar workers in strikes. Smaller companies (PYMEs) were still largely labor intensive and employed about one out of four workers in industry, but they were hard to unionize. Faced with the greater productivity of their larger competitors, the PYMEs struggled to survive, which also made jobs insecure. If threatened with unionization, they could always elect to hire *cuentapropistas* (black market labor). There were plenty of those, since unemployment was fairly high, and growing.[15]

Workers in commerce and services faced similar problems, since the average commercial enterprise in Argentina was, and is, very small. The Commercial Employees' Union had many members, but the great dispersal of its members among so many tiny establishments made for weak organization. Most of those members were also white-collar workers who identified more with the lower middle class than with the proletariat.

Cutting labor costs in the public sector was crucial to holding down inflation and controlling the fiscal deficit. As a Peronist, however, Menem had to worry about the political costs of confronting the trade unions. State enterprise employees did not submit quietly to Cavallo's plans. When Telefónica took over ENTel, it faced resistance in the form of a twenty-four-hour work stoppage that isolated Argentina from the rest of the world. The union was protecting the privileges it had won previously by similar tactics: guaranteed permanent employment, automatic wage adjustments, promotion by seniority, and a seven-hour workday. Instead of backing down, like the old political appointees in management, Telefónica fired over half the workforce, reducing it from 23,000 to 11,000 (of whom 5,000 were new hires). Union representatives no longer determined who was hired (such as their relatives and friends), the workday was raised from 7 to 8 hours, absenteeism dropped to a third of its former level, and the new management cracked down on the common practice of workers sabotaging telephone lines and then demanding bribes from customers to have them "repaired." YPF's privatization followed a similar pattern. The company had oil refineries in several provinces, chiefly in Patagonia and the northwest. At the time of privatization, it employed 50,000 people, but within a few years that was reduced drastically to only 5,000. Oil workers, backed by Ubaldini, the local Catholic clergy, and local businessmen fearful of the consequences of cutbacks, blocked streets and highways with protesting pickets in Salta and Neuquén. Such were the origins of the *piquetero* movement that would grow and spread throughout the 90s and beyond.[16]

Argentina's steel industry, located mainly in a small area north of the city of Buenos Aires and south of Rosario, Argentina's second city, had a long history of labor violence. The workforce belonged to the Metalworkers' Union (UOM), the country's largest and most powerful industrial union. The UOM's bully-boys had closed down the private mills and the state-owned SOMISA many times in the past when management resisted its terms. When Cavallo took over as economics minister, however, SOMISA was sold to the Technit conglomerate and renamed Aceros Paraná. Menem appointed his former labor minister, Jorge Triaca, as intervenor, with orders to make SOMISA more profitable for Technit by dismissing some 3,100 employees. The UOM called a strike, and thousands of workers took over the mills, whereupon Menem sent in the Gendarmerie (National

Guard) to expel the workers. When Technit finally assumed control, a weakened UOM was unable to stop a sweeping reorganization that in less than two years reduced employment at the San Nicolás and Ramallo plants by nearly half.[17]

Government employees' unions, like the Association of State Workers (ATE), the Union of Civil Personnel of the Nation (UPCN), and the teachers' Confederation of Educational Workers of the Argentine Republic (CTERA), were the real hotbeds of labor militancy. Well might they view Menem and Cavallo as their enemies. After being trimmed back by the Proceso, from just over 1.8 million under Isabel Perón to "only" 1.69 million, under Alfonsin they had grown to over 2 million, of whom slightly more than half were in the federal government administration, state enterprises and banks, public hospitals, and public schools. Cavallo intended to eliminate half of those jobs through (1) privatization; (2) transferring hospitals, health care, and schools to the provinces and the city of Buenos Aires; and (3) trimming back the bureaucracy.[18]

The ATE's strength used to reside in the state enterprises and the military-run companies, but privatization and closures left it with mostly provincial and municipal employees. However, those numbers actually grew as the result of the federal government transferring responsibility for health services and education to the provinces. The ATE and CTERA were both anti-Menem and, though nominally Peronist, were emotionally drawn to the more "classist" and "combative" left. They formed the core of Ubaldini's labor support and later would help to form the Frente Grande and its successor, FREPASO: political movements that combined radical socialists and left wing Peronist mavericks. By contrast, the UPCN backed Menem, in return for which it got the right to administer the public sector's health and recreational social aid funds (*obras sociales*). In the mid-1990s, ATE's membership was around 190,000; UPCN's around 300,000; and CTERA's around 189,000.[19]

Teachers alone were responsible for over 22 percent of all strikes, 29 percent of all participants in strikes, and 43 percent of the number of working days lost from strikes between 1984 and 1993. When civil servants at the federal, provincial, and municipal levels are added, the public sector accounted for 58 percent of all strikes, 57 percent of all strikers, and 75 percent of all working days lost. After Menem took office, most public sector strike activity occurred in the poorer provinces of the interior, "where wages were low, pay arrears rampant, private sector jobs scarce, and layoffs frequent."[20]

Although Cavallo indeed met his goal of downsizing the federal government's payroll by about half, many who lost their jobs soon turned up as employees of the provincial or municipal governments. For example, by devolving responsibility for health services and public education to the provinces, the Federal Ministry of Health was able to trim its staff by 88,129, and the Federal Ministry of Education reduced its staff by 118,173, for a total of 206,302 people dismissed from the federal payroll by 1995. As the provinces and municipalities assumed those responsibilities, however, they added 315,255 new jobs. Similarly, when the federal government laid off another 103,000 civil servants from other agencies, the provincial and municipal payrolls increased by 283,000.[21]

The Convertibility Plan's impact on the economy as a whole also presents a picture of contrasts. On the positive side, economic growth was very impressive. In 1989 the economy actually had shrunk by an alarming 6.2 percent, and in 1990 there was no growth at all. From 1991 through 1994, however, GNP growth averaged over 7.5 percent. Investment also grew, from 15.7 percent of GNP in 1989 to over 23 percent during 1994. Meanwhile, inflation dropped sharply, from 2,314 percent in 1990 to only 4.2 percent in 1994. The fiscal deficit also was brought under control: indeed, in 1992, 1993, and 1994 there actually was a small surplus. Exports rose significantly, but so did imports as investors sought to modernize their firms. After 1991 there was an unfavorable trade balance and a growing deficit in the balance of payments, which increased the need for loans. But that was considered to be an acceptable price for restoring growth. Modernization also meant rising unemployment, especially among unskilled workers, as technology eliminated many jobs. This was not a steady process. Unemployment actually declined between 1990 and 1993 from over 8 percent to under 7 percent of the labor force, but after that it quickly rose to double digits and remained high. Real wages also declined, even though inflation had come down. It had been assumed, originally, that there would be painful adjustments in the labor market in the early phase of economic modernization, but that these would end eventually when a healthy growing economy began to reabsorb workers. Unfortunately, that never happened. On balance, however, the economy at the end of 1994 seemed much improved over the dismal 1980s, and most Argentines looked cautiously forward to further gains.[22]

Chapter Five

The Underside of the System

Scandals erupted throughout Menem's first administration and escalated in terms of their seriousness. Bribery scandals were the least of them, although they forced Menem to shift his personnel. Jorge Triaca, former labor minister and interventor of SOMISA, was indicted for misappropriating funds from the interventor's office. Adelina de Viola, head of the National Mortgage Bank, resigned after being accused by Radicals in Congress of giving herself a $200 million loan and depositing it in a Cayman Islands bank. Julio Mera Figueroa, the interior minister, was discovered taking bribes from a French company bidding for the contract to print national identification cards. His successor, José Luis Manzano, also resigned for taking bribes from a company that provided uniforms for the Federal Police. The company's shirts were more expensive than those being sold at exclusive men's stores. Miguel Angel Vicco, Menem's private secretary, resigned after a company he owned sold contaminated milk to the Ministry of Health and Social Action for distribution to children's clinics. Raúl Granillo Ocampo, Menem's legal and technical secretary, was indicted for influence-peddling involving the construction of an aqueduct in La Rioja. Instead of going to jail, he went to Washington as ambassador to the United States. Even Domingo Cavallo, popular as he was, outraged public opinion by admitting that he took large "supplements to his income" from private corporations, in order (he said) to meet the high cost of living in Buenos Aires.

Government agencies that provided social services tended to be particularly lucrative plums for corrupt politicians. Luis Barrionuevo, the head of Social Security, was indicted in federal court for making people who claimed benefits "tip" the bureaucrats in order to get their claims processed. Social Security's Medical Aid Fund (PAMI) was heavily staffed with *ñoquis:* employees who never showed up except to collect a paycheck. Its agency heads also demanded kickbacks from contractors, who in turn were allowed to overcharge. Victor Alderete, Menem's first PAMI head, went to jail for "fraudulent administration." His successor, Matilde Menéndez, also was indicted for corruption and forced to resign. In addition to being badly managed, PAMI provided extremely poor services: filthy nursing homes, nonexistent ambulance services, falsified prescriptions, unusable dentures, impure medicines. Both PAMI and Social Security also issued thousands of payments to beneficiaries who were unqualified, and to some who were dead.[1] But however ugly those scandals were, they were minor compared to those involving people close to the president in narcotics trafficking, arms smuggling, and terrorism.

THE SYRIAN CONNECTION: "YOMAGATE"

To understand the origins of these more serious scandals, it is necessary to look back to August 1988, just after Menem had won his party's presidential nomination and was raising money for his forthcoming campaign. In that month he traveled to Syria with a small group of friends and political supporters, among whom was Oscar Spinoza Melo, a former ambassador to Saudi Arabia who would one day publish a description of what transpired on that trip. Ostensibly, Menem was on a holiday to visit Yabrud, his family's old hometown, and that of the Yomas, his in-laws, as well. According to Spinoza, another person they met in Yabrud was Monzer al-Kassar, who was related both to the Yomas and to Syria's dictator, Hafez al-Assad.[2] Al-Kassar was no ordinary neighbor: he had a long police record for automobile theft before Assad came to power and had spent time in Danish and British jails for selling hashish. Assad later put him to work raising money by cooperating with the Sicilian Mafia in smuggling drugs, arms, and stolen cars, and then funneling the proceeds to Middle Eastern terrorist groups.[3]

Through Al-Kassar, the Menem group got interviews with both President Assad and Vice President Abdul Halim Haddam. Spinoza alleges that during these conversations, oblique promises were exchanged: that in return for Syrian "investments" (i.e., support for Menem's campaign) Menem would, as president, facilitate "trade" (i.e., drugs and money laundering) between Argentina and Syria. But there was something even more important to be discussed. The Alfonsín government had promised back in 1984 to provide Condor missiles to Egypt and Iraq.[4] So far, Argentina's missile project was still in the development stage, but Syria was anxious to be involved in the deal. In a burst of generosity, Menem not only promised to send Syria the missiles but went further and promised to build it a nuclear reactor as well. Spinoza claims to have gone cold with shock when he heard this, and to have berated Menem afterwards for making a commitment that the United States would never allow him to fulfill. Menem shrugged it off and said that things would work out somehow.

Secret connections between Argentina and Syria revolved around Menem's sister-in-law and appointments secretary, Amalia Beatriz ("Amira") Yoma. Soon after Menem took office, Amira's former husband, Ibrahim al Ibrahim, a colonel in the Syrian army's intelligence branch, moved to Buenos Aires. Menem secured him an Argentine passport and citizenship, although he spoke no Spanish and, according to immigration laws, should have had to reside two years in the country before applying for citizenship. Moreover, Menem secured him an important position as co-director of the customhouse at the Ezeiza International Airport. That put him in charge of the customs warehouse, which happened to be managed by a company called Edcadassa that was owned jointly by the air force and a Syrian friend of Menem's, Alfredo Yabrán.

Another foreigner claiming Argentine citizenship and carrying an Argentine passport was none other than Monzer al Kassar. He and Amira had become lovers, and during his frequent visits to Argentina he stayed at her apartment, as did her ex-husband, Ibrahim.[5] Al Kassar now had a luxurious home in Marbella, Spain. He was in frequent contact with one of the chief bankrollers of the narcotics and arms trade, Jorge Antonio, a Syrian-Argentine "fixer" dating back to the Perón regime, who was sometimes thought to be the conduit for transferring Syrian money into Menem's political campaign chest. Antonio, who had a palatial villa in Torremolinos, was a friend of both the Menem and Yoma families. Amira's brothers, Karim and Emir, also acted as couriers between Argentina and Spain. Karim had once worked in the Spanish embassy in Damascus and so eventually was able to secure a position in the Middle Eastern section of the Spanish Foreign Ministry. Emir had resigned as special advisor to the president after the "Swiftgate" bribery scandal involving the Swift Meat-packing Company (see Chapter 3) but still was to be found frequently in the offices and corridors of the Casa Rosada. He also owned a leather factory in Marbella and had a summer home there. Another notable resident of Marbella was Rifat al Assad, the Syrian dictator's brother. He had been expelled from Switzerland because of his involvement in the illegal arms trade.[6]

Another contact was Mario Caserta, vice president of the Justicialist Party of Buenos Aires Province, who became undersecretary for Water Resources in the new administration. Caserta had been in the drug trade since the early 1980s, using his contacts with some of the more unsavory, corrupt officials in the Proceso. With the help of Cuban-Americans living in Buenos Aires, and carrying Argentine passports, he transported cocaine from Bolivia to Miami, by way of Ezeiza Airport. With Menem in office, his operations would blend in with those of Al Kassar. As drugs flowed into Miami and New York, it became essential to find a way to collect the payments and launder the money. Ibrahim and Amira, as government officials, could travel to the United States on diplomatic passports, and so they did—sometimes together, sometimes separately, and occasionally with Monzer al Kassar. From July 1989 to March 1991, it is estimated that they brought back around $11 million, stuffed into briefcases or in Amira's Samsonite luggage. Once the money was safely within the Ezeiza custom warehouse, it was under Ibrahim's protection. Then Mario Caserta's Cuban-American colleagues went into action. They owned a company that refurbished antique cars. The cash would be packed into the door panels of the cars, and the cars would be shipped by ferryboat to the Uruguayan port of Colonia. From there it would be transported to one of Uruguay's highly secret banks, safe from probing eyes.[7]

All went well until Rodolfo Etchegoyen, an air force officer in charge of the customhouse, began looking into what he thought were suspicious activities involving Edcadassa and some of his fellow officers. In September 1990 Etchegoyen was warned off by a retired air force general and advised to find another job, but it already was too late. Called away on the night of 12 December to an "urgent" meeting of customhouse officials, he was found dead in his office the next morning, There was a suicide note next to the body, complaining of "betrayal" and "pressure," but the pistol with which he presumably shot himself in the head had left no gunpowder marks on his hand, as would be usual in cases of suicide. The family insisted on a full investigation, but Etchegoyen's death was ruled a suicide. A friend of Yabrán's replaced him at the customhouse.[8]

The real scandal broke in March 1991 when a Spanish judge, Baltazar Garzón, accused Amira Yoma, her brother Karim, Mario Caserta, and Ibrahim al Ibrahim of being engaged in international drug smuggling and money laundering. To head off Judge Garzón's inevitable request for extradition, Menem and the Yomas decided to start a parallel "investigation" in Argentina that would claim priority. Menem's choice of an investigating magistrate was an appointee of his, María Servini de Cubría, who also was a friend of Jorge Antonio.[9] She previously had helped Menem get rid of another scandal involving his old friend, Eduardo Bauzá, who had been accused of taking kickbacks from a company that made the white laboratory coats that Buenos Aires schoolchildren are required to wear.

When Judge Garzón finally issued his extradition requests, Servini de Cubría stalled by alleging that they contained irregularities. She next requested an interview with him and flew to Madrid, ostensibly to discuss the case but really to discover just how much information the Spanish magistrate really had. It turned out that he had a great deal of information, much of it already published in a Spanish weekly magazine called *Cambio 16*. The Spanish authorities had arrested one of the Cuban Americans who lived in Spain and ran a dummy company that was used to launder the drug money. He not only confessed but provided so many details about the operations that the Uruguayan narcotics squad were able to arrest the other gang members and search their homes and offices. That turned up a notebook listing all the money that Amira and Ibrahim had brought back from New York and Miami during 1989 and 1990.

Meanwhile, Mario Caserta had been designated as the regime's "sacrificial lamb." Menem dismissed him from his government and stood aside while he was indicted and put under "preventative arrest." Anxious not to be next, Ibrahim began to give press interviews in which he accused Vice President Duhalde, Interior Minister Mera Figueroa, and President of the Chamber of Deputies Alberto Pierri of instructing him to meet certain passengers at Ezeiza and "take care of their luggage." That provoked loud denials from the accused.

By now Menem was thoroughly disgusted with the Yoma clan and wanted Amira to resign. But since she knew so much about affairs in the presidency, he didn't want to provoke her; so he decided to go on a "diplomatic trip" to Germany and leave Duhalde in charge of the situation. Once Menem was out of the country, Duhalde demanded Amira's resignation. The Yoma clan fought back. Zulema echoed Ibrahim's charges and said that it was Duhalde himself who was Argentina's narcotics boss. Emir seconded her, and Carlos Menem, Jr., wrote an open letter to Duhalde accusing him of betraying his father. Ibrahim also wrote an open letter, recalling that his appointment to the Ezeiza customhouse had been signed by Duhalde on a previous occasion when Menem was out of the country. The vice president retreated under this barrage, leaving it up to Menem to deal with the mess upon his return.[10]

When Menem got back to Buenos Aires, he had Amira check into a sanatorium and announced that she was resigning because of a nervous breakdown. Judge Servini de Cubría also had returned to Argentina in the meantime. Although she tried to ignore Garzón's extradition request, the press continued to harry her. Also, a Lebanese immigrant named Khalil Hussein Dib went to another magistrate to confess his involvement in the narcotics trade and provided additional evidence against Amira and Ibrahim. Amira was put under "preventative arrest," and Servini quickly set a date for her trial. The case was dismissed "for lack of evidence."

But it was not so easy to sweep "Yomagate" under the rug. Whistleblowers in Judge Servini's office went public with charges that she had destroyed evidence and tried to hide Judge Garzón's arrest orders. Carlos León Arslanián, the minister of justice, demanded her impeachment on the grounds of perjury and abuse of her judicial office and was backed in a public manifesto by 150 other federal judges and high court officials. The case went to Supreme Court Justice Rodolfo Barra, another Menem appointee. Servini was let off in March 1992 with a fine of 60 pesos, a risible penalty according to Horacio Verbitsky of *Página 12*. Instead of removing her from the bench, Judge Barra removed those of her staff who had leaked the truth about her. He also admonished Arslanián to be "more prudent" in his public statements. In the meantime, a new judge, Berraz de Vidal, had taken over the case, based on Hussein Dib's testimony, and began digging deeper. By the end of May, she had enough evidence to order the arrest of Amira, Caserta, and Ibrahim. Ibrahim fled to Syria. Once again Menem's stooges went into action to control the damage. The Justicialist majority in the Senate undertook to "reform" the judiciary. Over the next five months, four magistrates, including Berraz de Vidal, were moved to other jurisdictions, along with three prosecutors. A new judge released Amira from jail and declared her not guilty. Caserta got a four-year suspended sentence.[11]

THE SYRIAN CONNECTION: GUN-RUNNING

Illegal arms sales by the Argentine government date at least back to the Proceso, when the armed forces, in their eagerness to uproot the guerrillas' support networks, engaged criminal elements to help them locate underground supply routes. Before long, some military officers and their criminal accomplices were forming gangs to smuggle, kidnap people for ransom, and extort money or property from businessmen. Skimming off a certain amount of weapons, munitions, and explosives produced by Fabricaciones Militares and selling them abroad through dummy companies was but one of these flourishing rackets. At first, the sales were destined for the Nicaraguan Contras, with the connivance of the U.S. government, but soon there were other customers, such as Iran. Then the seemingly ubiquitous Monzer al Kassar became a major go-between, as he was also in the Iran-Contra affair that shocked the U.S. public in the late 1980s. Even before that, he had helped get Exocet missiles into Argentina during the 1982 Falkland Islands War after the United States cut off all military aid.[12]

Clandestine arms sales did not stop after civilian rule was restored. Sharp cuts in Fabricaciones Militares' budget made it strive harder to make up its losses. The outbreak of war between Iran and Iraq provided opportunities to sell arms to both sides, and again Monzer al Kassar was a convenient intermediary. Nor was Alfonsín's government innocent of all this. In 1985 Alfonsín signed a secret executive order allowing the air force to provide Iraq with parts for producing a missile, and two years later he signed another secret order setting up a factory in Córdoba Province to manufacture a solid, combustible fuel for launching long-range missiles. The actual work would be done by a German company, behind the façade of the Argentine air force. Saudi Arabia would put up most of the capital. The project was known as Condor II.[13]

Menem recognized the money-making potential of Condor II, and so he transferred the project to a civilian space agency, the better to control it. Even before his election, he had promised Syria missiles and a nuclear reactor; then, in February 1990, his brother-in-law, Karim Yoma, traveled to Iran as undersecretary of foreign affairs and made similar promises to President Rafsanjani.[14] None of those promises were to be fulfilled, because of U.S. pressure and Menem's desire to have good relations with the Americans.

Although Monzer al Kassar was still active in Argentina through his connections with Menem and the Yomas, the Argentine air force was also heavily involved in contraband trade through its control over Ezeiza's air cargo operations. A retired lieutenant colonel, Diego Palleros, ran a complex system of dummy companies designed to hide the flow of illegal arms. Fabricaciones Militares sold its weapons to a dummy Argentine company, which in turn shipped them to dummy companies in Uruguay and Panama. The first big sale, in mid-1991, was to Croatia, which was then at war with the militarily more powerful Serbia. Although the United Nations had declared an arms embargo against both sides, the United States, Germany, and the Vatican sympathized with Croatia and were willing to look the other way when the Argentines began sending it secret shipments. A very large shipment, valued at around $160 million, also was sent to Bosnia, whose large Muslim population was also being threatened by Serbia. This was paid for by Iran and Saudi Arabia, while the United States pretended not to notice.[15]

Antonio Erman González resigned as minister of defense in April 1993 and was replaced by Oscar Camillión, who had been minister of foreign affairs under the Proceso. At first Camillión opposed the illegal arms trade, but eventually he was brought round by Fabricaciones Militares' director, Luis Sarlenga, a crony of Menem's from La Rioja. Arms sales to Croatia continued. It was a bungled arms deal with Ecuador that finally caused a scandal and brought the whole underground operation into the open. War had broken out between Ecuador and Peru in January 1995. Since the United States and other Latin American countries had imposed an arms embargo on the belligerents, the Ecuadorians, being the weaker side, turned in desperation to the Argentines.

The Foreign Ministry opposed sending weapons to Ecuador, primarily because Argentina was a participant in a four-nation peacekeeping commission set up in 1942 to monitor border disputes between Peru and Ecuador. In addition, Peru and Argentina had long been allies in South American geopolitics against their common traditional enemies, Brazil and Chile. But greed trumped honor, so on 17 January Menem signed another secret executive order approving the sales. A private airline called Fine Air would carry the weapons, listing their destination as Venezuela but actually unloading them during a stop in the Ecuadorian port of Guayaquil. Two shipments were quickly made this way, but the pilot for the third run happened to be a Peruvian former air force officer who tipped off his government. The Peruvian authorities sent an angry note to the Argentine Foreign Ministry on 17 February, demanding that all further shipments be stopped. After some wrangling inside the government, the third flight was allowed to proceed, with a new pilot; but the Peruvians sent another note on 26 February, threatening to go to the Organization of American States, just as a fourth shipment was preparing to leave Ezeiza. This time the flight was cancelled, but by then journalists had gotten hold of the story. *Clarín* splashed it all over the front page of its 6 March edition.

The governments of Ecuador, Peru, and Venezuela were furious: Ecuador because it didn't get the weapons it had paid for, Peru because it had been betrayed by an old ally, and Venezuela because its name had been employed in a fraud. Their public statements fueled the scandal and led to an investigation by federal judge Jorge Urso and federal prosecutor Carlos Stornelli. In the meantime, Fabricaciones Militares was shut down, and all of its enterprises were put up for sale.

Urso and Stornelli faced strange obstacles to uncovering the entire story of the illegal arms trade. For example, on 3 November 1995 the army's munitions factory in Río Tercero, Córdoba, suddenly caught fire and disappeared in a massive explosion that rained shrapnel all over the surrounding town, killing seven people and destroying buildings. Although a police investigation declared it an accident, there was widespread suspicion that the explosion had been deliberately set off to destroy evidence.[16] Urso and Stornelli also had to face angry resistance and accusations of partisanship from high-level *menemistas* as they gradually uncovered more details about the scandal. Not until 2001, when Menem was out of office, were the leading figures indicted. The armed forces' commander Martín Balza, Foreign Minister Guido Di Tella, Luis Sarlenga, Antonio Erman González, Emir Yoma, and even Menem himself were put under arrest, pending trial. If convicted, they faced ten years in jail. Fortunately for them, however, Supreme Court justice Julio Nazareño, another Menem appointee from La Rioja, let them off for "insufficient evidence."

THE SYRIAN CONNECTION: TERRORISM

On 17 March 1992 a Ford pickup truck loaded with explosives and driven by a suicide bomber smashed through the front of the Israeli embassy in downtown Buenos Aires and detonated. The building was destroyed, 29 people were killed, and more than 250 were injured. Many of the dead and injured were Argentine children at a school across the street and some elderly inmates of a nearby nursing home. A Catholic church also suffered extensive damage from the blast. Two years later, on 18 July 1994, a Jewish community center, AMIA, was obliterated by another suicide bomber, driving a Renault van. This time 87 people died and over 300 were injured. Islamic Jihad, Hezbollah's military wing, claimed responsibility for both bombings. The suicide bomber in the embassy attack was never identified. Police quickly rushed to clean up the damage, trashing much of the evidence—including, according to some witnesses, the perpetrator's head. After many years of picking through scraps of evidence, Argentine prosecutors finally identified the AMIA bomber as Ibrahim Hussein Berro, a young Lebanese whose hometown had already glorified him by naming a plaza after him. But, as the suspense novelist Eric Ambler once wrote, in an assassination the important question is not who pulled the trigger but who paid for the bullet. If Hezbollah had carried out these deeds, who had ordered that they be done? Also, were any Argentine officials involved?

Hezbollah is a Shiite Muslim terrorist organization operating out of southern Lebanon with the support of both Iran and Syria. Either one of those countries, or both, could have ordered the attacks. Both had motives. On 16 February 1992, just a month before the embassy bombing, Israeli helicopters had attacked a motorcade in southern Lebanon, killing Hezbollah's leader, Sayed Abbas al Musawi, along with his wife, their son, and four other people. A simple desire for revenge may have prompted the attack on Israel's embassy, but why the one in Argentina? Some writers have speculated that this was because Menem had responded with an executive order, also in February 1992, to a request by the Simon Wiesenthal Center to release documents pertaining to the admission of Nazi escapees to Argentina after World War II. According to this theory, the Muslim militants were punishing Menem for his subservience to U.S. and Israeli pressure.[17]

A similar theory had the Syrians taking revenge on Menem for reneging on his promises to supply them with a nuclear reactor and Condor II missiles after they had invested so heavily in the project and in his presidential campaign.

Menem placed the investigation of the embassy bombing in the hands of the Supreme Court's chief justice, Ricardo Levene. Two years later Levene, a Menem appointee to the court, announced that he was closing the case for lack of evidence, despite much information provided by SIDE, Interpol, and the CIA.[18] Under prodding from the United States and Israel, the Supreme Court took over as a collective body and created a special task force to continue the investigation. However, the task force searched for clues in all the wrong places. Although photographic evidence showed a huge crater in the front of the embassy where the truck exploded, it preferred to follow up on interior minister José Manzano's hypothesis that the explosion had been set off from inside the building. Suspects were arrested, only to be released later.

In March 2000, when Menem was out of office, a new political party called *Acción por la República* published a report entitled "The Trail That Menem Fears" that criticized the ex-president for refusing to follow up on circumstantial evidence of Syria's connection to the embassy bombing. Specifically, the report noted that Monzer al Kassar was in Argentina at the time, and that he owned, under an assumed name, a factory in Spain that produced Sentex, the explosive used in the attack. Given his connection to Alfredo Yabrán, who ran the cargo operations at Ezeiza, it would have been easy for him to smuggle it into Argentina. The report also alleged that the money used to buy the Ford truck had been traced back to a currency exchange house owned by Al Kassar in the Lebanese city of Byblos. However, the report added, evidence about all this had mysteriously disappeared.[19] Before accepting such accusations, however, it should be noted that *Acción por la República's* main source was none other than its leader, Domingo Cavallo, who had quarreled with Menem. Still, the report is taken seriously by reputable Argentine political analysts such as Carlos Escudé, who observes that "The generalized perception of senior Argentine Foreign Ministry sources was that Syria had been an important co-sponsor of both the 1992 and 1994 bombings, but that it was in no one's interest to bring this out, except the victims' families organized in the non-governmental institution, *Memoria Activa*." Menem wanted to cover up his links to Monzer al Kassar and Assad. The United States and Israel—as well as some local Jewish leaders—also preferred to pursue an exclusively Iranian connection because they still hoped to win Syria's support for the Middle East peace process.[20]

The investigation that followed the AMIA bombing went somewhat further into the underground networks of cooperation between the Iranian embassy and local right wing elements in the security forces. Federal judge Juan José Galeano uncovered evidence that army officers at the Campo de Mayo base outside of Buenos Aires may have helped Hezbollah terrorists with explosives and information about the Jewish community center. Also, as in the embassy bombing, police guards were mysteriously withdrawn just before the attack. Nothing was done to question the army officers, but Galeano was able to trace the van used in the bombing to a car thief named Carlos Telledín. Rather than believe that Telledín had dealt directly with Hezbollah, he strongly suspected, from other witnesses, that the real nexus was Juan José Ribelli, a Buenos Aires Province police official who headed an underground criminal gang that specialized in car theft and extortion. At first, Telledín refused to name Ribelli, but he later did so. Unfortunately, a hidden camera in Galeano's office caught Galeano on videotape offering Telledín $400,000 to change his story. Galeano was removed from the case and impeached.

The investigation dragged on inconclusively; even after Menem left office, there was little encouragement for more vigorous digging. Nilda Garré, who headed Argentina's anti-terrorism office under Menem's successor, Fernando de la Rua, resigned in frustration in 2001, accusing the Federal Police and the State Intelligence Service (SIDE) of destroying and altering evidence. So far no one had been prosecuted successfully for either terrorist attack. Nevertheless, driblets of evidence continued to accumulate. In 1997 German authorities rounded up a terrorist cell that included Moshen Rabbani, the former cultural attaché at the Iranian embassy in Buenos Aires. The arrested men provided details about the planning and execution of the Israeli embassy bombing. The following year an intercepted telephone call from the Iranian embassy furnished more evidence of Iran's complicity in the 1992 attack. Six Iranian diplomats were expelled from the country, but no further action was taken. In 2000 Claudio Lifschitz, one of Judge Galeano's former secretaries, accused SIDE of pressuring his former boss into burying the case because the AMIA bombing had been a "sting" operation that had gone haywire. SIDE had infiltrated an Iranian terrorist cell with agents prova-cateurs, suggested AMIA as a target, and even provided logistical support, but then had lost control over the scheme. So, when the CIA, FBI, Mossad, and the German, French, and Spanish security services arrived to investigate, SIDE already had thwarted them. It even went so far as to leak the identity and a pho-tograph of the leading CIA investigator to the press, thus forcing him to flee the country. For revealing this, Lifschitz was himself indicted in a federal criminal court for exposing state secrets.[21]

Menem himself was accused of ordering the sabotage of the investigations, in return for a $10 million bribe from the Iranians, to be deposited into a Swiss bank account. He was forced to admit that he had such an account after a former mem-ber of Iran's intelligence services told German authorities details about the AMIA attack. The Iranian defector said that President Akbar Hashemi Rafsanjani had deposited the money into Menem's account after AMIA was destroyed. Swiss bank examiners confirmed that such a sum had indeed been paid into the account but could not (or would not) furnish information as to the date or the depositor.[22] Nonetheless, Menem was indicted in 2007 for tax fraud.

Indeed, it was not until Néstor Kirchner came to the presidency in 2003 and replaced many of Menem's judicial appointees that a really serious pursuit of the truth began, by which time many trails had gone cold. Even so, in November 2006 federal judge Rodolfo Canicobra Corral acted upon evidence supplied by an unidentified Iranian defector and issued indictments for Iran's ex-President Rafsanjani; its former intelligence chief, Ali Fallahian; leader of its Revolutionary

Guards, Moshen Rezai; Deputy Defense Minister Ahmad Vahidi, a Revolutionary Guards general; and Imad Mugniyah, a Lebanese commander of Hezbollah. Iran angrily rejected the charges, but, responding to the Argentine government's requests, Interpol issued "red notices" for these men, making them subject to arrest if they traveled outside their country.

"JUNIOR'S ACCIDENT"

Carlos Saúl Menem, Junior (Carlitos), died on 15 March 1995, at the age of twenty-six, when a helicopter he was piloting crashed. Silvio Olta, a racing car driver who was with him in the aircraft, also died. The two young men were heading to Santa Fe Province to attend an automobile race when the low-flying helicopter hit some power lines near the town of Ramallo, in northern Buenos Aires Province, and dove into the ground. Carlitos, like his father, loved to race automobiles, fly airplanes, and live high; but an autopsy found no evidence that he had been under the influence of drugs or alcohol. He had been in automobile accidents before, however. Just before his father was inaugurated as president, he had suffered such serious injuries from a crash that he had to be flown to the United States for emergency surgery.[23] Thus, it was plausible that his death might have been caused by careless handling of the helicopter.

Zulema Yoma rejected the police report calling the crash an accident and demanded a thorough investigation headed by a federal magistrate. Menem opposed the idea at first, but when she went to the media with allegations that Carlitos' death had been planned by high-ranking persons inside the Casa Rosada, he decided that it was better to go along. Zulema insisted that while she was living at the Presidential Residence in Olivos, she had seen many meetings being held between her husband and his cronies while they were being investigated for their involvement in the narcotics and arms trade. She said that Carlitos had told her that "those men are betraying *papi*" and that he was going to conduct his own investigation and expose them. Carlitos was known to be a friend of Mario Anello, one of the Cuban Americans deeply involved in the narcotics business. They ran with the young demimonde crowd in Buenos Aires at billiard parlors and fashionable cafes. Zulema concluded that Carlitos had been killed to prevent him from using Anello to get information about official contacts with the underworld.[24]

Zulema's accusations seemed credible at first, because some witnesses claimed to have heard an explosion just before the helicopter hit the power lines. Some also claimed to have seen a black car with three men inside, going down the highway beneath the helicopter as if following it. One woman said that someone in the car had fired at the helicopter. Most other witnesses near the scene saw none of these things, however. The Argentine *Gendarmería* recovered some 146 pieces of the helicopter and, upon examining them, reported that some pieces contained holes that might—or might not—be similar to bullet holes. On the other hand, the autopsies of Carlitos and Olta returned no evidence of bullet wounds. Vice Admiral (ret.) Juan Carlos Anchezar, SIDE's undersecretary, scoffed at the theory that the helicopter had been brought down by fire from a speeding car. It would have been an extremely unlikely and inconvenient way to assassinate the president's son, he said. Professionals would simply have secreted a bomb aboard the aircraft. However, two of the witnesses claiming to have heard or seen suspicious behavior just before the crash died soon afterwards, and that fueled rumors of a coverup.[25] It was not surprising that people believed in a conspiracy, given all the other revelations that were still coming out concerning the administration's connections to the international underworld.

Judge Carlos Villafuerte Ruzo agreed to conduct an investigation. The witnesses were questioned again, and the air force went over the helicopter's remains to inspect the "bullet holes." On 16 October 1998 Judge Villafuerte concluded that the crash was indeed accidental. The helicopter had been flying at a very low altitude when it hit the power lines. The great majority of witnesses, some of whom were at an Esso gas station just across the road from the accident, heard no explosions, saw no abnormal movement of the helicopter before it hit the power lines, heard no shots, nor saw any suspicious automobiles. The air force discredited the earlier investigation that claimed to have discovered bullet holes in the helicopter, and the mysterious deaths of the two witnesses who claimed either to have seen shots fired or heard explosions were found to be explicable.[26]

Zulema rejected these conclusions and appealed to the Supreme Court to take over the case. Federal Prosecutor Nicolás Becerra urged the court to approve Zulema's request so that the various theories and rumors circulating throughout the public concerning the case could finally be put to rest. Seven of the nine justices refused, however, on the grounds that a thorough investigation had been made and there was no new evidence since then to support her appeal.

INTIMIDATION OF THE PRESS

Menem had an antagonistic relationship with the media throughout his two terms as president. It was reporters, after all, who exposed the dark underside of his government, often at the risk of their lives. The Buenos Aires Press Workers Union (UTPBA) reported 1,283 cases of violent aggression against journalists between 1989 and 2001, including three murders. The worst years were 1993, when the narcotics, arms smuggling, and Israeli embassy bombing stories were filling the front pages of Argentine newspapers, and 1997, when the media was digging into the affairs of Menem's friend, Alfredo Yabrán, who was presumed to have ordered the murder of a press photographer, José Luis Cabezas.

The intimidation, and even murder, of too-intrusive journalists was nothing new in Argentina. It had happened frequently under Perón as well as under military governments. Heavy-handed regimes had many weapons to use for silencing the press. Some of those were considered to be legal, such as the Law of Disrespect *(desacato),* which could shut down publications and jail journalists for personal criticism of public officials. In the same vein, the law allowed public officials to sue reporters and editors for slander or libel. Even if the accused were found not guilty, the cost of defending the suit was a burden. Both Perón and the military dictatorships had simply closed down newspapers and broadcasting stations that offended them, but there were also more subtle "legal" devices to nudge journalists into line. Some governments rationed newsprint. A more common weapon, however, was to withdraw advertising by government agencies, which was an important source of revenue for the media.

Beyond "legal" methods lay another arsenal of criminal tactics, easily employed through underground networks to silence critics. Under the Proceso, the security forces had often used criminal gangs to help uncover the flow of aid to the guerrillas, and over time these rogue elements had gotten out of control. Some of their handlers in the police and military even joined them. Nor did their activities end with the Proceso. The Peronists also had their criminal gangs, recruited as bodyguards by corrupt politicians and labor leaders. Known as *patotas,* they could be used to control their organizations, eliminate rivals, and extort money. One of the most notorious *patotas* during the Menem era worked out of the Central Fruit and Vegetable Market and was under the control of Alberto Pierri, president of the Chamber of Deputies and political boss of a key industrial ward called (appropriately) Matanza, in Buenos Aires Province. These thugs had once been militants in a rightwing terrorist group called *Comando de Organización,* led by Alberto Brito Lima. Brito Lima became Menem's ambassador to Honduras.[27]

Pierri's *patota* was known as the *Batatas* (sweet potatoes), after their leader, Fidel "Batata" Juárez. He used them in election campaigns in Matanza to intimidate potential rivals, shake down the inhabitants for campaign contributions, pass out propaganda, paint slogans on walls, put up posters, and get Peronist voters to the polls. As a fervent supporter of Menem, Pierri was always ready to loan his *patota* to the president to silence any hecklers when he made one of his public appearances. One of the most notorious incidents of this sort came at the *Sociedad Rural Argentina's* 1993 annual fair, held in Palermo Park. The SRA's members were the country's *estanciero* elite, so it was customary for the president of the republic to address them on opening day. Menem was on the podium on 28 August, ready to address the crowd; but because many of the *estancieros* were known to disapprove of the government Pierri's *patota* were there to keep an eye on the audience. As soon as Menem started his speech, Carlos Negri, a builder of silos, began to boo from a nearby platform. Within seconds he was surrounded by young toughs who beat him and threw him to the ground. When reporters and cameramen converged on the scene, the thugs turned on them as well, driving them from the fairgrounds with kicks and blows.[28]

The government used the full range of its weapons against media critics. Menem's particular nemesis was the leftist muckraking daily newspaper *Página 12* and its star reporter, Horacio Verbitsky. He publicly called Verbitsky "a journalistic criminal" after *Página 12* broke the story about "Swiftgate," forcing a sweeping cabinet change. Menem liked to remind his listeners that Verbitsky had been a Montonero—conveniently ignoring the fact that he himself had welcomed the company of Montoneros once upon a time. When Verbitsky published in November 1991 his bestselling book, *Robo para la Corona* ("I Steal for the Crown"), about rampant corruption in the Menem government, several top officials including José Luis Manzano (whose flippant remark was the basis for the book's title), sued him in court for defamation. When found guilty, Verbitsky appealed to the OAS Human Rights Commission, claiming that Argentina was violating the Treaty of San José, which committed it to respecting speech and press freedom. Under OAS pressure, the Menem government backed down. Verbitsky then published another book, *Hacer la Corte,* which purported to tell the story of how Menem had packed the Supreme Court. Menem sued *Página 12* over an article by Verbitsky about the president's lack of moral authority as shown by his promotions of military officers tainted by their actions during the Proceso. The suit finally was dismissed in 1997 by a federal judge.

Other *Página 12* reporters suffered attacks. Hernán López Echagüe was badly beaten a week after the *Sociedad Rural* incident when he undertook to investigate "the batatas" and published an article about their links to Pierri and Eduardo Duhalde, the current governor of Buenos Aires Province. López was kidnapped in front of his home, shoved into a car by three big youths, and taken to a lonely spot, where he was punched and had his face slashed with a knife. Two weeks later he was attacked a second time. López Echagüe later received death threats after publishing an unauthorized biography of Duhalde. Other *Página 12* reporters also got death threats after publishing unflattering books about Menem and his entourage: Gabriela Cerruti, with her biography of Menem, *El Jefe;* and Román Lejtman with *Narcogate,* his exposure of the Yomas and their links to drug trafficking. But *Página 12* was not the only target. Olga Wornat, a reporter from *Somos,* a weekly magazine, got threatening phone calls after writing a story about the "batatas" she interviewed at the Central Fruit and Vegetable Market. Marcelo Bonelli, a reporter for *Clarín* and Radio Mitre, was beaten up after publishing stories about corruption in the Federal Police's anti-narcotics squad. *Clarín* also was sued by the Defense Ministry for violating state secrets when it began uncovering the government's illegal arms sales to Ecuador and Croatia. Some journalists paid with their lives for digging into corruption. Besides José Luis Cabezas, there were Mario Bonino and Ricardo Gangeme. Bonino was a reporter for the newspapers *Sur* and *Diario Popular,* in addition to being an official for the UTPBA, in charge of files concerning attacks on journalists. He disappeared on 11 November 1993, and his body was discovered four days later floating in the Río Riachuelo. Some years later an ex-Buenos Aires Province policeman claimed that some of his colleagues had committed the murder. Gangeme was the owner and editor of the local newspaper in Trelew, Chubut. He was shot on 13 May 1999, after running a series of stories about corruption in the local government. Six members of the Trelew Electricity Cooperative were arrested in connection with the murder.[29]

At the end of December 1997, *Periodistas,* the journal of the Argentine Association for the Defense of Independent Journalism, published a month-by-month survey of attacks on the media reported during the year.[30] There were four lawsuits for libel, all of the judgements suspended provided the journalists agreed to be silenced. In one case they agreed not to appeal a previous judgment to the Inter-American Human Rights Commission. Three other cases resulted in the cancellation of television specials about scandals in the Menem administration. But intimidation was more likely to be physical. The year began with the worst incident: the murder of José Luis Cabezas. Other reporters were threatened with a similar fate. By the end of December, some ninety-six death threats to reporters were recorded (some reporters got more than one). For example, not only was Antonio Fernández Llorente, a reporter covering the investigation of Cabezas' murder for Channel 13, threatened himself but there was a false bomb threat at a school his nephew attended. A week later his sister was attacked by three men who slashed her hand with a knife as she got out of a taxi in a residential area of Buenos Aires. Such knowledge about the whereabouts of Fernández Llorente's relatives suggests police involvement.

There were three kidnappings that might have might have resulted in grisly deaths like Cabezas', but fortunately didn't: Mario Ávila, a reporter in Tucumán; Carlos Suárez, a Buenos Aires journalist who was investigating links between Cuban American narcotics traffickers and Menem's interior minister José Luis Manzano; and Adolfo Scilingo, a former marine who had been the first to reveal, to *Página 12*'s Horacio Verbitsky, the Proceso's practice of throwing guerrilla prisoners into the South Atlantic from airplanes. Suárez was kept hooded for eight hours while he was interrogated about what he knew and whether he had passed it on to "that son-of-a-bitch Verbitsky." The procedure was very reminiscent of interrogations carried out by security forces under the Proceso. Scilingo was beaten and had his face carved with the names of three investigative journalists: Verbitsky, Mariano Grondona, and Magdalena Ruiz Guiñazú—all of whom had received death threats.

Periodistas recorded eleven other beatings. The police commonly beat up reporters and photographers covering protest demonstrations. Other journalists were victims of *patotas*. Sometimes the attacker was a prominent politician. Jorge César Humada, a Peronist senator from Misiones Province, injured a journalist in April by grabbing his neck and kicking him; and in October Jorge Rodríguez, the chief of Menem's cabinet (equivalent to Prime Minister), also sent a journalist to the hospital by kicking him. Shortly before that, Menem had encouraged citizens to apply "the law of the stick" against journalists who offended them. Apparently, some of his followers took him literally. But there were more serious attacks, too, as when Mario Domínguez, an investigative reporter for an FM station in Jujuy Province, was injured by a bullet after broadcasting a story accusing the local mayor of criminal activity. Arson destroyed much of a newspaper building, including its archives and photographic files, in Chubut Province. Unknown persons broke into the offices and set them afire after the paper published a series of stories about suspicious unsolved murders in the town of Esquel. Far more direct was the closure of two FM stations in the Buenos Aires area by the Federal

Police, who invaded their offices in broad daylight, without warrants. Their equipment was seized, and their two managers were abused: one was handcuffed and threatened with a gun; neither was allowed to call a lawyer. The police were acting upon a complaint by a rival FM station, owned by a friend of Menem's, whose broadcasting frequency was very close to those of the stations that were shut down.

In preparing its report, *Periodistas* expressed its conviction that "in a free and pluralistic society, independent journalism is an essential source of information and analysis and an instrument of control of government by civil society. All that tends to restrict freedom or to harass those who work in the press affects the freedom of citizens and democracy." Since almost everything that has become known about the vast underworld that seemed to permeate Argentina's government was revealed by journalists who took great risks (and sometimes paid a high cost for doing so), those sentiments appear well founded.

Chapter Six

Triumphs and Troubles

After the October 1993 midterm elections, the Peronist *Partido Justicialista (PJ)* increased its representation in the Chamber of Deputies from 61 to 64 seats, while its chief opponent, the *Unión Cívica Radical (UCR),* decreased its representation from 43 to 41 seats. The Peronists now had a one-vote absolute majority, and with help from allies among the scattering of minor and provincial parties, they would easily control the Chamber. Menem had worked hard for a decisive Peronist victory because it would strengthen his hand in his upcoming campaign to change the Constitution so as to permit his immediate re-election. As a measure of his success, the PJ carried 18 out of 24 provinces.[1] The post-election consensus among the media was that the 1993 results indeed constituted a popular endorsement of Menem and the Convertibility Plan.

Even so, there were small clouds on the political horizon that would grow bigger as the decade wore on. In the Federal District (the city of Buenos Aires), a new party calling itself the Frente Grande had managed to capture almost 14 percent of the vote and elect its two leaders, Carlos ("Chacho") Álvarez and Graciela Fernández Meijide, to Congress. Graciela Fernández Meijide had gained fame under the Proceso as a human rights activist. Álvarez was a film actor turned politician. As a left wing Peronist Congressman he, along with seven others, had broken with the PJ leadership in the Chamber of Deputies back in June 1990 and set up a "progressive" block of independents. Two of the other eight mavericks were (1) Germán Abdala, leader of the ATE's public sector workers in the Federal District, and (2) Juan Pablo Cafiero, son of Antonio Cafiero, the former governor of Buenos Aires Province. The elder Cafiero was, of course, an enemy of Menem, having been defeated by him for the JP's presidential nomination in 1988 and defeated a second time by Menem—indirectly—when he lost a referendum in 1990 to change the provincial constitution so as to allow him to run for immediate re-election.

These politicians started by opposing Menem's alliance with Bunge & Born and then became alarmed when he packed the Supreme Court, abolished the Tribunal of Accounts, and fired the administrative prosecutor (Ricardo Molinas, the targeted prosecutor, joined their group). The privatizations of the state companies provoked the final break. Soon this group gained the support of other left wing movements, such as the liberation theologists' Popular Christian Democratic Party and the Intransigent Party of former Buenos Aires governor Oscar Alende, who once led a radical left breakaway faction out of the UCR. Their first electoral attempt, in the 1991 midterm races, was a failure: they garnered only 1.4 percent of the Federal District vote. By 1993, however, they had attracted the backing of some of the factions of the old but badly divided Socialist Party. As the Frente Grande, they now had national representation. They were not yet a threat to Menem, but they had the potential to draw away some of the unions and intellectuals who were increasingly dismayed by Menem's seeming rejection of traditional Peronist principles. That might not happen so long as the economy kept growing, but any prolonged downturn could provoke serious desertions among the rank and file.[2]

CONVERTIBILITY'S POTENTIAL PROBLEMS

In January 1992 Cavallo eliminated the *austral*, which had been pegged to the dollar at 10,000 to one, and restored the old peso at a rate of one to one. Anyone with 10,000 *australes* could trade them in at the bank for either one peso or one dollar. This was no great change in the basics of the Convertibility Plan; what it mainly did was to simplify currency transactions. Argentines could freely trade pesos for dollars. The Central Bank still tied its printing of pesos to its holdings of exchange reserves.

Despite its obvious success in bringing down inflation, the Convertibility Plan drew criticism from the outset for linking Argentina's currency so closely to the dollar. Tying the peso to the dollar meant that if the dollar appreciated on the world market, so would the peso, making Argentina's exports more expensive and probably resulting in trade deficits. On the other hand, if the dollar depreciated, both dollars and pesos would tend to flow out to countries where interest rates were higher. The deregulation of capital transfers made it easy to send dollars out of the country. If that happened, the Central Bank's exchange reserves would shrink, requiring a tightening of the money supply. That would lead to a recession, in which case the Convertibility Plan would act like a straitjacket, because the government would not be allowed to try to stimulate an economic recovery through deficit spending. To preserve the parity between the peso and the dollar, the government had to either control its spending or continue attracting inflows of dollars through foreign investment, loans, or export earnings.

To keep the Convertibility Plan going in bad times as well as good, it was necessary to run budget surpluses so that there would be an ample cushion of reserves to fall back on. Instead, the Menem government spent lavishly. Small budget surpluses were recorded from 1992 through the end of 1994, but those were possible chiefly because the proceeds from privatizing the state companies were a way to cover what otherwise would have been deficits. That additional income gave the politicians inside the Cabinet a free hand to reward their political base. Even then the government raised additional money by selling bonds to foreign investors and negotiating more loans. Argentina's new positive image as an emerging capitalist economy and the fact that big international banks were awash in petrodollars from the rise in oil prices made all of that easy, in the short run. But it also drove up the foreign debt by almost $12 billion.[3]

Many critics also claimed that the fixed exchange rate was unrealistic and unsustainable. They argued that the original rate of 10,000 *australes* to the dollar overvalued the Argentine currency, and that the real rate should have been 11,000, 12,000, or even 15,000 to the dollar. Therefore, the one-to-one rate installed at the beginning of 1992 was also unrealistic, and unless there was a devaluation, Argentine exports would be overpriced and foreign imports would undersell domestic manufactures in the local market. Cavallo later admitted that he had been urged by economists in his ministry to quote the *austral* at a higher rate but had ignored them because he thought that anything above 10,000 would drive up prices and, besides, the public would adapt to the new system more easily if all they had to do was eliminate four zeroes.[4]

The Unión Industrial Argentina complained bitterly that manufacturers were being squeezed by the opening of Argentina to free trade, by an overvalued peso that encouraged cheap imports, by high interest rates, by rising energy prices from deregulation, and by higher taxes being levied at all levels of government. MERCOSUR, especially, came under attack for allowing an "avalanche" of Brazilian goods to enter the country. Unlike Argentina, Brazil periodically devalued its currency in order to boost its exports, while at the same time it was slow to open its own markets to other MERCOSUR members. Israel Mahler, the UIA's president, warned in 1993 that "We may be members of MERCOSUR, but we don't want to be its victims." Manuel Herrera, the UIA's secretary, called for a devaluation of the peso. He pointed out that the world's advanced capitalist nations had gotten ahead by protecting and nurturing their domestic industries.[5]

Neither Menem nor Cavallo had any intention of devaluing the peso, even if that meant running a trade deficit—which it did. From a surplus of $3.7 billion in 1991, the trade balance recorded a $2.6 billion deficit in 1992, $3.7 billion in 1993, and $5.8 billion in 1994. Nonetheless, the fixed rate of exchange was the cornerstone of the Convertibility Plan. Any attempt to modify it would destroy the plan's entire credibility. Cavallo had little sympathy and many harsh words for local industrialists. For years they had enjoyed a closed-off "hunting ground," he said, in which Argentine consumers were forced to buy high-priced, low-quality goods. Now local producers would have to face the discipline of open competition. The UIA's Mahler and Herrera were inclined to fight back, but many industrialists were afraid to provoke government reprisals, perhaps in the form of sudden tax audits. Also, the economy's resurgence following the Convertibility

Plan made it easier to swallow the new rules. On the other hand, Menem saw no advantage to alienating the industrialists. His political instincts led him to a compromise under which export-oriented local industries would pay lower taxes, receive export subsidies and easy credit, and get reimbursed for some of their expenses. Other local industries were encouraged to modernize by steep tariff reductions on their imports of machinery and equipment. All such concessions were justified on the grounds that they ultimately would help to narrow the trade deficit. Meanwhile, a mix of foreign investment and loans papered over the deficit for the time being.[6]

Table 6.1 shows another good reason why Menem and Cavallo strongly resisted devaluation. Most of Argentina's best-known companies were heavily in debt, far beyond their asset values. Those debts were figured mainly in dollars, so that any devaluation of the peso would plunge them deeper into debt and perhaps push them into default. Some Argentine industrialists, fearing foreign competition, had already begun selling off their heavily indebted firms. In 1994 Bunge & Born, now under yet another president, Ludwig Schmitt-Rhaden, began selling off parts of its conglomerate: Companía Química to Procter & Gamble; Atanor to Albaugh, a U.S. firm; Bunge Paints (formerly Alba) to ICI, a British-based multinational; and Grafa to a Brazilian textile company. Gilberto Montagna, the UIA's former president, sold his Terrabusi Biscuit Company to Nabisco. Terrabusi's main longtime competitor, the Bagley Biscuit Company, sold half of its stock to Danone, of France. Danone also bought the Villavicencio Mineral Water Company;

Table 6.1
Argentine Companies' Assets and Debts, January 1993

Company	Industry	Assets ($)	Debts ($)
Sevel	automotive	257,438,925	370,618,313
Pérez Companc	oil	99,376,955	111,227,361
Telefónica	telecommunications	81,562,932	196,146,249
Alpargatas	textiles, shoes	61,522,300	170,305,200
Siderca	steel tubes	56,602,973	145,127, 997
Telecom	telecommunications	28,955,435	197,293,982
Celulosa	paper	25,591,769	220,380,769
Particulares	cigarettes	23,091,000	38,006,100
Acindar	steel	14,625,900	266,097,300
Ipako	chemicals	13,619,102	31,620,265
Molinos R. Plata	food	10,788,893	172,825,987
Indupa	petrochemicals	10,345,826	189,562, 454
Comercial de Plata	Soldati holding co.	7,426,600	54,882,900
Atanor	chemicals	7,402,300	38,881,200
Editorial Atlantida	publishing	1,065,100	16,946,300

Source: Buenos Aires BOLSA, Comisión Nacional de Valores, cited in *Somos,* 4 January 1993, 58.

Lacteos Longchamps, a dairy; and Viñas del Sur. Garovagio & Zorraquín sold Cerro Castillo, its mining company, to the British firm, Lonhro. The Bridas Oil Company, under investigation for tax evasion, sold its paper company, Papel de Tucumán.

Most companies and conglomerates were still optimistic about the future, however, and Menem's flexible approach toward them paid off in the UIA's 1993 elections when Mahler and Herrera, the MIN "hardliners," lost out to a fusion list headed by Jorge Blanco Villegas, the owner of the local Philco franchise. Blanco Villegas was a *menemista* and a strong supporter of Convertibility. His backing came mainly from the conglomerates who were involved in buying the privatized state companies and from the export-oriented industries who were benefitting from government incentives.

The government had little to offer small and medium-sized firms (PYMEs) that produced just for the domestic market, however. The number of manufacturing enterprises operating in 1993 was 93,156, or fewer than half of those recorded in 1964. The decline had been steady, as Table 6.2 shows.

Table 6.2
Employment in Manufacturing versus Employment in Commerce and Services, 1954–1993

1. *Manufacturing*

Year	No. of firms	No. of employees	Average no. of employees per firm
1954	148,371	1,439,329	9.70
1964	190,862	1,370,486	7.18
1974	126,388	1,525,221	12.06
1985	109,376	1,175,001	10.75
1993	93,156	1,061,528	11.40

2. *Commerce and Services*

Year	No. of firms	No. of employees	Average no. of employees per firm
1954	389,750	467,700	1.2
1964	564,520	1,416,377	2.5
1974	696,910	1,845,488	2.6
1985	787,279	2,183,157	2.8
1993	810,839	2,490,308	3.1

Sources: Argentine Republic, Instituto Nacional de Estadística y Censos (INDEC), *Censo Nacional Económico,* 1964, 1974, 1994; INDEC, *Anuario Estadístico,* 1979–1980; INDEC, *Industria Manufacturera,* 1989.

From the end of the Perón era to 1964, the number of firms had increased, but their average size had decreased. By the time that Perón made his triumphant return to the presidency, however, political turmoil and economic stagnation had taken their toll on the weaker ones. Then came the Proceso with its attempts to liberalize the economy and encourage larger, more efficient companies. That was followed by stagflation under Alfonsín and the first years under Menem. The decline in enterprises affected all but a few branches of industry. Oil, petrochemicals, and plastics were the exceptions; otherwise, the industries that had characterized the "glory days" of import-substituting industrialization—clothing, textiles, and leather goods—offered many fewer jobs or opportunities for new entrepreneurs.[7] Where did the jobs and entrepreneurs go, then? Table 6.2 provides part of the answer. From the end of the Perón era down to 1993 the commercial and service sectors of the economy grew steadily, both in the number of establishments and the number of workers employed. Retail and wholesale trade, repair shops, hotels, restaurants, bars, cafes, corner groceries, drugstores, barbershops, beauty parlors, consulting firms, tourist agencies, private clinics, real estate agencies, taxi drivers, music stores, flower stalls, maid services and other services for the home—plumbers, carpenters, roofers, etc.—proliferated, while manufacturing became more capital-intensive. Wages and salaries were much lower than in manufacturing, however. An industrial worker in 1993 averaged $13,416 a year, or $1,118 a month. In the tertiary sector, the average was just over $5,000 a year, or about $428 a month.[8] To make ends meet, those workers had to hold more than one job. For the economy as a whole, productivity gains were more likely to be lower in the service sector than in manufacturing.

The 93,156 manufacturing firms recorded in 1993 were by no means all domestically owned, either. Between 1990 and 1994, foreigners invested around $3 billion in the private manufacturing sector, often taking over plants that had been idled during the long crisis of stagflation. They quickly changed the management style of their newly acquired firms, reorganized production, introduced new marketing schemes, and installed modern technology. Productivity per worker rose rapidly, partly because of new technology and organization, but also partly because so many redundant workers were fired. The incorporation of new technology also had mixed results for the trade balance. Although Argentina exported more, imports of machinery and equipment from abroad contributed greatly to the trade deficits that dogged the economy from 1992 on.[9]

MENEM'S RE-ELECTION

The Justicialist Party's decisive victory in the October 1993 elections indicated that Menem could be re-elected easily when his present term expired in 1995. However, the Constitution prohibited a president from serving two consecutive terms, so Menem would have to wait on the sidelines for another five years unless the Constitution was changed. He had tried before to get Congress to amend the Constitution to allow his immediate re-election, but opposition from left-wing

Peronists and Radicals prevented him from getting the necessary two-thirds majority in either the Senate or the Chamber of Deputies. But now, flushed with victory, he began campaigning for a constitutional convention.

Most of the JP, apart from the public sector unions, were willing to keep a popular Peronist in the presidency and ride on his coattails. The provincial parties, as Menem's unofficial allies, were also ready to go along. The strongest opposition came from the Radicals, of course. Former president Alfonsín was still the UCR's leader and a constant critic of Menem's government for what he perceived to be its "reactionary" economic and social programs. He was not adverse to changing the Constitution, having proposed to do so when he was president, but Alfonsín suspected Menem of wanting to increase executive power so much that, in reality, the president would be a dictator. Indeed, he thought that Menem already had claimed too many extraordinary powers. To prevent further erosion of democracy, Alfonsín wanted to create a European-style parliamentary system that would make the president mainly a ceremonial figure and transfer most of the executive powers to a prime minister removable from power by a majority vote in Congress.[10]

Menem got Alfonsín to cooperate by calling for a plebiscite on whether to hold a constitutional convention. Alfonsín could not easily oppose this end run around Congress, because he had himself resorted to plebiscites when he was president. He therefore accepted the idea of constitutional reform but tried to negotiate beforehand on some compromises. Menem was flexible, confident that he would get most of what he wanted and knowing that a pact with Alfonsín would make the reforms more legitimate. The two men, with their teams of advisors, began meeting at the presidential residence in Olivos. After signing the final agreement on 14 November, Menem called off the plebiscite as no longer necessary.

The "Pact of Olivos" allowed Menem the right of immediate re-election. In return he agreed to reduce the presidential term from six years to four, to limit the president's powers to issue decree laws "of necessity and urgency," to limit the president's ability to intervene in the provinces, and to create a "chief of cabinet" who would be like a prime minister, named by the president and removable either by him or by a congressional vote of censure. In addition, the president would be elected by a direct popular vote, instead by an electoral college. Senators, too, would be elected directly, instead of by provincial legislators. There would be three senators from each province, elected simultaneously, with two going to the majority party and the third to the runner-up. The city of Buenos Aires would be raised to the same status as a province, with its own directly elected mayor (intendant) and city council empowered to legislate without interference by the federal government. Congress would also have more control over the Executive's spending powers and more power to protect the independence of the judiciary.[11]

The April 1994 constitutional convention elections gave the Justicialists the most seats, but not enough for a majority. But, having already cut a deal with the Radicals, they had sufficient votes to control the sessions, which were presided over by Senator Eduardo Menem, the president's brother. "Chacho" Álvarez's

"Frente Grande" kept up a running attack on the proceedings and attracted a few defectors from the PJ, including Senator José Octavio Bordón from Mendoza, who had hoped to be the PJ's presidential nominee in 1995 but now saw his hopes dashed. On the UCR's side, its senator from the Federal District (soon to be the self-governing City of Buenos Aires), Fernando de la Rua, refused to attend the convention because he claimed that Alfonsín had betrayed the party by agreeing to a pact with Menem. Despite these sour notes, however, the new Constitution was duly approved on 22 August, and general elections were set for 14 May 1995. Menem would head the Justicialist ticket, with his most recent interior minister, Carlos Ruckauf, as his running mate.[12]

THE "TEQUILA EFFECT"

1994 had been another good year for the Argentine economy. Economic activity was still vigorous; economic growth was still at an 8 percent annual rate; per capita GDP was healthy; the consumer price index rose by only 4 percent; steady increases in investment made it possible to continue paying on loans, which made it possible to get more loans. But there were also some disquieting signs. Unemployment was over 12 percent and another estimated 10 percent of the workforce was underemployed. The trade deficit was almost double what it had been the year before, and the balance of payments deficit was rising too. Tax revenues chronically failed to match increased spending on pensions, social services, and transfer payments to the provinces, creating a nagging fiscal deficit. In the first years of the Menem administration, this had been obscured by the proceeds coming in from privatization, but now there was little left to privatize.[13]

The situation was manageable so long as foreign capital kept flowing in, either as investments or loans. But in December 1994, the Mexican government suddenly devalued its peso by 40 percent, setting off a panic among foreign investors in "emerging markets" and requiring an emergency bailout by the United States. Like Argentina, Mexico's strong economic growth with low inflation had attracted a lot of investors in the past four years; but when the U.S. Federal Reserve began raising interest rates in February 1994 much of that capital inflow proved to be ephemeral as investors pulled their money out of Mexico and bought U.S. Treasury bonds. The stampede out of Mexico quickly spread throughout Latin America and became known as the "tequila effect." In Argentina there was a sharp drop in bank deposits and foreign exchange holdings as people shifted their money to the United States. Argentine bonds found fewer buyers and share prices on the Buenos Aires Bolsa plummeted.

None of this prevented Menem from being re-elected with 45 percent of the vote, sufficient under the new Constitution to prevent a runoff. He had spent lavishly on his campaign: around $3 billion, according to one well-placed source.[14] The full impact of the "tequila effect" was not felt by May 1995, nor did most voters care deeply about the corruption scandals that the press had reported.

Years of official corruption and other abuses of power had made them cynical about politics. What mattered for them was that living standards were still better than they had been six years previously, and so they felt grateful to Menem and Cavallo. True, there was an indignant minority that swung behind the new party called FREPASO (*Frente para un País en Solidaridad*), which was a merger between the Frente Grande and some smaller left wing parties. Surprisingly, its candidates, José Octavio Bordón and Carlos "Chacho" Álvarez, came in second with 28 percent of the vote, ahead of the badly-divided Radicals whose candidates, Horacio Massaccesi and Antonio Hernández, garnered only 17 percent.[15] Later that year FREPASO would stun both the Justicialists and the UCR by winning the election in the City of Buenos Aires to choose a third senator.

ECONOMIC DAMAGE CONTROL

Even before the election, Cavallo was struggling to reverse the "tequila effect" and restore the economy's dynamism. He had ignored the IMF's warnings about the danger of fiscal and trade deficits in the past, and its urging of tax increases, spending cuts, and tighter credit. He viewed such a program as recessionary and certain to hurt Menem's chances for re-election. Because of his obvious success over the past three years, he was able to treat the IMF with a certain disdain, but now the "tequila effect" had shaken his confidence. Furthermore, his plans were disrupted by a series of judicial decisions. For years the government had sought to limit its budget shortfalls by withholding payments from pensioners and contractors. Now the courts declared that the government had to pay up, to the amount of around $7 billion, throwing Cavallo's budget estimates into turmoil. His original projection of a 900 million peso deficit in 1994 turned out to be 1.6 billion instead. A humbled Cavallo went to Washington in March 1995 to beg money from the IMF, World Bank, and private banks. He came back with $8 billion, but also committed to increasing the VAT tax, allowing more "flexibility" in the labor laws, reducing government salaries, privatizing the state's remaining companies, and suspending "additional payments" already promised to the provinces. Menem warned against any new social programs or increased spending for those already in place.[16]

The magic had gone out of Argentina's economy, which contracted by more than 4 percent during 1995, while unemployment rose to over 18 percent. The recession kept the rise in the consumer price index to only 1.6 percent, because consumer demand was way down. There was some good news: agricultural and oil exports rose, helping to produce a trade surplus; but that surplus was also the result of falling imports of machinery and equipment, which were in turn influenced by a drop in foreign investment. The recession also cut into tax receipts, making it impossible to reduce the fiscal deficit. Moreover, borrowing from abroad to cover the fall in revenues pushed the foreign debt up to $95.6 billion by the end of 1995. Payments on the principal and interest would become a crushing burden on the budget in the years to come.[17]

Years of lavish government spending, paid for by privatization, had dulled Menem and Cavallo to the need for fiscal discipline. Suddenly, the "tequila effect" had exposed the flaws in their strategy. But there were deeper underlying problems of a structural nature that might have destabilized a more responsible approach as well: the increasing burden of pension payouts and the constitutional requirement for federal revenue sharing.

Congress replaced Argentina's pension system in October 1993 with a scheme that was part public and part private. An ageing population was putting too much pressure on the Social Security Institute that Perón had created in the 1940s. Previously, retirees all drew the same pensions, regardless of how much they had contributed, while the state made up any deficits; but by the 1960s, falling birthrates and increasing longevity put the old system into financial difficulties. Raising the retirement age didn't solve the problem, so by the 1980s a bankrupt Social Security Institute stopped making payments, leaving retirees without coverage. There were loud street protests and many lawsuits. The courts regularly found in favor of the elderly, but not until Menem took office did the government start to settle the claims. Then the pensioners had to choose between accepting government bonds as payment or being paid in cash installments over fifteen years. Meanwhile, the old Social Security Institute was replaced by a new National Social Security Administration (ANSES) which would administer the reformed system. Argentines who were forty-five or older were now given a choice between staying in the government-funded, pay-as-you-go system or joining a private pension plan. Those under forty-five had to enlist in a private plan. All private accounts had to be approved by ANSES and were known as AFJPs (*Administradora de Fondos de Jubilaciones y Pensiones*). Unions were induced to support the plan by allowing them to set up their own AFJPs. Congress also raised the minimum retirement age and the number of years of work required to qualify for benefits.[18]

Initially, about an equal number of workers were in the pay-as-you-go option and the AFJPs. Those who failed to make a choice were randomly assigned to an AFJP. In all, some 5.7 million workers were covered out of an estimated 14 million. By the end of the decade, that had climbed to over 11 million, but the increase was not accompanied by a similar increase in the size of the pension funds' financial accounts. As the economy worsened, both employers and workers tended to evade their contributions. Also, many workers were in the underground economy. In 1994 the federal government was forced to take over the provinces' pension funds, which had run out of money, thus adding another burden to its budget. The provinces claimed, with some justification, that without federal relief they would suffer "a social explosion." At the same time, the federal government tried to encourage employers to hire more workers by reducing the rate of their required contributions. All these adjustments dramatically increased the pension system deficit from 3.75 billion pesos in 1995 to 21.4 billion (1995) pesos by the year 2000. Most of the AFJPs also had invested heavily in Argentine government bonds, which would soon be worthless. Rather than relieving the social security system's strain on the federal budget, the reforms actually increased it. By the end of the 1990s, fully half of the government's budget was being allocated to pensions.[19]

THE DYSFUNCTIONAL PROVINCES

Argentina's provinces ran large deficits every year, requiring frequent federal government bailouts. Yet the provinces resisted all attempts to discipline them. Article 75, Section 2 of the 1994 Constitution provided for revenue sharing between the federal government and the provinces, under agreements worked out in the Senate and ratified by both houses of Congress. The federal government collected three-fourths of all tax revenue, but then distributed 57 percent of that to the provinces "through political negotiations that often were hardly transparent and seldom objective."[20] The 1994 Constitution strengthened the provinces' bargaining position by providing for their equal representation in the Senate and the direct election of senators. Thus, Tierra del Fuego, with only 115,000 inhabitants, had the same number of senators as Buenos Aires Province with its 11 million. This led to a tremendous overrepresentation of the poorer, less-populated provinces of the interior. The four largest provinces—Buenos Aires, the City of Buenos Aires, Córdoba, and Santa Fe—accounted for 64 percent of Argentina's population, yet had only 17 percent of the Senate seats. The poorer provinces were often ruled by political bosses who needed federal funds to grease the wheels of their clientelistic political machines. Very often those political machines took the form of provincial political parties whose representation in the Senate prevented either the PJ or the UCR from claiming a majority, thus allowing them to determine the balance of power.[21]

Even the major parties were really coalitions of provincial organizations. The national leadership of the PJ or UCR exercised only nominal control over their provincial branches. The real power brokers in Argentine politics were the provincial governors who received the proceeds from revenue sharing and distributed the patronage among their municipal organizational leaders, who in turn distributed patronage among their ward captains. Although direct elections were the rule at all levels of government, voters voted for party lists drawn up by the provincial organizations. Thus, senators, federal deputies, provincial legislators, and local mayors and councilmen all owed their jobs to the leaders of the provincial party, not to the national leaders. And since these officials were rotated in and out of different posts, they were even more dependent on provincial leaders. Presidential aspirants had to cultivate good relations with the provincial governors, who controlled the nominating conventions. Not surprisingly, most presidential candidates were governors, usually from the more populous provinces. Once elected, however, they would have to deal with their colleagues from the marginal provinces.[22]

Menem and Cavallo were thus limited with respect to their ability to keep government spending under control. In the past, gross financial mismanagement by a province might have prompted the federal government to intervene and replace the irresponsible authorities. But although the 1994 Constitution retained, in Article 6, the federal government's right to intervene a province, this had been somewhat neutered by requiring Congress to take the initiative in calling for action. That was not likely to happen, and therefore Menem and Cavallo tried to find other ways to impose discipline. The new VAT tax provided the federal government with additional funds to cajole the governors into agreeing, in 1992 and 1993, to limit provincial spending, raise local taxes, and privatize their banks and utilities companies. In practice, however, there was no way to enforce those agreements, and few provinces actually made good on their promises, even though federal remittances to them more than doubled by 1995 to $14.5 billion. At the end of 1994, the combined deficits of all the provinces still added up to just under $2.7 billion. *The Review of the River Plate* reported that

most provincial governors have simply told the president that they have no intention of reducing expenditure, most of which goes to public employees, as long as widespread unemployment exists....They are not going to do it because the public sector is the only possible source of employment and of votes.

The poorer the province, the greater was the need to use the public sector to provide jobs and prevent emigration. One provincial governor admitted that his payroll was larded with superfluous employees, but defended the practice. "We give out public jobs to keep people from dying of hunger," he said, "because there's no other place to work. I'm fully aware that if I fire a fellow citizen I'm condemning him to poverty; and, what's more, I don't have the money to pay him welfare." Still, provincial and municipal payrolls often were padded with nonexistent employees (*ñoquis*) whose paychecks went to department heads or to people who showed up at work only on payday. Provincial legislators enjoyed lavish expense accounts and funds to hire their relatives and friends as "consultants."[23]

In Buenos Aires Province only 6 percent of the economically active population worked in the public sector, and in other relatively well-off provinces like Córdoba, Mendoza, and Santa Fé the proportion was still only 8 percent; but in peripheral provinces like La Rioja, Catamarca, and Formosa, more than one out of three people worked for the provincial or some municipal government. Public spending per capita was six and a half times greater in La Rioja than in Buenos Aires Province; yet La Rioja funded only 3 percent of its spending and depended on the Federal Treasury for the rest, whereas Buenos Aires funded 57 percent of its own expenditures.[24]

The expansion of provincial and municipal payrolls negated Cavallo's attempts to pare down public employment. Privatizations and downsizing reduced the number of federal employees by 445,935 from the end of 1990 to the end of 1997; but the provincial and municipal payrolls increased by 619,300.[25] It is true, however, that almost half of the cuts at the federal level were made possible by devolving responsibilities for education and health to the provincial level. The

Ministry of Education lost 118,173 employees between 1989 and 1995, and the Ministry of Health lost 88,129, for a total of 206,302 federal jobs eliminated, but the provinces added 315,255 new employees in those same two areas. That was more than half of their increase in public jobs.[26] Since job creation was the chief concern of provincial governments, most of the money (between 50 and 70 percent) allocated for those agencies went toward salaries instead of providing services. Consequently, hospitals and clinics were short of doctors, nurses, equipment, and medicines, but had an abundance of administrative and maintenance personnel. Local government employees often missed work, or else came late and left early. Sometimes services were contracted out to companies with political connections, who collected their money without doing the work. Argentina's public school system, once the best in Latin America, was an example. School buildings were dirty and crumbling because cleaning and maintenance were neglected. There were reports of schools in the provinces of Chaco, Formosa, Jujuy, and Salta, and in the city of Rosario, Argentina's second-largest, that had to be closed for unsanitary conditions or lack of drinking water. In some of the wards in the city of Buenos Aires, parents kept their children at home because the schools were swarming with rats. Classrooms were crowded, and many teachers were unqualified, having gotten their jobs through political patronage. School cafeterias were filthy, and the food was often inedible.[27]

Provincial governments complained that they were unable to meet their new responsibilities because the federal government failed to provide them with the necessary funding. La Rioja in 1993 got 20 million pesos a month from the federal government, yet by the end of the year was 70 million pesos in debt, of which 19 million was owed to the Banco de La Nación, which had given it advances on expected revenue sharing payments. The province ran monthly deficits of around 5 million pesos and was so short of funds by November that it couldn't pay its employees' salaries. Chaco Province got 36 million pesos a month in transfer payments but still ran deficits of between 7 and 9 million. Like La Rioja, it could not pay its employees, and its pension fund was bankrupt. Catamarca Province got 22 million a month but ran chronic deficits of about 4 million. Its total debt was about 45 million, and it couldn't pay either salaries or pensions. Salta Province got 35 million a month but owed back wages to its staff, and its pension fund was out of money. Corrientes Province also owed its employees back pay and couldn't pay its pensioners either. Its current problems stemmed largely from the fact that funds were diverted from the provincial government's budget to finance the governor's re-election campaign.[28]

Just as the federal government devolved new responsibilities upon the provinces, so the provinces, in turn, transferred some of their tasks to the municipal governments. To their traditional functions of street paving and cleaning, garbage collection and sewerage disposal, public lighting and the provision of running water, they now had to add some public health services, low-cost housing, soup kitchens for the poorest people, and employment bureaus. These local governments had neither the financial resources nor the technical and administrative experience to perform those functions. Their taxing powers were limited and tax evasion was widespread. In small towns the mayor and municipal council were elected and had to face their constituents daily, so there was little likelihood that they would apply the law harshly. Nor could they expect much help in the form of revenue sharing from the provincial government, except at election time. Like the provincial authorities, the town fathers simply let services deteriorate, ignored planning, and delayed paying their employees or their debts to providers.[29]

Calls by the federal government, the IMF, World Bank, and Inter-American Development Bank for the provincial governments to reduce their payrolls met with flat refusals and demands for emergency bailouts. If the federal government refused to come up with more money, the provinces took advantage of Article 125 of the Constitution, which allowed them to contract foreign loans. Although Menem might have prevented that, he did not consider it politically feasible. Instead, the federal government assumed the responsibility for repaying those loans when the provinces faced default. To further relieve the provinces' fiscal plight, the federal government also took over the responsibility for their pension systems. In brief, the provinces and the municipalities, with their administrative incapacity and fiscal irresponsibility, remained a fiscal drain that the federal government could not plug.[30]

THE DEMANDS OF CLIENTELISM

No Argentine politician better understood clientelistic politics than Carlos Menem, and no Peronist had a keener sense of how important patronage was to the Justicalist Party. A caudillo himself from a poor, distant province, his knowledge of the realities of Argentine grassroots politics enabled him to carry out a program that was openly at odds with Peronism's traditions. As a provincial caudillo, he understood that in the peripheral provinces political parties were essentially clusters of rival elite families, knit together more by personal loyalties than by principles. Each cluster was led by a family head, or *patrón*, who was expected to have a direct, personal relationship with those around him (sub-leaders, or *punteros*) and beneath him (clients). Those relationships were cemented by the careful distribution of favors or resources (jobs, welfare, graft). Since the peripheral provinces were poor, the *patrón* always sought to tap resources beyond his local district. Hence the importance of federal transfer payments, which would surely be greater if the national party organization controlled the Casa Rosada. Menem made certain that Peronist governors in the peripheral provinces were well treated, in return for which they used their overrepresentation in Congress to further his policies. He also courted conservative, non-Peronist provincial party machines to further ensure himself of congressional majorities.[31]

Urban politics was more class-conscious, since it rested on a mass base composed largely of the industrial workers and their families, but it too was clientelistic in nature. Its networks were complex and diverse, consisting of labor unions, social activists' clubs, neighborhood groups, squatters' movements, and even criminal gangs. Taken together, these networks constituted the Peronist Movement, which was broader and more informal than the Justicialist Party. The networks were not included in the party's statutes and operated largely outside of its control, but they had many different roots reaching into working-class society. The movement went underground when military governments came to power, allowing Peronism to survive; under democracy it acted in the open, mobilizing crowds for rallies, or to vote, to clog the streets with pickets and protestors, to close down businesses through strikes, or to run soup kitchens. As in the peripheral provinces, the governors of Buenos Aires, Santa Fé, or Córdoba tried to connect themselves to the *manzaneras* (block captains) of the "base units" (*unidades de base,* or UBs) through ward leaders and neighborhood leaders of *agrupaciones,* the equivalent of the poorer provinces' *punteros.* The movement's lower echelons had government jobs that paid them a salary without requiring them to work, thus leaving them free to devote themselves full-time to party tasks. In short, Peronism was a very loose, undisciplined organizational network lubricated by patronage.[32]

The "Fund for the Historical Restoration of Greater Buenos Aires" (*Fondo de Reparación Histórico del Conurbano Bonarense*) illustrates how the movement worked for the benefit of both Menem and Eduardo Duhalde, who resigned as vice president in 1991 to run successfully for the governorship of Buenos Aires Province. As governor of Argentina's largest province, Duhalde planned to run for president in 1995. He let it be known that he was an old-fashioned Peronist who believed in returning the party to its populist ideology, and therefore was not a *menemista.* Even then, however, Menem had plans to change the Constitution in order to serve another presidential term. Thus, the two men were natural opponents, although neither wanted to split the party. Finally, they made a deal by which a hefty portion of the federal government's taxes would be earmarked for social and public works programs to be carried out by a special "Fund for the Historical Restoration of Greater Buenos Aires," with Duhalde given complete discretion as to how the money would be used. In 1992, its first year, the fund received $400 million. That rose to $600 million in 1994 and $650 million in 1996. In addition, Duhalde agreed to support a second presidential term for Menem, while Menem, in return, would not oppose a second gubernatorial term for Duhalde and promised to support Duhalde for president in 1999. Shortly after Menem got the national Constitution changed in 1994, Duhalde succeeded in having the Buenos Aires constitution revised and was re-elected.[33]

Duhalde wisely targeted the fund's money to build schools, clinics, and sanitation works. With almost $2 million a day to spend, he bought a lot of popularity among contractors, workers, and a grateful public in the poorer *barrios.* The fund also allowed him to consolidate his political machine by rewarding his allies among the municipal politicians and withholding aid from those who opposed him. Every time a project was started, television cameras would be on hand to show the governor, his municipal allies, and their *punteros* giving it their blessing.

For Menem, this fund had the virtue of strengthening Peronism's hold in the industrial suburbs of Greater Buenos Aires, which were suffering from job losses brought on by privatization. It certainly helped to make the 1993 and 1995 electoral campaigns successful. On the other hand, it built up the power base of a potentially dangerous rival—especially since Menem, following his presidential re-election, began to plot for yet a third term! It also raised demands from other Peronist governors for more patronage. By the end of 1994 the federal government's budget, which had enjoyed surpluses since the Convertibility Plan went into effect, recorded its first deficit. From then on, there would be a tug-of-war between the need for budgetary responsibility and the demands of political necessity, and as it escalated under the stress of the "tequila effect," it would drive a wedge between Menem and Cavallo.

Chapter Seven

The Downward Slide

The year 1995 was a bad one for Argentina's economy. Growth was a negative 4.6 percent, and unemployment rose to over 18 percent. Spooked by the "tequila effect," about $10 billion of capital fled the country. Many private firms went out of business, while others teetered on the verge of bankruptcy. Inflation was a mere 1.6 percent, but the country was in a recession. There was a trade deficit of $5.8 billion and a balance of payments deficit of $9.4 billion carried over from 1994.[1]

Cavallo attacked the crisis with his usual vigor, but the Convertibility Plan's flaws were now painfully visible. Tax cuts and increased government spending to stimulate the economy were prohibited because they caused budget deficits. Of course, there had been deficits all along, but they had been covered by revenue from privatizations and from selling government bonds. There were still some petrochemical plants, electric power companies, and railway lines, worth about $5.2 billion, that could be sold, but that would be a one-time-only stopgap. There were fewer customers for Argentine government bonds, and they wanted higher interest rates. The trade deficit could be narrowed by restricting imports—but at the cost of slower growth. Devaluing the peso to increase exports was still unthinkable. Argentina's public debt rose from $70.7 billion in mid-1994 to $82 billion by mid-1995 and would reach $95.6 billion by the end of the year. Principal and interest payments absorbed almost one-fourth of all export earnings.[2]

The Convertibility Plan would require cuts in public spending. Now that more capital was leaving Argentina than was flowing in, it was necessary to reduce the amount of money in circulation. But then the government would have to choose between letting more businesses fail and watching unemployment rise further, or sharply cutting back its own spending. A worried IMF urged Cavallo to roll back government spending, but his ability to do so was limited. The federal government's payroll was trimmed a bit, salaries were reduced a little, and some public works projects were put on hold. Sales and VAT taxes were increased, and Menem vetoed several new social programs that Congress sent to him. Still, all that was not enough to offset the enormous drain of transfer payments to the provinces. Nor was it likely that Argentina would register sizeable trade surpluses so long as high labor costs and inefficiencies continued to make its industrial goods uncompetitive. In the meantime, higher taxes and reduced spending only made the recession worse.

Cavallo fought in cabinet meetings for reforms in revenue sharing and labor laws. He asked for emergency powers to control transfer payments and presented ample evidence to show how irresponsible the provinces were in handling their finances. Nevertheless, 1995 was an election year, so neither Menem nor Congress was willing to grant him the powers he demanded. To the contrary, "supplementary funds" were sent out to the provinces just before the elections to make sure that there were no Peronist defections. Menem knew that failure to appease the provincial governments could produce explosive riots, such as those that had erupted in Jujuy in November 1990 and in Santiago del Estero in December 1993. In the latter case, the provincial legislative hall, the provincial Supreme Court building, and about a dozen private homes belonging to prominent officials were sacked and set afire by a mob of civil servants, teachers, labor union militants, students, and pensioners. They were protesting unpaid salaries and pensions, the loss of jobs through downsizing, and the notorious corruption of top government people. The riot had been preceded by months of public protests against the federal government's insistence that the desperately poor province take on the financial responsibilities for public education, health, and sanitation while simultaneously trimming its own payroll and divesting itself of provincial banks and utilities. Although the riots led to federal intervention and the removal of local authorities, Menem also agreed to provide Santiago del Estero with more money to meet its new expenses. Neither Cavallo nor the IMF could dissuade him in 1993 because he was already angling for his re-election.[3] Now, having achieved re-election, he had not forgotten the lessons he had learned from Santiago del Estero.

While Cavallo and the IMF insisted that the federal government balance its budget by raising taxes and reducing expenditures, especially transfer payments to the provinces, the recession increased provincial demands for financial help. Powerful figures in the Justicialist Party argued that the party would fragment without federal patronage to hold it together. In this power struggle Cavallo gambled on his popularity, which at the height of the Convertibility Plan's success had rivaled even Menem's. Cavallo still was considered an economic wizard by the general public and a trusted ally by international bankers; he kept threatening to resign if he failed to get his way. He even presumed to exercise a veto over appointments to other executive departments besides the Economics Ministry if he thought the appointees were corrupt "mafiosos." "Either he goes, or I do," was his habitual way of forcing Menem to back down. Cavallo made it clear that he had a lot of information about payoffs from lobbyists who wanted to market products supposedly belonging to American companies under international patent law.[4]

What Cavallo failed to realize was that his attitude of indispensability and his popularity were an affront to Menem. Not surprisingly, Menem began to feel that Cavallo was beginning to usurp his authority. But what really caused the president's bucket of grievances to overflow was Cavallo's attack on an old friend and fellow Arab Argentine, Alfredo Enrique Hallib Yabrán.

CAVALLO VERSUS YABRÁN

Yabrán was a multimillionaire businessman, a first-generation Argentine born in Entre Ríos Province in 1944 to Syrian immigrants. He started as a delivery boy, selling his father's homemade ice cream from door to door. When still a teenager, he moved to Buenos Aires City, got a job with the Burroughs office equipment company, and eventually began his own mail courier business, which he named Ocasa. Those were the early days of the Proceso, when the government was trying to privatize or outsource many public services. Encotel, the postal and telegraph service, was so inefficient that General Videla encouraged Yabrán to expand his courier business into private mail delivery. There was competition, but Yabrán was ruthless about getting ahead. There was always a lawless element within the Proceso, and Yabrán recruited from it a bodyguard whom he put to work hijacking his competitors' cars and trucks as well as attacking their homes, offices, and employees. He even got control of the private mail carriers' labor union, which then refused to handle his competitors' mail. Using his contacts in the Proceso, Yabrán extended his operations to delivering bank documents in armored trucks. Eventually, Ocasa won a contract to transport the Banco de la Nación's documents to and from its various branches. Then it gained a monopoly on the distribution of bills and invoices issued by the federal government. Ocasa's fleet of yellow trucks, so commonly seen on the streets, soon earned Yabrán the nickname of "El Amarillo."[5]

Yabrán's friends in the air force paved the way for acquiring control of the Ezeiza airport's air cargo operations, under another company called Edcadassa. That, plus his underworld contacts, got him involved in facilitating the narcotics trade and money laundering. The "Yomagate" scandal did not touch him directly, and he continued to enjoy Menem's protection. Nor did the illegal arms trade scandal result in his arrest or his removal from Ezeiza. Instead, his company, Interbaires, was awarded control of the airport's duty-free shop, and another Yabrán company (called Intercargo) got control of the airport's custodial services. Not surprisingly, Yabrán was the largest financial contributor to Menem's campaign to change the Constitution in 1994 and also to his re-election a year later.

Yabrán's next target was Encotel, the state postal and telegraph company. He urged Menem to privatize it so that he could buy it and obtain a complete monopoly over all postal services in Argentina. Cavallo was determined to prevent that. Since the Economics Ministry had absorbed the functions of the old Public Works

Ministry, Cavallo had authority over Encotel. His first step was to replace its old management and outsource its responsibilities to many different private companies, other than Ocasa. Yabrán fought back with harassing lawsuits and violence. Judge María Servini de Cubría found Encotel's new manager, Abel Cuchietti, guilty of "fraud and abuse of authority." He had lowered a fee on foreign couriers, set by the previous management at Yabrán's request, and had made public a list of all of Encotel's concessionaires. A week later, a bomb exploded at Cuchietti's home and also at the offices of a new company that had replaced Ocasa as the courier for the Israelite Bank of Córdoba. A few months after that, Cuchietti was attacked by thugs and left with a broken leg. After Carlos Corach, then Menem's legal and technical secretary (and later to be his interior minister), hinted to Cuchietti that worse might be on the way, Cuchietti resigned.

Cavallo refused to back away from a fight. He reorganized Encotel as a new company, Encotesa, and appointed a new director, Haroldo Grisanti; but he too was battered by a series of lawsuits. One of those charged Encotesa with unfair competition because it had underbid Ocasa for the right to deliver documents for the Mortgage Bank (Banco Hipotecario). Yabrán also sued those of Cavallo's assistants who had prepared the decrees setting up Encotesa. Violence soon followed. Luis Cerolini, one of the Mortgage Bank's directors, came home from a vacation with his family in July 1994 to find the place vandalized and a note on his door threatening him with death if the bank did not reverse itself and rehire Ocasa. When the bank refused to cave in, Yabrán shrugged off his defeat: "I lost a battle, but the war isn't over."[6]

Cavallo intended to use the DGI (Internal Revenue Service) against Yabrán. The DGI discovered that all of Yabrán's companies were guilty of tax evasion, but before he could use this information, Cavallo found himself entangled in a scandal that weakened him both in the government and in public opinion. The scandal grew out of a project to computerize the operations of the Banco de la Nación, where Aldo Dadone, a lifelong friend of Cavallo's, was president. Another longtime friend, Hugo Gaggero, was vice president, and another close Cavallo associate, Alfredo Aldaco, was in charge of upgrading the bank's information system. IBM won the contract in February 1994, against six other competitors, although several of the bank's technicians pointed out that IBM's main advocate was Juan Carlos Cattaneo, a member of Menem's presidential staff, and that his brother Marcelo was one of the bank's directors. Some of these technicians were dismissed, others were transferred, and some were sent on forty-day mandatory vacations. But that didn't stop the press from digging, and in May 1994 La Nación carried a front-page story accusing IBM of obtaining its contract through bribery. The DGI launched an investigation, which led, in October 1995, to federal indictments of Dadone, Aldaco, and Juan Carlos Cattaneo. Dadone was eventually found guilty, as was Aldaco, who had been found to have an overseas bank account where he kept the bribe money. Cattaneo escaped, probably because his brother wasn't able to testify. Marcelo had been found hanged in his apartment, with a clipping from La Nación stuffed in his mouth: another of Argentina's curious "suicides." Santiago Pinetta, the reporter who first broke the story, was beaten up by a *patota* and had the letters "IBM" carved on his chest. IBM's home office fired all of the top officials in its Argentine branch, after an investigation by FBI agents convinced the company that the local office had indeed violated America's 1977 Foreign Corrupt Practices Act. The Banco de la Nación sued IBM to get its money back, and IBM sued the bank for breach of contract. IBM, however, was prohibited from ever bidding on any other Argentine government contracts.[7]

While none of this touched Cavallo directly, he was tarnished by the fact that some of the principals were his appointees. His own extravagant lifestyle, which he frequently flaunted, fueled suspicions that he too was taking bribes. In February 1996 a television news program revealed that Cavallo had paid only 5,000 pesos of income tax at a time when he was pursuing a campaign against tax evasion. Cavallo made things worse by trying to stop the program from being aired. Following that, a Radical congressman, Enrique Benedetti, filed charges against Cavallo for "illegal enrichment," and the DGI began an investigation into the economics minister's finances.[8] Suddenly Cavallo was very vulnerable.

Cavallo was convinced that Yabrán and Carlos Corach were behind the attacks on him. Following a press conference at the Economics Ministry, at which he accused Yabrán of using "mafia methods" to build up his empire and eventually take over the country's entire postal service, Cavallo was invited to appear before the Chamber of Deputies. He accepted, and on 23 August 1995 he spoke for eleven hours, describing with names, dates, facts, and figures the criminal methods Yabrán used to expand his business. As PJ deputies sat in silent gloom, Radicals fired a barrage of questions at him, which he answered in full.[9]

From that point on, Menem decided that Cavallo had to go. The two men had quarreled over Yabrán before, and Menem had threatened to fire him, but the president backed down after hearing protests from bankers, the Buenos Aires BOLSA, and the U.S. ambassador.[10] Now, however, the deepening economic crisis was taking a toll on the president's popularity, with polls showing his approval rating to be in the high 30 percent range and his government's economic policies in the low 30s. The CGT had called a general strike in February 1996 that was costing the already-slumping economy millions of dollars in lost production. Also, violent protests broke out in Neuquén Province in June over the forthcoming privatization of the state oil company, YPF, forcing the administration to send in the National Gendarmerie to restore order. Because the fiscal deficit was running far higher than the guidelines the government and the IMF had agreed to, Cavallo was talking about raising taxes and reducing family subsidies, both of which would increase the recession's painful consequences. On top of all this bad news came the results of the 30 June elections for mayor of Buenos Aires City, in which Fernando de la Rua led the Radicals to a victory, with 40 percent of the vote. Menem's hand-picked candidate, Jorge Domínguez, got only 18 percent and ran a distant third behind FREPASO's man, Norberto La Porta, with 27 percent.

Gustavo Beliz, a former *menemista* who had broken with the administration, in fourth place with 13 percent, got almost as many votes as Domíguez.

Menem was in an ugly mood when Cavallo came to see him to protest the appointment of Elias Jassan as the new minister of justice. Jassan had been responsible for finding compliant lawyers for Menem to appoint to the federal courts. He was a close friend of Carlos Corach, the new interior minister, who was Cavallo's most venomous enemy in the government. This time Cavallo's threat to resign was thrown back in his face. "I've had enough of your threats," Menem told him. "Don't threaten me again! If you want to quit, go!" So, on 26 July Cavallo offered his resignation, and Menem accepted it. Roque Fernández, the Central Bank president, became the new economics minister and promised to continue the Convertibility Plan.[11] In the end, neither Cavallo nor Yabrán won their "war." Menem sacrificed Cavallo, but Yabrán never got his monopoly of the postal and telegraph services, nor did he gain full control of the airports.

THE ROUT OF DOMESTIC CAPITALISM

Until the "tequila effect" sent Argentina into recession, local conglomerates and large independent companies had taken advantage of privatizations to expand and diversify their investments. They borrowed heavily to purchase shares in the former state companies, acquire new equipment, and absorb smaller firms, but the results pointed to the emergence of a true national capitalist leadership. Starting about 1995, however, local capitalists, frightened by the size of their debts, began liquidating their holdings in the privatized companies. Some, suspecting that the Convertibility Plan had run its course, even went so far as to sell a lot of their original industrial properties. Since they had made their companies more efficient, they had no trouble finding buyers. Thus, local capital began to recede in the industrial sector, and to some extent in the commercial and service sectors as well. It is estimated that these Argentine capitalists sent around $100 million out of the country; other sums were invested in farmland or agro-businesses, where the country's natural advantages made them relatively safe investments.[12]

As domestic capital receded, foreign capital became more dominant, but the pattern of direct foreign investment changed. The peak year for acquiring shares in privatized industries was 1993; after that, foreign capital came in mainly as new companies in the private sector, or more frequently as takeovers of existing Argentine firms.

The Economic Commission for Latin America and the Caribbean listed 467 major company buyouts in Argentina between 1995 and 1999. Of those, 251 (54 percent) involved foreign capital buying out national firms. The next-largest category (80 cases, or 17 percent) consisted of Argentine conglomerates acquiring other national firms' properties. In another 56 cases (12 percent), foreign companies acquired other foreign companies' Argentine holdings. Argentine companies buying out foreigners accounted for 16 cases (3 percent). That left 64 buyouts (14 percent) that involved consortia in which it was impossible for ECLAC to disentangle foreign from domestic capital.[13]

The greatest amount of activity took place from 1997 to 1999. Up to 1995, the United States was the chief source of foreign direct investment, accounting for about one-third of the total. After that, European inflows became more important, with Spain, France, and the Netherlands leading the way. In 1997, when foreign direct investment hit a peak of $63 billion, fully half of that was from Spanish investors. Those included Repsol, which became the leading oil company in Argentina; the Banco de Bilbao y Vizcaya; the Banco de Santander, and Telefónica de España. Oil and gas, banking, telecommunications, electric power, large-scale merchandising, and export-oriented agro-industry attracted most of the foreign capital. Also, despite Argentina's limited market, Ford, General Motors, Fiat, and Volkswagon invested heavily in the automotive industry in order to gain access to MERCOSUR.[14]

The opening of Argentina to global trade and investment was rapidly changing the character of its economy. The old state-owned industrial sector all but disappeared after 1990. Big foreign companies and conglomerates, sometimes investing on their own and at other times joining with Argentine capital to form consortia, now accounted for approximately two-thirds of the sales of the country's 200 largest firms. Among strictly Argentine-owned companies, there was a relentless trend toward fewer and bigger ones, as PYMEs were squeezed out and some of the old traditional conglomerates sold off their properties to new, aggressive conglomerates and either paid off their debts or sent their profits overseas.[15]

By the end of the 1990s, many of the most powerful names from the early days of Argentina's industrial development were either gone from the scene or were much reduced in importance. Fabril Financiera, once the holding company of an empire that included the country's leading paper, textile, chemical, banking, and publishing industries, went out of business in 1995. It had been struggling with debt and had been selling off its companies, one by one, since the 1980s. The Roberts Group, another big conglomerate from the nineteenth century, had been divesting itself of holdings since the 1980s and finally sold its holding company, the Banco Roberts, to the Shanghai Banking Corporation, acting through the London-based HSBC, in 1997. The Tornquist Group, formerly the most powerful in Argentina, lasted until 2000, when its Banco Tornquist was sold to Spain's Banco Santander. Another huge conglomerate from the past, the Braun-Menéndez "Sociedad Importadora y Exportadora de la Patagonia," survived under its president, Federico Braun. Still, it was only one player out of many in the supermarket business, and not the largest one. Alpargatas, formerly the country's largest textile and shoe manufactory, was heavily in debt and losing its share of the local market to cheap Asian imports. Similarly, Garovaglio & Zorraquín was deeply in debt and barely holding on. Its biggest holding, the Ipako petrochemicals company, had sold off its polypropylene and plastics divisions, and its shares in the Bahía Blanca Petrochemical Complex, to Dow Chemicals in 1995; its Cerro Castillo mining company to the British Lonhro in 1996; and its leather company to U.S. Leather in 1998. Eventually, Repsol would acquire Ipako. Repsol also bought out Astra, the country's largest private oil company, from the Gruneisen family in 1996, after which the Gruneissens retired to live on their stocks and bonds. The troubled Bridas conglomerate sold 60 percent of its oil business to British Petroleum and Amoco in 1997. The merger resulted in a new entity, Pan American Energy, with Bulgheroni as its chairman.

Two Argentine conglomerates may serve as examples of what had gone on in the local business world to bring about such changes, which shattered the hopes of those like Domingo Cavallo who had expected to nurture a domestic capitalist elite capable of competing in the global economy. The first example is Bunge & Born, the grandest of Argentina's traditional conglomerates, and a multinational company besides. Following the purge that ousted Jorge Born from the presidency in 1991, B&B underwent a restructuring of its operations. Starting with Brazil, which had been suffering from a recession since 1989, the new management whittled down its 170 different companies to only 30. The number of employees fell from 30,000 to 20,000, while some 400 managers were dismissed. Then it turned to its Argentine operations and began selling them off: Companía Química to Procter & Gamble in 1993; the Centenera container company in 1995 to Córpora, a Chilean company; the Alba paint company to Imperial Chemicals in 1996; Petroquímica Río Tercero to Pieso, a local company, in 1996; Atanor, a factory producing herbicides and pesticides, to the Iowa-based Albaugh in 1997; and Textiles Grafa to Santista, a Brazilian manufacturer. The most shocking news came when B&B sold its largest food-processing company, Molinos Río de la Plata, to the Pérez Companc Group in 1999. Molinos was Argentina's leading producer of flour, pasta, and edible oils. It had even expanded its operations in 1997 by acquiring Granja del Sol from Cargill, one of B&B's global competitors in the agro-business sector. Despite its size and versatility, however, the company had been losing money for many years, and not just because of the recession. Like many of the other B&B companies, Molinos failed to change its family-oriented management style or adopt new production methods. It rose to its dominant position in the Argentine market at a time when food retailing was handled almost entirely by many small grocers, and therefore had been able to fix prices. In recent years, though, Argentina had seen the rise of supermarket chains that had buying power and were able to force down food prices.[16]

Molinos' downward slide coincided with a growing sense of frustration among the far-flung shareholders, who were tired of declining profits. According to one anonymous B&B executive, many shareholders no longer felt themselves to be part of an extended family. They didn't really know one another all that well and felt that they would prefer to sell off B&B's properties and use the money to pursue their own private interests. None of them felt up to the task of taking over B&B's huge worldwide empire and streamlining it. Many were convinced that closely held family businesses had no future in the global competition from transnational private equity firms. Accordingly, in May 1998, over one hundred shareholders in Bunge, Ltd., the Bermuda-based holding company, met at New York's Rihga Royal Hotel. They came from South America, Europe, and the United States to decide the conglomerate's future, and after vigorous discussions they agreed to sell off all of B&B's industrial enterprises, including Molinos, and return B&B to its original core business of the processing and exporting of grains.[17]

The second example is the Soldati Group and its holding company, Sociedad Comercial de la Plata. About the same time that Cavallo launched the Convertibility Plan, the Soldati Group underwent a change of its top leadership. Francisco ("Pancho") Soldati died in a polo accident in May 1991, leaving his son Santiago a diverse empire whose net worth he had increased in twenty-five years from $23 million to $129 million. The holdings ranged from petroleum and industrial chemicals to pharmaceuticals, radio and television stations, and even a railway line. Santiago went further, borrowing heavily to join foreign multinationals and other Argentine conglomerates in buying up privatized oilfields, gas pipeline companies, electric power plants, water and sanitation works, and another railway line—the Tren de la Costa, a luxury line taking passengers to a resort on the Paraná Delta where the Soldatis planned to build a hotel, theme park, and upscale shopping mall. All of this was expensive, but might have been affordable if the "tequila effect" had not brought on the recession. By 1997, however, the Soldati Group owed an estimated $700 million to various banks, and the burden of carrying such a debt had become intolerable. Throughout that year and the next, the Group divested itself of some of its gas and oil properties to Repsol and Shell; some of its power plants to Entergy, Duke Power, and National Grid (UK), and also to the Pérez Companc Group; its construction company to a Mexican firm; its waterworks to Suez Lyonnaise de Eaux; and its insurance company to the British Bristol Group. By late 1998 *Página 12* was asking whether the Soldati Group

will follow more the path of, for example, the Macri Group, which narrowed itself to specific areas (food, postal services, construction) by selling off Sevel [motorcars]; or whether it would be broken up like Garovaglio & Zorraquín, or Bunge & Born, which ended up suffocated by debts or unable to find a growth strategy in the new economic scene. Or whether its fate will be like the Gruneisen family which, with the sale of Astra, divided up the profits and got out of the oil business. Or like the Terrabusis, who after selling their biscuit factory to foreigners, decided just to manage an investment portfolio.[18]

Some Argentine conglomerates bucked the trend and, in the short run, consolidated their positions in the economy. Three of those were Technit, the Pérez Companc Group, and the Macri Group. Technit's core investments were in the steel industry, in which it gained a dominant position with its purchase of SOMISA, the state's big steel mill. Its other major interests were in the related fields of engineering and construction. In the first phases of privatization, Technit had diversified a little by buying a small share of Telefónica; a somewhat larger share of Edelap, a company that distributed electric power; a gas pipeline company, and a railway line that ran through the steel belt north of Buenos Aires. It divested itself of Telefónica in 1997, however, and of Edelap in 1998, preferring to concentrate on steel production, where its main strength lay. The gas pipeline and railway were retained to provide energy for its mills and transport its finished products to market. Technit sought to branch out beyond Argentina or even MERCOSUR, buying up large steel plants in Venezuela, Mexico, Brazil, and the United States. It also projected its engineering and construction companies, which specialized in building and equipping industrial plants, into the global economy and acquired a stake in Argentina's privatized oil industry. Soon its subsidiary, Tecpetrol, had branches in Bolivia, Brazil, Ecuador, Mexico, and Peru. Originally founded with Italian capital, Technit had another subsidiary in Milan that built and managed hospitals throughout Italy and funded medical research.[19]

Pérez Companc's traditional focus was the oil and gas industries, in addition to which it owned the Banco Río de La Plata, Argentina's largest private bank. As state enterprises were privatized, "Goyo" Pérez Companc went into a frenzy of buying, acquiring shares of companies in a bewildering variety of areas: telephones (both Telefónica and Telecom), food processing, electronic communications, mining, fisheries, construction, supermarkets, shopping malls, warehousing, metallurgical factories, farm machinery, cement, dairies, gas distribution, electric power generation and transmission, insurance, and plastics. Some of these were bought directly from the state, while others were acquired from rival conglomerates like the Soldati Group or Bunge & Born. Pérez Companc's purchase of Transener from the Soldati Group in 1997 gave it control of an electric power company that had been distributing almost 98 percent of Argentina's electricity; and its 1999 purchase of Molinos Río de La Plata, when combined with other purchases in the food-processing sector, made it the country's largest food conglomerate. Pérez Companc, like Technit, also sought to expand beyond the La Plata region by buying up oil properties in the United States, Venezuela, Bolivia, and Guatemala. This sort of expansion was expensive, however, so the conglomerate also sold many of its companies as it went along, in order to raise sufficient capital without going too heavily into debt. Its biggest sale was that of the Banco Río de La Plata to Spain's Banco Santander. The sale proceeded in stages. The Spaniards paid $649 million for 35 percent of Banco Río's stock in 1997, then bought an additional 45 percent in 1998 for an undisclosed sum.[20] By doing so, the Banco Santander also acquired an interest, along with the Bank of Tokyo and the British Midland Bank, in the Argentine Private Development Trust Company (APDT). Headquartered in the Cayman Islands, the APDT held around $100 million in Argentine government debt that it used to buy up property in the country through a subsidiary, the Corporation for Investment and Privatization. The sale was beneficial to Banco Santander inasmuch as it facilitated getting Spanish money into (and out of) Argentina, but it may not have been a wise business deal for Pérez Companc.

Francisco ("Franco") Macri, who in 1995 was probably the richest man in Argentina, pursued an investment strategy different from either Technit or Pérez

Companc. Like other big Argentine capitalists, he had bought into the privatized state companies. He also cultivated Menem and lesser politicians to obtain public franchises and used his contacts in his native Italy to raise the capital to buy the Sevel motor company, which manufactured Fiat and Peugeot cars. From 1995 on, however, Macri's Argentine investments began to go sour. First, Fiat and Peugeot decided to re-enter the Argentine market, producing cars under their own names. While Fiat built a new plant, Peugeot bought Sevel from Macri. Macri also began to sell off his gas and electricity shares. On the other hand, in 1997 he acquired a dairy company and a construction company that he merged with SIDECO. He also beat out Alfredo Yabrán to take over Encotesa and renamed it Correo Argentino, S.A. (CASA). This last move was a mistake. Although Encotesa had annual revenues of nearly $500 million, it also had $258 million in outstanding debts. It had run a deficit of $23 million the year before, and in 1997 it lost another $50 million. Macri spent another $40 million trying to improve mail sorting and processing and fired about half of the 25,700 employees. Nothing that he did worked to make the company profitable, and Menem refused to renegotiate the terms of the concession. Nor would he act to suppress the clandestine postal services, like Yabrán's, that were a large part of the problem. Disillusioned and bitter, Macri began diverting his investments to Brazil. He bought food-processing plants and started an offshoot of SIDECO, his construction company, to build roads and high-tension power lines. That switch was to save his fortune.[21]

THE RAIDERS

In Argentina's open economy, foreign companies had a great advantage over domestic companies, not simply because of their greater efficiency but also because of their better access to credit. Foreign banks doing business in Argentina naturally preferred lending to companies of their same nationality. What is more, those foreign banks were larger and better capitalized than the local ones. Some forty-six domestic banks went out of business when the "tequila effect" hit Argentina between November 1994 and November 1995, as depositors fled to the supposed safety of larger banks. Co-op banks, provincial banks and municipal banks were the hardest hit; foreign banks were the biggest gainers. From 1995 through 1998, there was a flurry of mergers and takeovers by foreign banks. Spain's Banco de Bilbao & Vizcaya and the Banco de Santander led the way. The BBV bought the Banco Francés del Río de la Plata (which despite its name was locally owned) and the Banco de Crédito Argentino, both major domestic banking institutions; Santander absorbed, as we have seen, the Banco Río de La Plata, which at the time was Argentina's largest private bank. American capital was not far behind. The Bank of Boston bought out the local branch of the Germans' Deutsches Bank; Citibank of New York took over the Banco Mayo, which in turn had just merged with the Banco Patricios; and Bankers' Trust absorbed the Banco Liniers Sudamericano. British capital, operating through HSBC and the Shangai

Banking Corp., acquired the Banco Roberts, as noted above, and also its many investments; Lloyd's Bank bought the Banco de Tres Arroyos; and the Bank of Nova Scotia took over the Banco de Quilmes. France's Banque Crédit Agricole bought 30 percent of the Banco Bisel's shares; and even Chile, operating through its Banco Transandino, got a useful piece of the Argentine banking community by acquiring control of the Banco de Crédito de Cuyo, just on the other side of the mountains. In an analysis of current investment flows at the end of 1997, the Argentine Embassy in Washington noted that, of the largest ten banks in Argentina, only one—the Banco de Galicia—was still fully under domestic ownership. During the following year, however, the Banco de Galicia sold 10 percent of its shares to the Banco Santander.[22]

One foreign bank, Citibank's Argentine branch, went way beyond just the financing of other companies and became a major investor itself. Citibank held Argentine government bonds that had a total face value of over $1 billion, which it had been accumulating since the start of the Proceso. Those had become almost worthless, losing almost 90 percent of their real market value during the 1980s, especially after the Alfonsín government stopped paying interest. When Carlos Menem became president and announced his intention to privatize the state enterprises, Citibank's local CEO Richard Handley saw an opportunity to recoup the bank's losses. With the approval of Citicorp president John Reed, whom he had known since their childhood days in Buenos Aires, Handley set up Citicorp Equity Investments (CEI) in 1990 and began negotiating swaps of Argentine government debt for stock in certain privatized companies. CEI acquired a large interest in Telefónica and, later, after its reorganization, in its holding company, Cointel. It also bought up a gas pipeline from Gas del Estado, a steel mill in Jujuy (Aceros Zapla), and some paper mills. Over the next five years, CEI shifted its investments, selling off most of its original acquisitions, except for Telefónica, and began building a communications empire that included telephone service, cable and satellite television, Channel 9, and Editorial Atlántida.[23] At the end of 1993, CEI was worth an estimated $1.5 billion.

Back in the United States, however, Citibank was coming under pressure from bank regulators to begin selling some of CEI's investments. American banking laws required banks to dispose of their majority holdings in companies within ten years, and preferably sooner. So Handley began reducing Citibank's share of CEI to only 40 percent in order to get out from under U.S. regulation. Some of his closest associates at CEI were given enormous pay packages that enabled them to turn around and acquire CEI shares at bargain prices. The Banco Mercantil, a subsidiary of the Werthein Group, bought a block of shares, as did George Soros, who was interested in Argentine real estate and who partnered with CEI to buy the luxurious state-run Hotel Llao-Llao in the mountain resort of Bariloche. But the biggest single investor was Raúl Moneta, owner of the Banco República, in Mendoza, who bought up about 35 percent of CEI's stock. Moneta was another one of Handley's childhood friends, having gone to prep school with him in Buenos Aires.[24]

By 1998 CEI's assets were estimated at around $4 billion, but all was not well. Like those of most other Argentine companies, CEI's investments were going sour. As the recession continued, and even deepened, telephone and cable subscribers either cancelled their contracts or stopped paying their bills. CEI's shares fell in value on the BOLSA, and the company faced a serious financial crisis. Citibank wanted to sell out, but BOLSA investors were not buying. Finally, a "white knight" appeared in August, in the form of a Texas buyout company called Hicks, Muse, Tate & Furst, which bought about half of Citibank's stock, after which Handley announced his retirement. Then trouble erupted in June 1999, when Raúl Moneta, CEI's new president, failed to show up in court to answer charges of financial malfeasance and tax evasion.

Ever since Moneta joined CEI in 1992, he had been pulling sums of money out of Telefónica and other investments he had in Mendoza Province and transferring them to an account at Citibank in New York, held under the name of "American Exchange," from which they were then sent to a "Federal Bank" located in the Bahamas. As a U.S. Senate investigation in money laundering would show in 2001, both "American Exchange" and "Federal Bank" were phantom enterprises that existed only on paper so as to hide Moneta's illegal transfers of money out of the country to evade taxes. The scam came to light only gradually, however, and only because the recession brought about by the "tequila effect" suddenly caused the Banco República to fail, in April 1999, leaving its depositors defrauded. Worse yet, the Banco República previously had taken over Mendoza's provincial bank and pension fund, which now were also found to be empty of cash. For the next seven months, Moneta was a fugitive from justice, until his good friend Carlos Menem was able to get his appointees on the Supreme Court to overrule the lower court and have the charges dropped. While he was on the run, however, the hard-pressed Moneta sold most of his shares in CEI to Hicks, Muse, Tate & Furst, giving them effective control. (Later, he would try to repudiate this deal and get his shares back, but without success.) In the end, CEI was dissolved, and its media empire was divided between Hicks, Muse, Tate & Furst, and Telefónica de España.[25]

In 1997 the Exxel Group was second only to Telefónica as the largest foreign enterprise in Argentina. Its president, Juan Navarro, had worked under Handley at CEI, helping him in his early debt-for-equity swaps in privatized state companies, but in 1991 he decided to branch out on his own. Unlike CEI, Exxel was not the offshoot of a bank, although it did start with a bank loan, and it preferred to buy private companies rather than shares in state enterprises. Many Argentine businessmen, pessimistic about surviving in the new era of open competition, were willing to sell. At the same time, interest rates in the United States were so low in the early 1990s that Navarro had little trouble finding people willing to invest in Argentina. Financial circles already were buzzing about the bold new initiatives being taken by Menem and Cavallo, and were predicting high returns on investments there.

One of Navarro's first clients was Oppenheimer & Company, an investment bank, which provided him with $47 million with which to scout for good properties to buy. He bought three companies that produced various kinds of cleaning products, merged and reorganized them, and sold them three years later to Clorox for $95 million. This success attracted more capital from Oppenheimer that was profitably invested in paper, pharmaceutical, and electric companies. By 1995 Exxel's reputation was so strong among American investors that it was no longer dependent on Oppenheimer exclusively, but was handling investments from Aetna, Allstate, the Rockefeller Foundation, the Ford Foundation, the Getty Family Trust, General Electric's Pension Fund Trust, the General Motors Investment Management Corporation, the New York State and California public employees' retirement systems, and pension funds from several universities, including Princeton, Brown, M.I.T., and Columbia. In addition to those funds, it also used loans from Citibank and the issuance of high-interest "junk bonds" from some of its companies to leverage its buyouts of other companies. Its investment accounts were all located in such "financial paradises" as the Cayman Islands, the British Virgin Islands, and Panama, where they would be away from the purview of the U.S. Treasury and Internal Revenue Service.[26]

Exxel's investments embraced some seventy-three companies by 1998, valued at almost $4 billion: energy companies, credit card services, supermarkets, music store chains, insurance companies, bakeries, and ice cream parlors. Exxel seldom quibbled over price. It was willing to pay high because it then could raise the company's book value. Once Exxel bought a company, it immediately began cutting costs by firing employees, closing down operations it considered "marginal," and using the savings to modernize the plant. New assets were always valued at the highest possible figure and added to the company's already-inflated book value. Then the reorganized firm would be resold, at a profit. In many cases Navarro made additional profits from the issuance of his junk bonds. Under Argentine law, interest payments were tax deductible and could be subtracted from the company's profits. Moreover, in the heated atmosphere of the early 1990s, bondholders paid no taxes on the interest they earned, so not only were Exxel companies' bonds eagerly snatched up, but these companies would often buy their own bonds and make tax-free profits.[27]

Exxel's rise was spectacular, but the company soon declined as the protracted recession upset its financing strategy. Heavily leveraged buyouts of overvalued properties and the floating of great numbers of high-interest bonds were no longer feasible when there were no buyers for the reorganized companies. As interest rates rose in the United States and the "tequila effect" made emerging markets unattractive, investors pulled their money from Exxel's accounts to place it elsewhere. Suddenly, Exxel was forced to sharply reduce its asking prices and to scramble for money to pay off its loans. Then, in desperation, it made a bad mistake. In 1997 it arranged to buy up all of Alfredo Yabrán's properties. Yabrán was in serious legal difficulties, having been accused of ordering the murder of a photographer/reporter who had been investigating his affairs. He was planning to flee the country and was looking for some way to transfer his fortune abroad as well. Exxel's holding companies in the West Indies offered Yabrán an opportunity.

Navarro opened up a new account in the Cayman Islands, called Capital Partners V, with money from Yabrán that was funneled through a secret, Panamanian-based holding company. However, enough facts about the deal leaked out to set off a congressional investigation of money laundering. That pushed Exxel ever closer to bankruptcy.[28] By the time its largest creditor, Deutsche Bank, took it over in 2003, it was reduced to only six companies.

SUMMARY

The "Menem Decade" began with the government's intention of throwing off the restrictive corporatist practices of the past and opening up Argentina to free markets and free trade. In doing so, it hoped to transform Argentina's "hothouse capitalists" into modern businessmen capable of competing in the global economy. By the end of the decade, however, most Argentine capitalists had disappeared, along with local companies whose goods and services had been familiar to Argentines for generations. They had either gone bankrupt or been bought up by foreign capital.

There was plenty of blame to go around for this debacle. Some analysts pointed to Argentina's corrupt political institutions as failing to provide the legal framework essential for a capitalist system to work properly. Others argued that Menem and Cavallo failed to adjust their policies in the face of recession, by modifying the Convertibility Plan, controlling capital transfers more carefully, or, more drastically, by "dollarizing the economy." Some blamed the IMF and the ultra-orthodox "Washington Consensus" outlook for imposing laissez-faire ideological blinders on the Argentine government. Still others insisted that Argentine businessmen lacked a true capitalist spirit, having been protected from competition for so long by the state. They had not developed modern management skills, and they had no notion of putting aside reserves to carry them through capitalism's periodic recessions. Besides, their foreign competitors had better access to credit. Thrown suddenly into the icy waters of globalization, local businessmen were easily numbed and overwhelmed. Yet others saw predatory global financiers as the villains.

There is, perhaps, an element of truth in all those views, although I think that none fully encompasses the whole problem. In any case, for the great majority of Argentines today, all such discussion is moot. The spectacular crash that finally occurred after Menem left office hardened the public's attitude against free enterprise and free trade for the foreseeable future.

Chapter Eight

Challenges

Whether 1997 was a good year for Argentina, or a bad one, depends on one's perspective. On the positive side, the GDP grew by slightly over 8 percent, and consumer prices rose by less than 1 percent. Foreign capital inflows resumed, with over $2 billion in new investments by Kraft Foods, Monsanto, Levi Strauss, Reynolds Aluminum, General Motors, and Chrysler, to name the most prominent. Wal-Mart, Lockheed, Repsol, and others invested another $2.6 billion in buying up existing companies. Exports were on the rise, but their returns were limited by a fall in world prices for grains and oil. Meanwhile, imports of machinery and equipment resulted in a $12 billion trade deficit. Fortunately, that and the $15 billion balance of payments deficit were offset by capital inflows from foreign direct investments, the sale of government bonds, and foreign loans. The Central Bank's foreign exchange reserves were at a comfortable level of just over $3 billion. Thus, the situation was sustainable, so long as investment capital or loans kept coming in. There were disturbing signs, however, that another global financial crisis might be approaching. In July, Thailand, the Philippines, and Malaysia, which—like Argentina—had pegged their currencies to the dollar, devalued. In November, South Korea defaulted on its debt payments, setting off a flurry of capital flight from that country.[1]

On the negative side, all the loans and government bonds sold abroad had pushed up the foreign debt to almost $75 billion, much of which was dollar denominated. The debt represented about 40 percent of the annual GDP, and financing it was becoming the largest line item in the government's budget. Even more worrisome was the public's growing disillusion with the free market economy. Although unemployment dropped slightly in 1997, at 14 percent it was still too high. Many industrial firms had closed their doors since the onset of the "tequila effect." The survivors, especially those bought by foreign investors, were raising productivity by installing modern machinery, but also were eliminating jobs. Argentina's rigid labor laws also made it harder for the unemployed to find new jobs. Some did manage to do so in the service sector, or as self-employed *cuentapropistas,* but at much lower wages and greater insecurity of employment. By the end of 1997, it was estimated that about 29 percent of Argentina's families lived below the poverty level, unable to afford basic goods and services. Many had no unemployment insurance or medical coverage. Unskilled and semi-skilled workers suffered the most, but the middle classes were hard hit too. Many of them, even highly skilled workers and university-educated professionals, were living precariously.[2]

There was a growing number of violent mass protests during which people blocked roads, attacked government buildings, and occasionally took officials as hostages. This phenomenon had begun earlier in the Menem period, in places like Santiago del Estero and Neuquén, usually with at least partial success in getting the authorities to pay attention and modify their policies. This was different from the often violent strikes of the Argentine industrial unions. With the decline of manufacturing, the industrial trade unions were reduced in importance, but the public sector unions had become larger and more militant, especially in the provinces. The latter were more likely to represent white-collar workers, rather than blue-collar workers, and not just office clerks or school teachers. Often they included professionals such as doctors and lawyers, who were no less willing to engage in mass action to preserve their jobs. Their violent protests were neither irrational nor anarchistic but were well-orchestrated examples of political theater, designed to create the greatest possible impact on the media. The protesters often were supported by the Catholic clergy, and usually by a sympathetic public well aware that the government had failed to pay salaries or supply public institutions with necessities, while at the same time funneling money to its friends or relatives. Indeed, when Menem and his cabinet ministers attended the traditional Te Deum Mass on Independence Day, 25 May, they were forced to listen to a sermon by Bishop Raúl Rossi, castigating them for the uncontrolled corruption that was generating widespread contempt for Argentina's political institutions.[3]

MURDER'S RED TRAIL

Argentina's political institutions were shaken by the discovery, on 25 January, of the body of José Luis Cabezas, a photographer for the Buenos Aires weekly magazine *Notícias.* He had been kidnapped the night before, after leaving a late-night party in the beach resort of Pinamar. According to a coroner's report, he had been handcuffed, beaten brutally (his jaw and ribs were broken), and murdered with two shots in his neck. Then his body was driven, in his own car, to a sand pit outside of town. There the car was set afire. An employee from a neighboring ranch found the half-burned corpse the next morning and called the police. According to witnesses and reporters, the policemen seemed intent on obliterating much of remaining evidence. Since the Buenos Aires Provincial Police were notoriously corrupt, there were suspicions of a coverup. *Notícias* affirmed that Cabezas had been investigating the actions of criminal gangs along the province's southern resort coast, where he himself had grown up. He felt certain that the gangs were being protected by the police, and also that they were connected to drug and money-laundering operations controlled by Alfredo Yabrán. Cabezas had even succeeded in taking a photograph of the publicity-shy Yabrán.[4]

In addition to being a heinous crime, the murder had implications for the political ambitions of President Menem and Governor Eduardo Duhalde, both of whom were seeking the Justicialist Party's presidential nomination for 1999. Although Menem was forbidden by the 1994 Constitution from running for immediate re-election, he was used to circumventing constitutional prohibitions. Already his ex-brother-in-law, Jorge Yoma, was leading a campaign in the Senate for a popular referendum that would modify the Constitution. Given Menem's vast patronage resources as president, he was confident of gaining the support of most of the Peronist governors, along with their allies in Congress.

Duhalde had been disappointed back in 1994, when Menem had begun his drive for a second term. As former vice president and head of Argentina's largest province, Duhalde had considered himself to be the next in line. However, he swallowed his pride and, assured that he would get the party's nomination in 1999, agreed to back Menem's re-election. Now it was clear that the *turco* was going to betray him again, but this time Duhalde intended to fight back—and he had resources of his own. First, his style was more traditionally Peronist. He was a natural-born populist and a believer in the strong regulatory welfare state. Even as vice president he had felt uncomfortable with Menem's radical free market policies. Second, his hold on Buenos Aires Province seemed unshakeable. He still had the huge public works slush fund (Fund for the Historic Restoration of Greater Buenos Aires) that guaranteed his hold on the municipal Peronist machines. He also had a food distribution program for the poorest *barrios:* the *"Plan Vida,"* headed by his wife, Hilda "Chiche" Duhalde, under which unpaid volunteers called *manzaneras,* or "block captains," set up soup kitchens for the unemployed families, and also distributed milk, rice, and eggs to young children and pregnant mothers. The *manzaneras* were almost always highly sympathetic women who knew their neighbors in the *barrios* and could sometimes help them, as go-betweens with Peronist ward leaders, to find jobs, secure medicines, or get help with legal problems. Mrs. Duhalde occasionally toured the *barrios,* encouraging the *manzaneras* and listening to the woes of the residents. Needless to say, the public works fund and the *Plan Vida* helped to turn out the votes on election day.[5]

The Cabezas murder exposed the slimy side of Buenos Aires politics. Not only did the police act unprofessionally at the crime scene, but it quickly became clear that they intended to divert the investigation by coaching a "witness" to place the blame on a small-time prostitution ring. The press corps was stirred up, and Duhalde immediately understood that unless he got the investigation back on track, his presidential hopes would be destroyed. He notified all 48,000 officers of the provincial police that they were liable for criminal charges unless the real culprits were soon found, and then reorganized the province's top detective bureau. Orders went out to cooperate completely with Judge José Luis Macchi, the investigating magistrate. Thus motivated, the detectives soon found new leads by interviewing Cabezas's neighbors, some of whom identified the men who had been waiting in a car near his home. Detectives then raided Pinamar's police station and began going over its telephone records, which led to the arrest of members of the "Los Hornos" gang. They quickly confessed their part in Cabezas's murder and also revealed a longtime arrangement with the local police to share the profits from drug dealing, car thefts, and burglaries of vacation homes. Their main contact was chief inspector Gustavo Prellezo, who, they said, had hired them to silence Cabezas.

After taking Prellezo into custody, Chief Detective Victor Fogelman examined his cell phone records, using a method known as Excalibur. Those revealed that Prellezo had gotten about fifty calls from Gregorio Ríos, an ex-cop who headed the squad of bodyguards that surrounded Alfredo Yabrán, many of them drawn from the sinister "task forces" used under the Proceso. Even more startling was the great number of calls from Ríos and from various Yabrán business offices to high officials in Menem's government between the time of Cabezas's murder and the end of June: 102 to justice minister Elías Jassan, 17 to interior minister Carlos Corach, and one to cabinet coordinator Jorge Rodríguez. There were also several calls to Senator Eduardo Menem, to Alberto Kohan, Menem's private secretary, and to Menem's private line at the Casa Rosada.

Judge Macchi called in Yabrán for questioning. Confronted with the evidence of so many telephone calls between himself and Prellezo, he was forced to admit that he knew the murderer. Still, he denied any involvement in Cabezas's death, or that he had ever discussed Cabezas with his chief bodyguard, Ríos. If any of the other bodyguards had participated in killing Cabezas, they had done so on Ríos's orders, not his. Menem publicly declared his support for Yabrán after the interrogation, but the scandal forced the shady businessman to withdraw his bid to buy the newly privatized Encotesa postal service. Yabrán also appeared before Congress to defend his business practices, but even some of the diehard Peronists were so skeptical that they voted to set up an Anti-Mafia Commission to investigate him.

All this was mortifying to the publicity-shy Yabrán, but Duhalde was shocked and outraged at what he perceived to be a ploy by Menem to discredit him. It was well known that Yabrán had clashed with Duhalde when the latter had vetoed his project to build a deep-water port along the resort coast. Now, Duhalde exclaimed, "they've thrown a corpse at me!"

THE OCTOBER 1997 ELECTIONS

The 26 October congressional elections found the Justicialist Party badly divided. Menem and Duhalde, formerly allies, no longer appeared together or spoke to each other. Attempts at a truce had barely papered over their quarrel.

Conversely, the opposition Radicals and FREPASO had come together to form an Alliance. The election results brought bad news to the PJ. In the national totals, the Alliance edged ahead of the Peronists with 36.4 percent of the vote to 36.2 percent. To the Alliance's total, however, should be added another 6.8 percent won by the UCR and 2.4 percent won by FREPASO when running on separate tickets in certain provinces. That would have given it 45.4 percent. As it was, the PJ came in first in only eight peripheral provinces: Formosa, Jujuy, La Pampa, La Rioja, Salta, San Juan, Santa Cruz, and Tierra del Fuego. In Buenos Aires City the Alliance demolished the PJ, with 55 percent of the vote to the latter's 17.5 percent.

For Duhalde, the defeat of his wife, Hilda "Chiche" Duhalde for a congressional seat by the Alliance's Graciela Fernández Meijide was the really bad news. As head of the *Plan Vida,* "Chiche" had a network of *manzaneras* working to get out a big vote for her. She aspired to be another Evita Perón and carefully groomed herself to look like her role model. Graciela was a human rights activist who got into politics after her teenage son "disappeared" under the Proceso. Her style was unpretentious, and her message was simple: Argentina had to adopt higher moral values. There could be no more "impunity" for political criminals. That was in tune with the Alliance's chief campaign theme: to end corruption and bring the corrupt to justice. The PJ waged an intense campaign against Graciela, calling her an "outsider" because she resided in Buenos Aires City, not in the province. She was a *porteña,* not a *provinciana,* they told the voters, and didn't understand local problems. Pre-election polls showed "Chiche" ahead, but when the votes were counted, Graciela won. Moreover, the Alliance beat the PJ throughout the province, with 48 percent of the votes to 41.[6]

THE PERONISTS SPLIT

This setback for Duhalde encouraged Menem to believe that the path now was clear for his third presidential bid. Nevertheless, his ambitions provoked opposition from prominent PJ politicians in addition to Duhalde. Carlos Ruckauf, Menem's new vice president, made a deal with Duhalde to run for governor of Buenos Aires after Duhalde secured the PJ's presidential nomination. Felipe Solá, Menem's agriculture secretary and a friend of both Ruckauf and Duhalde, hoped to be Buenos Aires Province's next lieutenant governor. Carlos Reutemann, the popular governor of Santa Fe, also opposed Menem's ambition to be president-for-life; and Néstor Kirchner, the governor of Santa Fe made it clear that he wanted to bring Peronism back to its traditional populism. Meanwhile, the investigation into Yabrán's connection to Cabezas's murder continued; and when Juan Pablo Caficro, a member of Congress's Anti-Mafia Commission, accused Yabrán of heading an organized crime syndicate, people were reminded of Domingo Cavallo's accusations, just a year and a half earlier. All of this was beginning to cost Menem politically. Against the background of a deepening recession, his darting about the highways in his red Ferrari, the gift of an Italian lobbyist, was no longer amusing. Another scandal erupted when government censors prevented the showing of a television documentary about Menem's new Spanish colonial mansion in Anillaco, complete with a nearby landing strip long enough to accommodate jets. It was not clear where the money for these projects had come from.[7]

As the recent elections showed, fighting corruption was a popular theme. Duhalde sought to improve his image by hiring a highly regarded former federal criminal court judge, León Arslanián, to conduct a purge of the Buenos Aires Provincial Police. He also warned that yet another Menem re-election would be the equivalent of a "juridical coup d'état."[8]

The year 1998 was to be even worse for Menem than 1997 had been. Economic growth slowed as the inflow of foreign capital declined to a trickle. During the course of the year, Indonesia and Russia would default on their foreign debts and devalue their currencies, triggering a new flight of investors from "emerging markets." In Argentina, slow growth meant more unemployment, which rose to 18 percent of the potential workforce. The government's popularity plummeted. Even Peronist voters were turning against it, with fewer than 13 percent expressing approval of the economic program.[9] Menem's unpopularity and the PJ's election of Duhalde to be the party's president in January made a third term more unlikely.

There was no sign of a reconciliation between Duhalde and Menem, although the president insisted that his differences with the governor were "merely formal." In February he stated that, while he did not really seek re-election, he was willing to be drafted "if the public wanted it." Others in the Casa Rosada, like Corach and Kohan, spoke openly of changing the Constitution through a referendum to permit Menem a third term. Menem supporters submitted a petition to the Superior Electoral Court in March, requesting it to change the eligibility law by decree, but that tribunal refused jurisdiction and instructed the petitioners to seek redress from the Supreme Court.

Unsavory events involving his old friend, Yabrán, added to Menem's unpopularity. A *menemista* majority on the Anti-Mafia Commission effectively blocked any serious probe into Yabrán's dealings and, indeed, issued a report, over loud protests from the opposition minority, saying that there was "insufficient evidence" to link Yabrán to any crimes. On 12 May, however, Louis Freeh, the U.S. FBI chief, met with Menem to report on his agency's investigation of money laundering by various Argentine businesses. Yabrán figured prominently in Freeh's report. Three days later, Gustavo Prellezo's ex-wife testified before Judge Macchi that her former husband had confessed to her back in March 1997 that Yabrán had ordered Cabezas's murder because Cabezas had followed him and taken photographs.[10] Judge Macchi issued a warrant for Yabran's arrest and asked for Interpol's cooperation in the event that Yabrán fled the country. Yabrán went into hiding while his lawyers sought to get the Supreme Court to move his case from Judge Macchi's jurisdiction and into a federal court, on the grounds that Macchi was too close politically to Duhalde. The opposition Alliance loudly accused the Menem government of protecting Yabrán. *La Nación* opined that

"The Yabrán case has extremely serious institutional implications, given that members of the three branches of government are strongly suspected of providing protection to the businessman in question."

On 18 May, defense minister Jorge Domínguez, speaking for Menem, announced that the government would not protect Yabrán. By then Yabrán, who was at his ranch in Entre Ríos, knew that his situation was hopeless. Rather than submit to arrest, he fired a shotgun into his mouth, disfiguring his face so badly that at first the police were not sure that the body really was his. The first news stories about the suicide questioned the police report and suggested that Yabrán had escaped after all, leaving somebody else's corpse in his place. To restore calm, Judge Macchi ordered that the body not be cremated until DNA testing confirmed its identity.

Despite all this bad publicity, and the fact that polls showed that only about 25 percent of the public favored a third term for Menem, the *menemistas* continued to press their campaign. Senator Yoma persisted with his idea of calling a referendum to change the Constitution, but after introducing his bill in the Senate, he discovered that he lacked the necessary two-thirds majority to pass it. The next ploy was to convoke a national PJ convention that would endorse Menem's candidacy. Duhalde refused to attend, claiming that Menem had packed it with his own loyalists. Antonio Cafiero and Carlos Ruckauf also boycotted it. Still, the attending delegates seemed ready to steamroller through a motion to nominate Menem as the party's presidential nominee when Carlos Reutemann, the popular governor of Santa Fe, rose to speak. Menem, he said, was dividing the party, making it unlikely that any Peronist candidate would defeat the Alliance next year for the presidency. Then he and his supporters also withdrew. Barely half of the seats in the convention hall were occupied, but the *menemistas* went ahead anyway and, by a unanimous vote, picked the president as their choice for 1999. It was a lukewarm endorsement that left many PJ politicians secretly agreeing with Reutemann. Sensing their gloom, Menem announced on 22 July that he would not run for a third term.

He didn't really mean it, though. One last attempt came on 4 March 1999, when a federal judge in Córdoba decreed that the constitutional prohibition violated the citizenry's right to elect whomever they wished. Congress immediately took up the issue, and a week later the Chamber of Deputies voted, by 159 votes out of 257, to nullify the judge's decree. That put an end to the *menemista* campaign, for Menem definitively withdrew the next day.

Though out of the contest at last, Menem left Duhalde with bleak prospects. The GDP fell by 3.4 percent during 1999. Tax revenues also shrank, but government spending did not. Political campaigning during 1998–1999 cost over $5 billion. Years later, former economics minister Roque Fernández estimated that Menem alone spent around $3 billion in attempting to win a third term, most of it on propaganda and subsidizing public works for Peronist governors. The funds were mainly diverted from the Economics Ministry to the presidential office, where spending was more discretionary. There was a record federal deficit of

$7.1 billion in 1999, which sent the IMF into a panic. Unless the Argentine government got spending under control, investors would quickly lose confidence in it and shift their capital elsewhere. After a string of losses in Asia and Russia, the IMF needed Argentina as a success story.[11]

The deficit had to be covered somehow, but how? Tariff receipts were down because the peso was pegged to the dollar, and the dollar had continued to appreciate, pricing Argentina's exports out of world markets. Trade deficits since 1997 hovered between 12 and 15 billion dollars a year. The government continued to issue bonds, but now had to offer interest rates of between 11 and 13 percent as potential investors began to worry about the risk of a default. Their concern had been growing throughout the Asian crisis and the Russian default, but was heightened especially in January 1999 when Brazil announced that it was devaluing its currency. There had been no prior consultation with its MERCOSUR partners: the action was purely unilateral. Since Brazil was Argentina's largest market, the devaluation was a horrible blow. Not only did Argentina's exports to Brazil drop precipitously, but cheap Brazilian goods poured into Argentine markets, with fatal results for many Argentine companies already weakened by the deepening recession. Meanwhile, the sale of new bonds drove up the foreign debt from $75 billion in 1997 to over $85 billion by the end of 1999.[12]

Duhalde persevered, trying to disassociate himself from Menem's failed policies. He promised, if elected president, to negotiate with foreign bondholders to forgive Argentina's debt. No one believed him, since he had been not far behind Menem in lavish spending to win support for his presidential bid. Refusing to be discouraged, Duhalde even went to the Vatican to get John Paul II's support for the debt cancellation idea, but got only fifteen minutes of the Pope's time and no commitment. Still, there were bright spots. On 9 May Duhalde's candidate, Ruckauf, trounced Menem's candidate, Antonio Cafiero, in the PJ gubernatorial primary with 80 percent of the vote. Then, on 16 June, a PJ national convention nominated Duhalde as its presidential candidate, without the need to hold a primary election. To placate the *menemistas* and unify the party the delegates picked a Menem protege, Ramón "Palito" Ortega, a popular crooner and ex-governor of Tucumán, to be his running mate.[13]

THE ALLIANCE ROLLS FORWARD

The opposition alliance, whose full name was the Alliance for Justice, Jobs, and Education *(Alianza por la Justicia, el Trabajo, y la Educación)* was a loose coalition of groups whose principal (perhaps only) connection was a desire to oust the Peronists from power. The alliance had come into being only a few days before the close of the registration period for the October 1997 legislative elections, when ex-president Raúl Alfonsín, of the UCR, and Carlos "Chacho" Álvarez, of The Front for a Country in Solidarity (FREPASO), agreed to merge their electoral lists. Each side brought to the bargaining table evidence of strength. In 1995, when Menem was re-elected, FREPASO's ticket had come in second, well ahead of the Radicals. Then in 1996, Fernando De la Rua of the UCR won election for mayor of Buenos Aires city by a long margin over both the FREPASO and PJ candidates. On the other hand, FREPASO's Graciela Fernández Meijide had been elected senator from the city the previous year. As we have seen, the new Alliance won more votes and congressional seats than the Peronists in 1997. "Chacho" Álvarez was elected to Congress from Buenos Aires City, and Fernández Meijide beat Duhalde's wife for a seat in Congress from Buenos Aires Province.

There was no doubt that the Alliance would hold together for the October 1999 general election, but who would be its presidential and vice presidential candidates? Both the UCR and FREPASO were loose coalitions. The Radicals were split into a social democratic left wing that was affiliated with the European socialist parties and an orthodox liberal right wing. The left was headed, nominally, by Alfonsín, but its driving force was a team of more orthodox socialists that included ex-foreign minister Dante Caputo and two Buenos Aires Province congressmen: Federico Storani and Leopoldo Moreau. The Radicals' right wing leader was De la Rua, a veteran who had served various terms in the national Senate and Chamber of Deputies. Back in 1973 he had been the vice presidential running mate of Ricardo Balbín, who lost to Perón. De la Rua was Balbín's protégé, and when Alfonsín finally replaced his mentor as UCR leader De la Rua assumed the leadership of the party's classical liberal wing and became Alfonsín's gadfly. He severely attacked the UCR leader for signing the Pact of Olivos that allowed Menem to have a second term, and when he won the mayoralty election for Buenos Aires City, he succeeded at last in bringing his faction to ascendancy in the party.

FREPASO was even more divided. Having started as a group of dissident Peronists from Congress and public employee unions, it had gradually incorporated liberation theology Christian Democrats, left wing socialists, human rights activists, and a variety of independent leftists. It was a volatile mix that frequently lost bits and pieces of its following. José Octavio Bordón, its 1995 presidential candidate, quit when FREPASO's executive committee refused membership to his friend, Gustavo Beliz. The latter had been Menem's interior minister for a brief period, but resigned, he said, when his attempts to clean up corruption were blocked. Most of FREPASO's leaders didn't trust him, however, and suspected that he would be a spy for Menem. Another split occurred when Fernando "Pino" Solanos, a film actor and leader of a "hard-left" militant faction, failed to stop "Chacho" Álvarez from meeting with Alfonsín to discuss the creation of an alliance. Besides its tendency to fragment, FREPASO's electoral support was largely confined to the Greater Buenos Aires metropolitan area. Argentine political scientist Marcos Novaro considered it a transient political phenomenon, "a force with little organization or territorial base, that has achieved its success based largely on a handful of prestigious leaders" like Carlos "Chacho" Álvarez and Graciela Fernández Meijide. Its rise was due to the weakening of traditional party loyalties within the PJ and UCR. During the course of the 1990s, the electorate had become disillusioned with party politics. The Radicals had ceased to reflect the middle classes' interests faithfully, and the PJ could no longer take labor for granted. Oscar Landi, another Argentine political scientist, observed a high level of abstentions at election time and noted that opinion polls indicated that abstention rates would be even higher if voting were not obligatory. Thus, FREPASO could be seen as chiefly a protest movement.[14]

Nevertheless, FREPASO saw itself, and was seen by many observers, as a vigorous new force in Argentine politics, with a track record of impressive successes. To underline its modern, innovative character, it proposed Graciela Fernández Meijide as the Alliance's presidential candidate. The Radicals countered by insisting on Fernando De la Rua. To avoid a split, the two sides agreed to hold a primary in November 1998. The winning candidate would choose his vice presidential running mate from the other party. When De la Rua won that primary, with 64 percent of the vote to Graciela's 36 percent, he complied with the previous agreement and offered her the second place on his ticket. Instead, she chose to run for governor of Buenos Aires province, so the offer was then made to Carlos "Chacho" Álvarez, who accepted.

The 1999 presidential campaign was essentially a three-way race. De la Rua ran a quiet, subdued campaign, saying little but appearing calm and confident. There was absolutely nothing charismatic about his personality, but after ten frenetic years under Menem, that did not seem to bother the voters. He assured them that he would not make any radical policy changes but would get rid of corruption. Duhalde, by contrast, promised to return to old-style populism. The people, he said, could not continue to "adjust, adjust, adjust." In addition to cancelling the foreign debt, he proposed to call all the major interest groups—business, labor, the Catholic Church, estancieros—together to establish a "social pact" that would control wages, prices, trade, and investment. It was a traditional Peronist approach to economic crises, but this time around it got little support. When he promised to attack corruption, he invited the rather obvious question of why he hadn't done more to clean up Buenos Aires Province during the eight years of his governorship, and why he was so friendly with the notorious boss of La Matanza and patota kingpin, Alberto Pierri. The third candidate in the race was Domingo Cavallo, who had formed his own free market party, Acción para la República. For his running mate he chose Armando Caro Figueroa, Menem's labor minister in 1997, who had been a strong proponent of "flexibilization" laws to break the unions' power. Cavallo's entry into the race signaled an end to the old Menem coalition of Peronists and conservatives. Throughout the campaign Duhalde tried, unsuccessfully, to restore that coalition by getting Cavallo to drop his candidacy and endorse him, but the most that Cavallo would agree to was to back Carlos Ruckauf for Buenos Aires governor.

When the voters went to the polls on 24 October, they gave De la Rua a resounding victory. He got 48.4 percent of the vote and carried 20 of 24 provinces, including Duhalde's home base, Buenos Aires Province. In 13 of the 20 provinces he won, De la Rua got 50 percent or more of the vote. Duhalde trailed badly with only 38.3 percent, and since there was more than a 10 percentage-point difference between them there would be no need for a runoff. The PJ ticket won only in poor, marginal provinces like Santiago del Estero, Misiones, Jujuy, and La Rioja (where Menem managed to deliver some 60 percent of the vote). Cavallo garnered a respectable 2 million votes, or 10.2 percent. The remaining 3 percent was scattered among several minor and provincial parties.

With half of the Chamber of Deputies up for re-election, the Alliance picked up 63 seats out of 130, for a gain of 17; the PJ got 50 seats, for a loss of 1; *Acción por la República* won 9 seats, for a gain of 6. Minor parties won the remaining 8 seats. But if Peronists ran poorly in legislative contests, they did much better at electing governors by retaining control of 14 out of 24 provinces. Apparently, the voters, having shed any strong party identification, were willing to split their ballots. Out of 24 million registered voters, over 19 million (81 percent) went out to vote. Blank or spoiled ballots were only 4 percent of all those cast, a sign of continued support for the political system.

It was the end of the Menem era and a temporary setback for the Peronists, who for only the second time in Argentina's history had lost a presidential contest. The Alliance had the Casa Rosada and a majority of the Chamber of Deputies, but the Peronists still controlled the Senate. Moreover, they had won in the pivotal province of Buenos Aires, where, thanks to Cavallo's support, Carlos Ruckauf beat Graciela Fernández Meijide for the Buenos Aires governorship, with 48 percent of the vote to her 41 percent. The Alliance was not securely in power, and the Peronists were far from vanquished. Much would depend on Fernando De la Rua's skill in leading Argentina out of its grim, prolonged economic crisis, and on how solid the Alliance would prove to be under pressure.

Chapter Nine

The Crash

President Fernando De la Rua had to tread carefully, upon taking office, for there was no great popular enthusiasm for his government. The Alliance was swept into office by the severe recession that had begun in mid-1998 and by the Peronists' rampant corruption that seemed to mock the public. A 16 percent official unemployment rate, a black market economy that absorbed half the labor force at low wages, an increasing resort to child labor by desperate lower-income families, and deteriorating educational, health, and pension systems combined to produce a public mood that was increasingly impatient with politicians. Although a poll taken in February 2000 found that 71 percent of the respondents thought that democracy was preferable to any other form of government, only 46 percent were satisfied with the way democracy was functioning in Argentina. Two-thirds said they had "little or no confidence" in Congress; over three-fourths said they had "little or no" confidence in Menem; and 80 percent said they had "little or no" confidence in political parties. President De la Rua came off a little better: 53 percent said they had "some or much" confidence in him, but 43 percent expressed "little or none," and 4 percent were undecided.[1] His political honeymoon would be brief.

De la Rua began his presidency from a weak position due to his narrow base of support. He was not the unquestioned leader of his own party, the UCR; Alfonsín had more support among the Radicals, and his social democrat orientation was in direct conflict with De la Rua's preference for free market polices. Nor could De la Rua count on FREPASO, his partner in the Alliance. While Vice President Álvarez shared his commitment to the Convertibility Plan, "Chacho's" views did not reflect the majority of FREPASO activists, who were much further to the left. His leadership rested mainly on his personal popularity and excellent communication skills, which might not be enough if the government ran into hard times.

De la Rua's personality was sober, to the point of being boring. He had risen to the top of the UCR through hard work and tenacity.

Still, the new cabinet promised well. Rodolfo Terragno, a prominent Radical intellectual became the chief of cabinet. A journalist and author of books on contemporary Argentina, he held a doctorate in philosophy from the University of London, had been in exile under the Proceso, and served as public works minister under Alfonsín. As minister, he proposed privatizing most of the state enterprises, but failed to get his way.[2] José Luis Machinea, the new economics minister, held a doctorate in economics from the University of Minnesota and had taught economics at the Universidad Católica. After serving as a consultant to the Economics Ministry under Generals Ongania and Levingston (1970–1971), he later held various important positions in the Central Bank during the Proceso and became the bank's president under Alfonsín. During the Menem decade, he headed his own private consulting firm and numbered many large Argentine companies, such as Technit, among his clients—along with the World Bank and the Inter-American Development Bank. He also had been director of research for the industrialists' UIA, and had developed close ties to the more nationalistic MIN faction. As De la Rua's minister, he put Technit executives into key positions involving industrial policy, trade, and investment.[3]

The remaining cabinet ministers reflected De la Rua's desire to broaden his political base. Ricardo López Murphy (Defense), Adalberto Rodríguez Giavarini (Foreign Affairs), Juan Llach (Education), and Fernando de Santibañes, the head of State Intelligence (SIDE) joined Machinea as part of an orthodox, free market clique. López Murphy was a University of Chicago-trained economist, and Rodríguez Giavarini and Llach were economists as well. Santibañes was a millionaire banker and a longtime friend of the president. Opposing them was a group composed of Alfonsín's followers. Federico Storani (Interior) represented the UCR's left wing. Beginning as a student activist in the 1970s, he was one of Alfonsín's earliest supporters and eventually became the leader of the UCR block in the Chamber of Deputies. Nicolás Gallo (Infrastructure and Housing) had been an *alfonsinista* senator and also had served both as president of Buenos Aires City's subway company and as general manager of ENTel. Ricardo Gil Lavedra (Justice) won fame as the presiding judge in the trial of the Proceso's leaders, after which he served as Alfonsín's vice minister of interior. Héctor Lombardo (Health) was a physician who had once headed the public hospital system of Buenos Aires City.

FREPASO's cabinet ministers were divided too. Graciela Fernández Meijide had been compensated for her recent defeats with the Social Development and Environment Ministry, but some observers believed that she aspired to replace "Chacho" as head of the party. She was often combative toward both De la Rua and Álvarez in cabinet meetings. On the other hand, the new FREPASO labor minister, Alberto Flamarique, supported Álvarez and fought hard to get Congress to make Argentina's labor laws more "flexible." Unfortunately, as it turned out, he fought *too* hard. Such a cabinet needed strong leadership to make it work efficiently, but De la Rua failed to use the presidential "bully pulpit" to outline a clear program and keep public opinion on his side. Instead, he preferred to isolate himself behind trusted family members, like his brother Jorge, who as general secretary to the president screened him from outsiders, and old cronies like Santibañes. That was the wrong approach, given the public mood.

THE ALLIANCE BREAKS UP

The voters expected the new government to quickly repair the rapidly deteriorating economy, not realizing that Menem had left behind a fiscal deficit impossible to close without extremely unpopular measures. The nominal deficit was $7.1 billion, which was bad enough, but that value did not include other obligations that would more than double it in real terms. For example, the provincial governments had a combined debt of around $4.2 billion, which the federal government would be expected to shoulder. In addition, the health care system for the elderly, PAMI, owed about $500 million to service providers which it had failed to pay the year before. On top of that, Argentina would be trying to roll over part of its $140 billion foreign debt at rapidly rising interest rates that hovered around 12 percent. Payments on the principal and interest were projected to cost more than $12 billion. Despite that, the government continued to borrow nearly $6 billion by selling dollar-denominated bonds, and borrowed another $4 billion in euro-denominated bonds.[4]

None of the options available to President De la Rua for restoring fiscal solvency were palatable. If the trade deficit could be turned into a surplus, it might be possible to balance the budget, and perhaps reduce the foreign debt. To make Argentine goods more competitive meant cutting labor costs, so the Labor Ministry started a new campaign to push "flexibilization" through the Peronist-controlled Senate. Out in the streets, the CGT prepared to do violent battle. Another option was to raise taxes and prune government expenditures. De la Rua didn't want to increase sales taxes, however, because that would squeeze the Alliance's middle-class base. Conversely, raising VAT, export, or corporate taxes would hurt Argentina's competitiveness. In the end, De la Rua settled for increased income taxes on Argentine society's richest 10 percent; but since those were also the people who constituted most of the investor class, that tax soon put an end to the faint glimmerings of an economic recovery that had begun late in 1999. By computerizing data on social spending, the DGI uncovered about $51 million of fraudulent claims for the past year, a laudable beginning but far from sufficient to close the budget gap.

Cutting government expenditures was equally challenging. There was little or nothing left to privatize. Political considerations made De la Rua back away from a sharp crackdown on provincial profligate spending. The most that Machinea could achieve was a compromise by which the provinces agreed to accept a fixed sum of money, amounting to about $1.4 million a month, as their share of the national revenues. The economics minister originally thought the bargain to be a good one because he expected the economy to improve. When, instead, the economy dipped further he was unable to get the provinces to accept less, and Congress backed them up. De la Rua ordered salary reductions of 12 to 15 percent for all federal employees and threatened to refuse any provincial requests for bailouts. He also put all new public works spending on hold, a move that angered Nicolás Gallo, his minister of infrastructure. From the sidelines, Alfonsín sided with Gallo and publicly castigated both the IMF and the administration for their conservative economic policies. The ex-president wanted a unilateral halt to all payments on the foreign debt. Terragno wobbled between the two sides, but suggested that perhaps Argentina might be better off taking a more hardline position with the IMF.[5]

De la Rua turned to Vice President Álvarez, who also presided over the Senate, to steer his program through Congress. It would be a homeric task, even for someone as likeable and persuasive as "Chacho." The Peronists had a majority of the Senate and, with the help of provincial parties, could prevent a quorum in the Chamber of Deputies. Furthermore, 14 of the 24 provinces were headed by Peronist governors, and the Supreme Court was still packed with Menem's appointees. Nevertheless, for a brief period in the first half of 2000, it seemed possible that De la Rua might work his way through the crisis. The "labor flexibilization" bill was his first big initiative. Labor Minister Alberto Flamarique argued that rigid labor laws governing hiring, dismissals, seniority, severance pay, closed shops, and industry-wide collective bargaining were adding excessive costs to production. The so-called *costo argentino* not only made the country's goods uncompetitive but also discouraged investment and the hiring of new employees. To this the Peronists replied that the way to bring down the price of Argentine goods was to abandon Convertibility, with its peg to the steadily appreciating dollar, just as the Brazilians had done. With the end of Convertibility, the Central Bank would be free to print more pesos, which then could be spent to stimulate the economy, rather than deepening the recession with more taxes and tight money. The government rejected that option. Too many Argentine private borrowers had taken out dollar-denominated loans, even though their incomes were in pesos. Abandoning Convertibility would lead to an avalanche of bankruptcies. With the provinces in turmoil and the CGT threatening a general strike, both sides became intransigent. Santibañes, at SIDE, and Flamarique, at the Labor Ministry, decided to go on the offensive.

Caught in a tug-of-war, the "flexibilization" bill appeared to be dead. Although Álvarez lobbied hard, the Alliance lacked the votes in Congress. Then, surprisingly, the Senate passed the labor reform bill at the end of April, and the Chamber of Deputies approved it in mid-May.[6] It seemed like a major breakthrough for the Alliance, especially as it followed other heartening news. On 7 May, just four days before the labor reform law finally passed Congress, the Alliance ticket scored a big victory in the City of Buenos Aires by electing Aníbal Ibarra as mayor and Cecelia Felgueras as vice mayor. Ibarra was a FREPASO member and a supporter of Álvarez; Felgueras was an actress who was recruited by De la Rua to run for the UCR. Their win, in such a crucial district, demonstrated that public opinion was still behind the Alliance. "Chacho" Álvarez quickly seized the initiative and, as a former Peronist who continued to have useful contacts in the PJ, began to canvass the opposition for support. Since Carlos Menem was already promising a comeback in 2004, "Chacho" especially sought out those Peronists who were anti-Menem and succeeded in convincing three powerful Peronist governors—Carlos Ruckauf of Buenos Aires Province, Carlos Reutemann of Santa Fe, and José Manuel De la Sota of Córdoba—to use their influence in getting De la Rua's first budget through Congress.

No sooner had the austerity budget passed than riots began in several provinces. In Salta and Neuquén they erupted over the closure of oil refineries. In Tucumán, Santiago del Estero, Formosa, Chaco, and Tierra del Fuego, the prospect of provincial belt-tightening due to the federal government's refusal to help threatened to raise their already high unemployment rates. The Peronist governors were cowed, and Peronist senators prepared to claw back many of the budgetary concessions they had agreed to. In June, they restored the salaries of federal employees to their previous levels. The Senate, composed of sixty-eight members, also resisted Álvarez's attempts to reduce its staff of 3,200. Many of those were highly paid *ñoquis:* friends and family members who regularly collected paychecks but never showed up for work. The press picked up the story, however, and the embarrassing publicity finally forced the senators to agree to lay off 500 of the most egregious cases.

That, however, turned out to be the administration's last big success. *La Nación's* chief investigative reporter, Joaquín Morales Solá, had been exploring rumors that some Peronist senators had been bribed to support the labor flexibilization bill. Some of the senators he interviewed confirmed the rumors, which prompted a series of articles on corruption in the Senate. There was no great outcry at first, because Menem often had bribed senators to get his legislation passed; but in July Senator Antonio Cafiero demanded an investigation into *La Nación's* charges. "Chacho" Álvarez, as the Senate's presiding officer, backed him up. He had not been a party to any bribery deals, and now he was both embarrassed and angry that someone in the Alliance government had gone behind his back to corrupt the legislators. He suspected that either labor minister Flamarique or SIDE chief Santibañes had passed over the money.[7] In meetings with De la Rua, however, Álvarez found only tepid support for an investigation. The president expressed skepticism about the charges and suggested that the Peronists were just trying to soil the Alliance's image. Nonetheless, he would go along because Rodolfo Terragno, the Chief of Cabinet, strongly favored an investigation too.

After launching his investigation on 31 August, Álvarez ran into fierce resistance. The Peronists had been on the defensive, since a few of them had admitted to taking bribes and had even named Augusto Alasino, the leader of their senatorial block, as the distributor of bribe money; but now they decided to fight back by claiming that Flamarique and Santibañes had acted as De la Rua's go-betweens. Meanwhile, the UCR senators were furious at "Chacho" because now the scandal was not only damaging the Senate's image, but threatening the administration as well.

Interior Minister Storani urged De la Rua to shuffle his cabinet, in order to give the impression of "cleaning house," rather than just drifting. It would give him the moral authority to demand that the Peronists expel some of their own senators. Rather than a complete shakeup, however, on 6 October De la Rua made just a few changes that fell far short of cleaning house. His targets were those ministers who had supported Álvarez. Chrystián Colombo, who had been head of the Banco de la Nación, replaced Rodolfo Terragno as Chief of Cabinet. Terragno did not take his dismissal amicably. If there were bribes made, he told the press, then De la Rua must have known about them. Jorge De la Rua, the president's brother, replaced Ricardo Gil Lavedra at Justice. Nicolás Gallo, the infrastructure and housing minister, was dismissed, and his portfolio was absorbed by economics minister José Luis Machinea. Another of Álvarez's supporters in the cabinet, education minister Juan Llach, had resigned a week earlier when De la Rua failed to back his school reform program because of opposition from the powerful teachers' union, CTERA.[8] Alberto Flamarique moved from the Labor Ministry to the president's staff in the place of Jorge De la Rua, and Patricia Bullrich took on the Labor portfolio. Ms. Bullrich, a descendant of one of Argentina's richest families, was nevertheless a Peronist and a former Montonera. A human rights activist, she had been picked by Dr. Gil Lavedra to head the Justice Ministry's penitentiary system. Fernando de Santibañes remained in place as the chief of SIDE. The Peronist senators were unimpressed by those changes and felt no compunction to resign their seats. "If the guilty ones on the other side have been rewarded, why should we pay?" they demanded. "Or maybe the bribes just fell out of the sky?"

On the other hand, Carlos "Chacho" Álvarez did resign as vice president on the same day that the cabinet changes were announced. Without support from the president, and ostracized by the Senate, he felt that his situation was hopeless. Rather than continuing to participate in "the game of lies and evasions that form part of the everyday rules of Argentine politics," he returned to private life.[9] Although his enemies in the administration no doubt celebrated his departure, his leaving not only wrecked the Alliance but also dealt the government a mortal blow. In the uproar that followed, Flamarique resigned from the presidential staff, and De la Rua finally had to remove the now too-controversial Santibañes as a political liability. As for the bribery charges, those were finally buried in the courts, as usual, "for lack of evidence."

TROUBLES AND TURMOIL

The economic recession worsened as the year 2000 drew to an end. The GDP shriveled, and the fiscal deficit widened, despite earlier budget cuts. There remained some hope of an eventual turnaround, since Argentina's exchange reserves and bank deposits were still plentiful, but the government's seeming inability to close the budget gap was beginning to generate serious concern at the

IMF and among private international creditors. The latter were willing to go on lending, however, so long as the IMF continued to give Argentina its support. The IMF, in turn, was fearful of cutting off aid so long as there was even a slim chance of Argentina showing some fiscal responsibility. The alternative would surely lead to a default and the collapse of the country's economy. The IMF had rushed in after vice president Álvarez's resignation with a $14 billion emergency loan to help calm jittery investors. Then, in December 2000, the IMF, the World Bank, the Inter-American Development bank, a consortium of private foreign banks, and Argentine institutional investors agreed to a $39.7 billion financial aid package involving the rollover of old bonds for new ones and the extension of new lines of credit that allowed the Argentine government to meet its current financial obligations. By that time, however, the "spread" on Argentine loans was about 7.5 percentage points above the rate for U.S. Treasury bonds, or about 13.5 percent. As usual, the IMF insisted that the Argentine government meet certain quarterly "benchmarks" toward resolving its fiscal deficit as a condition for the loans; but the IMF had been loaning Argentina money for years without "benchmarks" ever having been met, so no one took them very seriously.[10]

Economics minister José Luis Machinea trumpeted the loan package as the acquisition of "financial armor" (*blindaje financiero*) and promised that it would lead to a quick improvement in the economy. Instead, the new year brought more bad economic news. In February, Turkey defaulted on its foreign debt, once again undermining investor confidence in "emerging markets." Argentina suffered from the rippling effects as investors withdrew some of their money. With the economy resuming its downward course, Machinea looked for more budget lines to cut. He got no help from Congress, which turned down all his proposals to reduce spending on government salaries, retirement pensions, highway maintenance, police, health care, or education. Nor would the provinces cooperate. As usual, their expenditures exceeded their income, leading to demands for federal emergency aid. In Buenos Aires Province alone, Governor Carlos Ruckauf had increased spending by $312 million in order to add 11,255 people to the payroll, despite having signed an agreement with the federal government to freeze spending and balance his budget.[11]

Blocked on every front, his popularity in decline, and knowing that both foreign investors and political rivals were scheming for his removal, Machinea resigned on 2 March. Three days later Ricardo López Murphy replaced Machinea, while the Defense Ministry was turned over to Horacio Juanarena, an old UCR stalwart who had held the same post under Alfonsín. López Murphy lasted only two weeks in office. On 16 March he presented a drastic austerity plan that would slash government spending by $2 billion. Half of the cuts would come from transfer payments to the provinces and the other half from social programs like PAMI and aid to education. To sweeten the pill, he held out the promise of tax cuts, once the fiscal deficit was eliminated. It did no good. His plan was attacked from every quarter. Not even the Radicals in Congress would support him. Alfonsín dismissed his proposals as "market fundamentalism," and even

Rodolfo Terragno observed that this was not the sort of program the public had voted for. Inside the cabinet Federico Storani and López Murphy screamed insults at each other. When President De la Rua seemed inclined to back up his new economics minister, Storani resigned—as did Graciela Fernández Meijide, the last FREPASO minister. In the face of such mounting opposition, the president finally caved in and replaced López Murphy with the man whom most international bankers and businessmen had been lobbying for: Domingo Cavallo. He was the man, they said, who could salvage Argentina's sinking fortunes and turn the country around with his genius and his magical touch. But at the IMF, Michael Mussa, who headed the organization's research department, saw the change as a death knell for the administration. For Mussa, López Murphy was the only economics minister so far to have seriously attempted to end runaway government spending. The storm of opposition to his austerity plan and De la Rua's failure to continue backing him showed that the Argentine political system was unwilling to change its profligate ways, even under conditions of extreme crisis. Sophisticated Argentines with money in the bank began quietly withdrawing it, and there was an increase in tax evasion. Default was only a matter of time.[12]

RETURN OF THE "WIZARD"

Domingo Cavallo demanded, and got, extraordinary powers to deal with the economy. Nostalgia for the good times of the early 1990s gave him an aura that temporarily silenced all opposition to his schemes. Even his enemies were afraid to deny him the powers he demanded, because they would be blamed if the economy collapsed. He was now the government's key man, overshadowing even the president. Such adulation would turn anyone's head, and Cavallo was no exception. His hobnobbing with foreign presidents, kings, and prime ministers had convinced him that he was a genius. *La Nación*'s economics reporter observed that Cavallo's "long-noticed pride had...swelled his ego to immeasurable proportions."[13]

His first big victory was to convince Brazil's president, Fernando Henrique Cardoso, to sharply reduce tariffs on Argentina's exports in order to save MERCOSUR. That was worth an estimated $800 million a year in additional sales. He followed that up by providing subsidies to exporters, as well as to importers of certain capital goods. To help pay for those, he placed a tax on financial transactions, and also raised other taxes. His first big mistake was to revise the Convertibility Plan to include the euro, along with the dollar, as the peg for the peso. That upset foreign creditors as well as Argentine businessmen with dollar-denominated debts, who feared that Cavallo was inching toward a devaluation. It also brought him into conflict with Pedro Pou, the Central Bank president, who opposed any modification of Convertibility unless it increased financial discipline by "dollarizing" the economy: i.e., by abolishing the peso altogether and using only dollars as the medium of exchange.

Pou was a Menem appointee whom De la Rua had kept in place. Thus, he had few friends in the government, or in the Radicals' congressional block. Even among Peronists he was supported only by die-hard *menemistas,* since Menem himself had recently declared his own support for "dollarization" as a way to set limits on spending. Earlier in the year Machinea had also clashed with Pou over loosening the money supply. Convertibility required the Central Bank to have on hand dollar reserves equal to the amount of money in circulation plus the amount of money that Argentina's private banks were required to keep on deposit at the Central Bank. Machinea, and now Cavallo, wanted Pou to allow private banks to withdraw some of their deposits from the Central Bank for lending purposes, in order to stimulate the economy. Pou resisted them, arguing that it was necessary to keep large reserves at the Central Bank in case of a financial panic. The Argentine Bankers' Association agreed with him and warned De la Rua that any changes in the rules would threaten the financial system by making it vulnerable to large-scale capital flight.[14]

Pou's enemies got him out of office by accusing him of deliberately failing to prevent certain banks from money laundering. Soon after the Alliance government took office, Elisa Carrió, a UCR congresswoman, began an investigation into corruption and money laundering under Menem. With the help of Gustavo Gutierrez, a Conservative (*Partido Demócrata*) deputy from Mendoza, she began uncovering a multi-billion-dollar network for laundering money from narcotics and arms smuggling. Carrió accused some of the country's leading bankers, including Citibank-Argentina, of collaborating with foreign criminals and corrupt officials. She and Gutierrez also charged Pedro Pou with covering up those schemes and demanded that President De la Rua fire him. When De la Rua refused, the two representatives went to Washington with their evidence and turned it over to the Senate Permanent Subcommittee on Investigations, which also was looking into the role of U.S. banks in facilitating money laundering by international drug dealers, especially the Mexican drug cartel and its corrupt accomplices at the highest levels of the Mexican government. The Argentine deputies were able to link their investigations to those of the U.S. Senate by showing how Mexican drug money was brought into Argentina with the connivance of officials in Menem's government, and then was laundered back out through Citibank accounts in New York to dummy banks in the Bahamas, Panama, and the Cayman Islands. At the beginning of February 2001, the Senate subcommittee's Democratic staff issued a minority report detailing the operations of a worldwide money laundering cabal in which some prominent Argentine financiers were involved. Some were former high civilian officials under the Proceso, and one was Menem's own banker, Raúl Moneta. Since Pou was both a banker and a *menemista,* Carrió and Gutierrez assumed he was guilty, by association, of abetting the operation and called for his prosecution.[15]

On the same day that the U.S. Senate subcommittee issued its report, Isidro Mariano Losanovsky Perel and his wife, Rosa Berta, were found murdered in their cabin at an Argentine beach resort called Cariló, each with a bullet in the back of the neck. The killers had used a silencer, so no one heard the shots. The police found an underlined newspaper clipping about the money laundering investigations and a message from the killers left on Lovanovsky Perel's laptop, which read: "I am a gringo who collaborates with Citibank, and am dead for not turning over Citibank's bribes." It turned out that Lovanovsky Perel worked for a firm called Antfactory Latin America that was jointly owned by Citicorp Venture Capital and Antfactory, Ltd., a London-based venture capital company.[16] This double murder, coming on the heels of the U.S. Senate subcommittee's revelations created such an uproar that President De la Rua ordered an investigation into Citibank-Argentina; Mercado Abierto, an Argentine-owned bank chartered in the Cayman Islands; and Moneta's Banco República, which had operated a dummy subsidiary called Federal Bank in the Bahamas. Both Mercado Abierto and Banco República had been laundering money out of Argentina through correspondent accounts held at Citibank. Moneta also had been a lifelong friend of Richard Handley and had presided over CEI-Citicorp, until his Banco República collapsed in 1999 under suspicious circumstances, and he had been indicted for financial malfeasance.

Thus, when Pedro Pou tried to resist Cavallo's orders to modify the Convertibility Plan, he found himself politically isolated. Menem, his former *patrón,* was now under indictment and house arrest in connection with the illegal arms sales scandal. De la Rua, not knowing whether Pou might indeed be connected to the money laundering operations, would no longer back him. On 26 April Pou finally gave up and resigned, to be replaced by a Cavallo designee, Roque Maccarone. De la Rua then followed this up by revising the Central Bank's charter to allow it more discretion regarding the size of its reserve holdings. It was another victory for Cavallo, but a pyrrhic one this time. The Central Bank's independence was compromised. Foreign lenders, already disturbed by Cavallo's inclusion of the euro as part of Convertibility without consulting them, perceived that the bank would no longer be free from political pressure. Confidence in the government by domestic businessmen and bankers also took a plunge.

Cavallo dismissed his critics as "myopic" and turned next to the problem of Argentina's foreign debt, whose servicing consumed far more than Argentina's export revenues and weighed heavily on the government's budget. Some $12 billion of old bonds were set to mature in 2001, but there weren't enough dollars in the Treasury to redeem them. In May the Credit Suisse-First Boston bank sold Cavallo on a scheme that would become known as the "mega-swap," to temporarily relieve the pressure. Credit Suisse-First Boston and seven other banks formed a consortium that would offer to swap new Argentine government bonds bearing much higher interest rates for the old bonds that were about to mature. Under this "restructuring" of the debt, principal and interest payments would be postponed until 2006, giving Argentina a bit of breathing room. That is to say, instead of some $15 billion in payments that would have come due between 2001 and 2005, it would have to make no payments at all. But after that, for the almost $30 billion in new bonds that the consortium sold, another $65 billion would be added to Argentina's debt. Meanwhile, the consortium collected a total of $137 million in brokers' fees, of which $90 million went to Credit-Suisse-Boston. Cavallo heralded the "mega-swap" as yet another personal victory, but it was really just the act of a desperate debtor who promises to pay anything in the long run, so long as he can wriggle out of his current tight spot. In effect, both the bankers and the Argentine government knew that a default was coming.[17]

Why would the big international bankers agree to such a deal, knowing in advance that Argentina would never pay up? The composition of Argentina's creditors had changed. Back in the early 1990s, when Cavallo first became economics minister, he had had to deal with only a handful of powerful financiers to get what he wanted. Brokerage firms like Goldman-Sachs, Morgan-Stanley, and Credit-Suisse-Boston had competed to manage the sale of Argentine government bonds, while big mutual fund and pension fund managers in the United States were eager to buy. By the end of the Menem period, however, those fund managers were becoming leery of Argentina's prospects, so the big brokerage houses turned to Europe, where regulations protecting small investors were less strict. There, most individual investors bought stocks and bonds through their local banks. Those banks, having less information than the research units at big U.S. mutual fund companies like Fidelity or Vanguard, were more easily taken in by glowing reports about Argentina's future prospects, and passed them on to their customers. Thus, the big international brokerage houses succeeded in "atomizing" the risk of default by spreading it among literally hundreds of thousands of small investors in Italy, Germany, and the rest of Europe (and Japan), who bought into high-interest-bearing "emerging market" mutual funds through their pension plans. "That's what kept Argentina going," said an emerging market bond manager at Metropolitan Life Insurance Company. "Those poor suckers didn't have a clue as to what they were buying."[18]

FREE FALL

Argentine capitalists were not fooled about the state of the economy. Stocks plunged on the Buenos Aires Bolsa. At mid-year the GDP had already contracted by over 5 percent, and both Moody's and Standard & Poor downgraded Argentina's bond ratings. There were rumors that De la Rua might resign. Money was discretely drawn out of bank accounts and deposited overseas. Cavallo attempted a show of strength by announcing a "zero-deficit" program that mandated across-the-board cuts in wages, pensions, and transfer payments to the provinces. A nervous Congress approved them in principle, although whether they could actually be implemented was a matter for some skepticism. Instead of calming the private sector, such measures indicated that the government was suffering a severe liquidity crisis. That intensified the drain on bank deposits. The IMF came to the rescue with another emergency loan in August, but the relief was only temporary. The run on the banks began again, after provincial governors rejected any cutbacks in transfer payments.

Legislative elections were held on 14 October for all the Senate seats and half of the Chamber seats. The Alliance got 5 million fewer votes than it had in 1999, while the Peronists won majorities in both houses of Congress. Eduardo Duhalde easily won the governor's race in Buenos Aires Province and became the acknowledged leader of the *Partido Justicialista;* but many voters split their ballots in that province and elected Raúl Alfonsín to the Senate as well. Elisa Carrió broke away from the UCR, set up her own "Alternative for a Republic of Equals" (ARI) and easily won re-election to the Chamber from Chaco Province. The press also noted an unusually large protest vote (*voto bronca*). Over 26 percent of the eligible voters failed to show up at the polls, even though voting was obligatory. Of those who did vote, over 20 percent cast blank or spoiled ballots. *Clarín* interviewed some of the voters in a poll taken the next day in Greater Buenos Aires. The great majority who said they cast blank ballots were young and highly educated. Their blank votes were an expression of anger at all politicians.

After the election, De la Rua's government was unable to raise any more foreign loans. By then the United States was preparing for the "War on Terror," following Al Qaida's 11 September attacks on the Twin Towers, and "had no interest in...a geopolitically insignificant country that was busily, stupidly, destroying itself." When Cavallo went to Washington in October to seek more financial aid, U.S. Treasury Secretary Paul O'Neill turned him down, saying that when a country like Argentina paid 300 base points over LIBOR to get a loan, it was "a certain candidate for a payments crisis."[19] Nor would the IMF provide any more bailouts. Its internal reports noted that Argentina's debt load had become unsustainable, that there was little hope of an increase in its exports, that foreign capital was leaving the country, and that there was no likelihood of overcoming the political stalemate that prevented fiscal discipline.

Unable to get foreign help, in November a desperate Cavallo put pressure on Argentine banks and pension funds (AFJP) to buy the government's bonds, at below-market interest rates. The bonds were payable in dollars and (theoretically) backed by the federal government's tax receipts. Although the deal was said to be "voluntary," the banks knew that, in the current atmosphere of hostility toward finance, they would surely face heavy penalties if they refused. They also knew that the so-called backing for the bonds was illusory: the government was broke and already was refusing to pay its debts to suppliers. Even if there was some money in the treasury, past experience showed that it would be spent on the politicians' clientele, rather than to pay off the bondholders. The bankers were further disheartened by the knowledge that they would not easily rid themselves of the bonds, because there simply was no secondary market for them, even at a big discount.

By the end of the month, thousands of depositors, fearful that their banks might collapse, or that a snap devaluation might make their peso accounts worthless, pulled some $3.6 billion dollars out of the banks, on top of around $10 billion that had left Argentina since the June "mega-swap." Thanks to Cavallo's liberalizing the Central Bank's deposit requirements, much of the money the IMF and others had loaned to Argentina flowed out to the private banks and then to overseas accounts. Not just Argentine businessmen and other private citizens, but leading foreign companies had transferred enormous sums, facilitated by big foreign banks like Credit-Suisse-First Boston, Morgan Guaranty, Barclay's, and Banesto of Spain.[20]

To stop this hemorrhaging, on 1 December Cavallo froze bank deposits and prohibited money transfers abroad. With few exceptions, no one could withdraw more than $250 or 1,000 pesos a week from any account. All dollar deposits were converted into pesos. "We have to stop capital flight," he explained, in defense of this extreme measure, which became known as the *corralito*. Reactions to the *corralito* differed widely. Carlos Heller, general manager of the Banco Credicoop defended it as the only way to stop a financial stampede. Julio Macchi, former president of the Buenos Aires Bolsa, shrugged it off. "If people don't need the money it's better that they keep it in the bank. Otherwise, I'd advise them to do like in the old days: hide it under the mattress." By contrast, Juan Luis Bour, of the pro-business Foundation for Research on Free Markets (FIEL), predicted that it would undermine people's confidence in the banking system. Jorge Ávila, an economist at the Centro de Estudios Macroeconómicos de la Argentina, agreed: "I think it's horrible. I never in my life thought I'd see such a breakdown....They're violating the rights of property." Still, some depositors managed to evade the ban and funnel another $2.7 billion out of Argentina after Cavallo's decree, through "obscure channels." "The *corralito* trapped the little guys [*perejiles*]," one banker observed. "The big players already knew what was going to happen and got out ahead of time."[21]

The IMF added to Cavallo's woes on 5 December by cancelling a scheduled $1.3 billion loan on the grounds that Argentina failed to stop its chronic fiscal deficits. On the following day Cavallo seized all private pension funds, replacing the money with government bonds and transferring the sequestered sums to the treasury's account at the Banco de la Nación. That would temporarily allow the administration to pay its bills.

The *corralito* was the "wizard's" last magic trick, and it backfired disastrously. Depositors lined up outside the banks, and as they were turned away, there were sporadic protests, while in nearby alleys and arcades some were changing pesos for dollars with black marketeers at steep discounts. By the second week of December, public anger was mounting dangerously. Unemployment figures for October came out on the 13th, showing that the official jobless rate was at a new high of 18.3 percent. Treasury Secretary Daniel Marx resigned. The CGT called for a general strike. On the 17th the government presented its budget for 2002, with projected spending cuts of almost 20 percent.

Two days later, violent protests broke out against Cavallo's policies. They began in Rosario, just as they had back in 1989, and quickly spread through the interior to Santa Fe, Córdoba, La Plata, and Mendoza; then down into the Buenos Aires suburbs of Avellaneda, Moreno, La Tablada, Lanús, and Ramos Mejía. In the capital, the area around Plaza Constitución was the first to erupt, after which the violence quickly spread. Mobs gathered outside of groceries, supermarkets, and other retail stores, and eventually forced their way in. Chinese and Korean merchants seemed to be favorite targets. In some cases the merchants tried to defend their property with guns or knives, but were overwhelmed. Sometimes the police stood by and refused to intervene; at other times they tried to stop the rioters, whereupon there were bloody battles.

Were the riots spontaneous, or organized? According to press observers, they were both. Many of the rioters, especially those in working-class neighborhoods, were experienced agitators from far-left organizations like the CTA, the CGT's combative left wing; the Communist Party's *Corriente Clasista y Combativa;* the trotskyite *Asamblea Piquetera* and *Bloque Piquetero;* and the *Izquierda Unida.* But in many cases the rioters were middle class—unemployed white-collar types, ruined small businessmen, pensioners, people whose bank accounts were frozen by the *corralito*—the sort of people who never before in their lives had taken part in a protest. They first went out into the streets, beating on pots and pans to call attention to their plight. Then they began heading, in cars and on foot, toward the Plaza de Mayo to demand Cavallo's ouster and De la Rua's resignation. There they were met by the palace guard and the police, who stopped them with tear gas and then went on the attack, chasing and clubbing the slower demonstrators, many of them women and elderly people. The guards also turned on the television cameramen who were recording the event. The originally peaceful demonstration turned into a full-scale riot as groups of young left wing militants, eager to take advantage of the situation, struck back violently. As the battle of the Plaza raged back and forth, the CGT's Hugo Moyano sent in "tough guys" to back up the leftists. Meanwhile, out in the industrial suburbs, it was rumored that Governor Carlos Ruckauf had joined with Moyano to encourage riots and sackings of stores to bring down the De la Rua government. Some journalists reported seeing PJ organizers going through the streets distributing crude maps showing which shops were to be attacked and communicating with one another by cell phones.[22]

De la Rua declared a state of emergency and gave the police special powers to restore order, but the violence escalated. Late in the evening of 20 December, he resigned as president after the PJ refused his call for a national unity government. Cavallo had resigned the day before and was now locked in his apartment on the Avenida Libertador, afraid to go out for fear he'd be lynched. While private police held off mobs of demonstrators outside the building, his wife was on the verge of a nervous breakdown. Cavallo himself was under judicial order not to attempt to leave the country. As the dawn rose on 21 December the city of Buenos Aires "presented a scene never witnessed before," according to *La Nación.* Banks, shops, and restaurants lay in ruins, some of them in flames. Burnt-out cars blocked the streets. The Plaza de Mayo was littered with cartridges, rocks, and garbage. In the working-class *barrios* on the city's southern side, the scene looked like a hurricane had passed through. The streets were littered with glass, spilled food, and broken boxes. There was a strong smell of alcohol and the sound of sirens. There were similar scenes of devastation in the interior of Argentina, where riots had flared up in 11 of the 24 provinces. Twenty-eight people had died during the two-day riots, hundreds more were badly injured, and over 2,000 were under arrest.[23]

Ramón Puerta, the Senate's president, was De la Rua's proper successor under the Constitution, but the triumphant Peronists in Congress quickly called a joint session of the two houses and replaced him with Adolfo Rodríguez Saá, the governor of San Luis Province. Rodríguez Saá announced a suspension on all foreign debt payments and promised to call a general election on 3 March. Meanwhile, new public works programs would create jobs. "Everything for social justice!" he proclaimed.

In fact, Rodríguez Saá lasted only a week in office. His failure to lift the *corralito* led to a middle-class protest march on the Plaza de Mayo on Friday, 28 December. However, the peaceful demonstration was taken over by gangs of young toughs from La Plata and La Matanza who broke into the Congress building on their way down the Avenida de Mayo and vandalized it. Then they tried to invade the Casa Rosada but were driven off by the police, after which they turned their fury on nearby banks and fast-food joints. The next day Peronist governors Ruckauf, Reutemann, and De la Sota met with congressional leaders and decided that Rodríguez Saá had to go. He already had been filling his government with cronies, without consulting anyone, and was showing signs of wanting to run as the PJ's official presidential candidate in March. On Sunday, 30 December, Congress replaced him with Ramón Puerta, who this time arranged for Eduardo Oscar Camaño, the president of the Chamber of Deputies, to assume the presidency *ad interim*. Camaño was a Duhalde supporter, and by Tuesday, 1 January, he had lined up sufficient support for a joint session to pick Eduardo Duhalde to fill out the remainder of De la Rua's term. The previously scheduled March elections were cancelled, and new ones were set for 10 December 2003. As a condition of his appointment, Duhalde had to promise not to be a candidate.

Chapter Ten

The Retreat to Populism

Eduardo Duhalde finally attained the presidency, only to find himself bogged down in an economic morass. Argentina's foreign debts totaled some $214 billion, of which the federal government owed $132 billion, the provinces $22 billion, and the private sector around $60 billion. Most of that was payable in foreign currency, usually dollars. By itself, the federal government's share was equivalent to around 45 percent of the country's annual GDP and nearly five times the total value of all exports. In his inaugural speech Duhalde admitted that the country was broke. His choice to head the Economics Ministry, Jorge Remes Lenicov, did little to inspire confidence that he would fix things. Lenicov had been Duhalde's provincial economics minister and had left the economy in a shambles, with a debt that had more than doubled and huge, chronic budget deficits. After Duhalde's two terms in office as governor, his successor, Carlos Ruckauf, had to issue scrip, called *patacones,* in order to pay the salaries of government workers.[1] In brief, Duhalde signaled a return to traditional Peronist populism.

Events quickly bore this out. The new president began by announcing that Rodríguez Saá's moratorium on debt payments would remain in place. Those principal and interest payments had become the largest single drain on the federal budget, even surpassing revenue sharing with the provinces. Now the money would go to financing public works and social welfare programs. Duhalde was alarmed at the rising levels of unemployment and underemployment, which totaled almost 35 percent of the labor force, and the widespread poverty that resulted. It was estimated at the end of 2001 that over 40 percent of the population now lived below the poverty line.[2] The December riots seemed to presage more social explosions if something was not done. A poll conducted in January found that a third of the Argentines interviewed would emigrate if they could.

Indeed, many Argentines were lining up at foreign consulates to ask for visas. Most of them were young professionals with a dim view of the country's future. The longest line was to be found at the Spanish consulate, where some 3,000 people—descendants of Spanish immigrants—were camped out, having brought chairs and food to accommodate the wait. Almost as many Argentines lined up outside the Italian consulate, whose officials were processing at least 17,000 applications for immigrant status. Many other European consulates also were besieged by visa applicants. Israeli officials, operating out of the Jewish Community Center in downtown Buenos Aires, were handling hundreds of applications daily. "We have Argentines who aren't even Jewish calling us up," one embassy official said. "We have to explain to them that this program only applies to Argentine Jews." Those who were accepted as immigrants would get free plane tickets, relocation expenses, health and educational benefits, help in obtaining mortgages, and, if necessary, job training. The United States embassy was busy too, processing a large number of requests for temporary work visas and passport applications for the Argentine wives and children of U.S. citizens.[3]

Duhalde outlined a series of emergency steps to meet the crisis. Because the economy had contracted by over 8 percent under De la Rua, tax receipts were way down, which meant that a deficit of perhaps $2.7 billion would be unavoidable. Nevertheless, he immediately allocated $350 million for more soup kitchens, to be administered by "Chiche" Duhalde. Another $1 billion would be spent on job creation projects, with preference in hiring going to the heads of families. Duhalde also restored the year-end "bonus" (aguinaldo) of an extra month's wage for public employees. All of this would be expensive, he admitted, but his budget would be more "realistic" than the zero-deficit budget that Cavallo had announced a month before.[4]

Duhalde also took the bold, though controversial, step of ending the Convertibility Plan with its fixed one-to-one dollar/peso exchange rate. The peso was devalued by 30 percent for foreign currency earned from exports; otherwise, it was allowed to float. An exception was made in favor of "small debtors" whose debts amounted to less than $100,000. They could still pay in pesos at a one-to-one rate. Meanwhile, dollar-denominated bank accounts and obligations were converted into pesos at the rate of 1.4 pesos to the dollar. Congress also passed a bankruptcy law at the end of January that placed a 180-day moratorium on the collection of debts and required banks to write off loans as "uncollectible" if they and the debtors failed to agree on new terms within 90 days. The banks calculated that this would cost them about $15 billion, although the government argued that their losses would be closer to only $10 billion. In any case, Duhalde promised to compensate the banks with 5-year government bonds.[5]

Devaluation and "peso-fication" greatly relieved debtors, who could now repay their local creditors with cheap dollars, but it penalized prudent savers who had put their money away in dollar accounts. It also did irreparable harm to the banking system, inasmuch as it discouraged future would-be depositors. It also hurt foreign investors who acquired properties by paying in dollars, for those properties were now valued in pesos whose worth kept falling. Foreign companies also lost money because the machinery and equipment they imported had to be bought with dollars, which in turn had to be acquired at the bank with more pesos than before. The same was true when they turned pesos into dollars in order to repatriate profits to their home countries. Not surprisingly, European and American direct investment in Argentina dropped off sharply. By contrast, local conglomerates who took out big peso loans to buy into the privatized state enterprises back in the 90s now found some relief from their debts. Those that had stashed dollars abroad could even profit hugely from the new exchange rate. Local farmers and ranchers producing for export also were helped by the devaluation. Still, devaluation and peso-fication were not popular with the general public, which feared a return to hyper-inflation. Polls showed that 78 percent of those interviewed disapproved of the measures, and 81 percent expressed no confidence in the government's general economic program.[6] The government had estimated that the floating peso would finally stabilize at around 2 to 1, and so it did in the Buenos Aires *cambios* throughout February (although it already was being quoted at 3 to 1 across the river in Montevideo). In March, though, the peso began to slide, ending at 4 to 1.

Indeed, the populist financial reforms brought few benefits to the general public, although they aimed to offer relief to "the little fellow." Arisó and Jacobo note that: "Of the nearly five and a half million physical or juridical persons indebted to the banks, some twelve hundred represented 51 percent of the obligations. And they were not exactly PYMEs." In fact, PYMEs only accounted for a little over 15 percent of the banks' debtors. Small wonder that the UIA and the Cámara de Comercio strongly supported the new government. Peso-fication benefitted the big local industrialists and merchants. "Of the approximately twelve thousand companies exporting from the country, the largest five hundred controlled 90 percent of the output. In other words, five hundred companies got 90 percent of the benefits." Otherwise, "unemployment and poverty increased, wages fell, exports didn't rise, and no new markets were gained. Afterwards we were all poorer, except for those who had positioned themselves in dollars, warned beforehand about what was about to happen." People who had dollar debts or mortgage payments in dollars were ruined. Their combined losses were estimated at over $66 billion. Another $19 billion found surreptitious ways to flee the country.[7]

Such capital flight prompted the government to send investigators into several banks to look for evidence of "economic subversion." The Banco General de Negocios' general manager was arrested on 23 January as he boarded a flight to Zurich. His bank, in turn, was controlled by Credit Suisse-Banco de Boston, Dresdner Bank, and J.P. Morgan-Chase Bank, so their Argentine branches were investigated by the Justice Ministry as well. So were those of Citibank, Banco de Quilmes, Banco de Nova Scotia, Sudamerica Bank, and the Banco de Galicia. Their records were seized for incriminating evidence that they had helped clients to get their deposits out of the country after the *corralito* was imposed. The banks' top executives were forbidden to leave the country and were forced to open their clients' safety deposit boxes so that they could be examined. Fearful that the government would try to make the banks the chief villains of Argentina's woes, the Association of Argentine Banks took out large advertisements in Buenos Aires' newspapers, calling for an end to the "witch hunt" that threatened to destroy the whole banking system.[8]

The banks had to be thankful, however, that the government kept the *corralito* in place. Without it, their depositors would have left their coffers empty. Indeed, some depositors went to extreme lengths to get their money out. On 23 January Norberto Roglich, a sixty-two-year-old retiree, went to his local bank in Tandil and asked to close his account of some $22,000. The manager told him it could not be done. "I just want what's mine," Roglich insisted. He was a diabetic, he explained, and needed to money to guarantee a steady supply of insulin. When he was refused a second time, he took a grenade out of his pocket. "Give me all the money in my account," he told the manager, "otherwise, I'll pull the pin." The manager told the teller to hand over the cash. Roglich took his money and left, but of course was arrested later at his home and charged with extortion and the illegal possession of a dangerous weapon.[9]

As a *Buenos Aires Herald* editorial noted on 27 January,

Contrary to government propaganda and media outcry, the banks have not until now been the prime factor in pulling money out because they need as much as possible within the financial system in order to have a business: the sad truth is that everybody's hero, the people themselves, have been the most frantic to pull out money because of their total lack of confidence, but nobody wants to admit this.

On the previous day, in fact, there had been a massive demonstration in the Plaza de Mayo of middle-class depositors banging pots and waving placards to protest the *corralito*. One placard read: "We put our money in the banks to keep it safe, not so they could steal it." That was but one demonstration out of many that would take place over the next few weeks. Under such a constant barrage of criticism, the government began making exceptions to the freeze, loosening the requirements for the elderly, the unemployed, people convalescing from serious illnesses, people about to undergo major surgery, and widows and widowers cashing in life insurance policies. Wage and pension checks could also be cashed for any amount. The courts broadened the exceptions further by including lawyers who incurred legal costs or were claiming legal fees.

Duhalde also got Congress to amend the Central Bank's charter, allowing it to print pesos without requiring the currency to be backed by foreign exchange. Another emergency decree froze the rates on electricity, gas, water, telephone, subway, and commuter train services. His decree also unilaterally revised the privatized utilities by requiring their fees to be paid in newly-devalued pesos. Duhalde also brought back price controls for "essential goods" such as fuels and medicines. And to halt the rise in unemployment, a new labor law forbade layoffs for three months, unless first approved by the government.

Duhalde's rate freezes affected companies that were owned by Spanish, Italian, French, American, and British capital, which caused a notable lack of confidence in Argentina among European and U.S. investors. Duhalde stirred up more protests when, in a frantic search for revenue, he imposed 20 percent export taxes on agricultural goods as well as on nontraditional exports, including oil and gas. The Argentine Rural Confederation (CRA), which represented small and medium-sized farmers and ranchers, responded with a strike. In Patagonia, oil workers joined with the companies in protesting the "retentions" and threatened to seize the wells and oil rigs unless they were rescinded. Their strike disrupted daily life in the capital when the privately-owned buses (*colectivos*) announced that they were reducing their services because of a lack of gasoline. In the end, Duhalde had to back down on the "retentions," but then sought to substitute a new tax on the country's largest companies, purportedly to aid the PYMEs.

THE CONFLICT WITH THE COURTS

Since Cavallo first decreed the *corralito,* there had been lawsuits challenging it as an unconstitutional seizure of private property. By early February there was a daily average of some 1,200 suits being filed, reaching 2,000 on 14 February and 10,000 on 20 February. The Federal Supreme Court already had declared the *corralito* to be unconstitutional, but Duhalde had issued an executive decree suspending all judicial judgments about the matter for 180 days. At the Federal Courthouse in downtown Buenos Aires, a line of lawyers and petitioners stretched for twelve blocks. Lower courts already had in many cases called on the banks to return their depositors' money, although different courts disagreed as to procedures regarding dollar-denominated accounts. Some ordered the money returned in dollars; others allowed payments in pesos. Some allowed the peso reimbursements to be at the official 1.4 to 1 rate; others insisted on the more generous free market rate. The banks already were feeling under siege by the frequent *escraches:* depositors violently banging on their doors and windows with hammers and crowbars, attacks on their armored cars, and government investigations into their role in capital flight. They protested to the courts through the Association of Argentine Banks (ADEBA) that they could not act in the absence of a single, common judicial norm. On 12 March ADEBA petitioned the Supreme Court to suspend its earlier decision about the *corralito's* unconstitutionality, arguing that the *corralito* was the only way to prevent massive withdrawals that would cause a complete collapse of Argentina's banking system. The ADEBA's petition was contested by the Buenos Aires Bar Association, which argued that the *corralito* violated the citizenry's property rights and created a situation of "juridical insecurity." The Supreme Court took the lawyers' side, reaffirming its decision that the *corralito* was unconstitutional and adding that Duhalde's decree suspending judicial action on it was unconstitutional as well.[10]

Duhalde struck back at the court by asking the Chamber of Deputies to begin impeachment proceedings against all nine of the justices. They were accused of failing to uphold the law by not investigating with sufficient rigor the cases of illegal arms sales to Croatia and Ecuador, and by not punishing those in the Menem government who had obstructed justice in the Israeli Embassy bombing investigations.[11] Duhalde also issued another executive decree "of necessity and urgency" prohibiting the justices from taking steps that would upset the government's banking policies. Eduardo Ratti, the Economic Ministry's legal and technical secretary, told a press conference on 15 April that it was not Duhalde's intention to interfere with the judiciary's constitutional powers, but to protect the vast majority of depositors who had not sued in court and to protect the banks from being financially drained by the 160,000 or so lawsuits filed against them. Meanwhile, the banks were offering interest rates as high as 50 percent on savings accounts in order to attract new deposits. One bank executive admitted sadly: "We have to offer interest rates that would be shocking in any First World country, but that's the only way we have to get people to once again put their money into our banks."[12]

Public opinion was cross-pressured on the subject of Duhalde's struggle with the court. Lots of people wanted to get their money out of the banks; on the other hand, the charges against the Menem-appointed justices seemed well founded. The *Buenos Aires Herald* reflected this ambivalence in an 8 February editorial that criticized both the court and Duhalde. The former's actions were "badly timed," the *Herald* opined, but Duhalde also displayed a "wanton disregard for property rights and the process of law." Impeaching all, or just some, of the justices would constitute "a vendetta subordinating justice to political expediency" and open Argentina to mob rule. Even the government itself was internally divided. Mario Blejer, the Central Bank president, wanted to lift the *corralito,* but economics minister Jorge Remes Lenicov overruled him. Blejer argued that the IMF was insisting on the return of the deposits as a prerequisite for any future aid. Having worked at the IMF for 20 years before presiding over the Central Bank, he was in a position to know. Nonetheless, Remes Lenicov stood firm.

On 19 April the severe shortage of dollars prompted the government to decree the "indefinite" closure of all banks and exchange houses. Earlier in the day, Blejer had been forced to close down Scotiabank-Quilmes, the local branch of the Bank of Nova Scotia, because the parent bank had refused to send down any more cash. As frantic depositors piled into the Scotiabank's lobby in the vain hope of withdrawing their funds, the bank's employees passed out leaflets that read: "Canada: Fork Over the Money!" Remes Lenicov's solution to the lack of liquidity was the usual ploy of issuing ten-year government bonds to depositors in lieu of cash. This was being done already in the cash-strapped provinces, where local governments were paying their wages and debts in bonds, or scrip. Local business and provincial banks were required to accept this scrip as legal tender, although it could not be used to pay one's taxes. In the private sector, a black market had grown up to evade the *corralito.* Throughout the downtown financial district *cuevas,* or *mesas del dinero,* had sprung up. These were clandestine offices, usually sponsored by one of the banks but disguised as other kinds of businesses, that dealt in selling dollars, at an estimated rate of $30 million to $50 million a day. The most common operation was called the *cheque móvil,* or "mobile check." This usually involved a certified check, which the holder would sign over to the *cueva* in return for an equivalent amount in dollars, minus about a 12 percent commission. The dollars would not be paid over immediately, however. First, the check would have to be cleared by a bank or sold to a third party. So if the face value of the check was $10,000, the owner would turn over $1,200 to the *cueva* and would receive $8,800 about two days later. The cueva might then sell the check to a third party at an 8 percent discount. That third party would then own a $10,000 check for a payment of only $9,200, while the *cueva* would have made $2,000 on the entire operation. The third party might then use the check to pay off a creditor, or sell it to a fourth party. In this way, millions of dollars circulated outside the regular banking system.[13]

Remes Lenicov's bond-swapping plan required congressional approval, but as soon as the bill was submitted, angry crowds of frustrated depositors surrounded the heavily guarded Congress building, chanting "Bonds, no! Bonds, no!" They waved banners and placards that insulted politicians and bankers, and they harassed everyone who entered or left, kicking at cars and giving the legislators a taste of what they could expect if they passed the bill. Congressmen showing up for the sessions had to be escorted by police. The presidential residence in Olivos was similarly besieged, requiring Duhalde to enter and leave by a secret rear entrance. Throughout the country there were wildcat strikes, street protests, and blockades of highways by pickets. After two days of debate, Congress turned down the bill, and on 27 April Remes Lenicov resigned. In the meantime, an IMF team had arrived in Argentina to meet with Duhalde and his top economic officials. One result of the visit was to convince the president to back down on his campaign to impeach the Supreme Court.

ECONOMIC AGONY

Roberto Lavagna replaced Remes Lenicov at the Economics Ministry. He had served previously in second-level positions in that ministry under Peronist, military, and Radical governments. At the time of his appointment, he was ambassador to the European Union. After a few weeks in his new job, Lavagna reopened the issue of bonds for cash but allowed each bank to decide for itself whether to offer its clients cash or government bonds. The IMF reluctantly supported the scheme, fearing that otherwise the government would start printing money in such huge quantities as to bring back hyper-inflation. With that imprimatur, Congress approved the bill, following which Mario Blejer resigned from the Central Bank. In the weeks that followed, it became clear that few depositors were willing to accept bonds. "There is no way that I would accept a government bond instead of my money," one man, whose life savings had been frozen, told the *Herald.* "Who in their right mind would trust the politicians we have to set things right? With a bond, you'll never get your money back."[14] By October, this relaxation of the *corralito* had resulted in total bank deposits falling from some $70 billion at the beginning of 2002 to only $2.9 billion. As their capital shrank, the banks closed 210 branches throughout the country and laid off 9,500 employees.

Despite his stirring calls for "patriotic collaboration," Duhalde was attacked by all groups and classes as more businesses failed, unemployment rose, and over half of the population sank below the poverty line. By the end of 2002, the economy shrank by just over 10 percent, having already shrunk by over 20 percent since 1998.[15] At the same time, consumer prices rose by an average of 18 percent, with food prices rising by 29 percent. The overall rise would have been higher but for the freeze on utilities' rates.

During just the first four months of 2002, more than 100,000 commercial establishments closed down, throwing some 280,000 people out of work, according to Fedecámaras, the retailers' confederation. Sales were down by about 40 percent, sending ripples throughout the construction industry as plans for new shopping centers and supermarkets were put on hold. Manufacturing was suffering as well, with many of the country's largest firms finding themselves unable to pay their dollar-denominated debts with devalued pesos. Acindar, once the largest private steel company, had never recovered from the collapse of Argentina's automotive industry following Brazil's devaluation of its currency in 1999. Brazil had been Argentina's biggest market for cars and trucks, and devaluation priced those vehicles out of range. The drop in automotive sales caused cutbacks in steel purchases, pushing Acindar to the verge of bankruptcy. Its founding family, the Acevedos, sold their controlling interest to Brazil's Belgo Minera in 2001. At the end of 2001 Alpargatas, the largest textile company, filed for bankruptcy. It would be taken over by Camargo Correa, a Brazilian conglomerate that already had acquired Alpargatas' Brazilian branch. Camargo Correa also eventually acquired Loma Negra, Argentina's leading cement company. In April, 2002, Amalia Lacroze Fortabat, Loma Negra's president, declared the company bankrupt. The deal with Camargo Correa was sealed three years later for $1 billion. Brazilians also took over the Quilmes Beer Company, Argentina's largest. The new owner was AmBev, a holding company that also owned Brahma, Brazil's most popular beer. By mid-2002 Pérez Companc, the energy giant, was unable to pay on over $2 billion of accumulated debt and began takeover negotiations with Petrobras. The Pescarmona Group and the Soldati Group were kept from bankruptcy only by reaching agreements with their creditors to reschedule their debts and sell off their greatest money-losing properties. The recently privatized telecommunications company, Telecom, which served northern Argentina, declared itself in bankruptcy in April 2002. It had lost a long, costly battle in the courts over government freezes on its rates; moreover, many of its customers, suffering from the prolonged recession, had either cancelled their services or simply were not paying their bills.[16]

Argentines were shocked by the large number of impoverished middle-class families who had to sell their businesses, cars, furniture, clothes—even their homes. These "newly poor" cut back on services, deferred payments on others, and sometimes defaulted on debts. They stopped going to movies and restaurants, and ate cheaper food at home. They had to take their children out of private schools and could no longer afford to send the older ones to university. Not accustomed to thinking of themselves as poor, they were ashamed when forced to resort to the same charitable organizations to which they once were donors. More and more they joined protest demonstrations, beating pots and pans in the Plaza de Mayo to dramatize their plight.

The traditional working class was better organized, though no better off. Those who still had jobs had their labor unions and the CGT, which pressured the government to retain price controls on essential goods, guarantee job security, and take a hard line with the country's foreign creditors. For the unemployed, or the underemployed with extremely low wages, the options were charity, crime, or picking through garbage in the streets at night. All three were on the rise in Buenos Aires, which once was a safe, beautiful, chic metropolis. There were more abandoned children (*pibes de la calle*), more beggars on the streets and in the subways, more people selling cheap little items to patrons of bars and cafes. One depressing sign of the growing desperation was the widespread phenomenon of *cartoneros:* people, sometimes families, going through the streets and alleys of downtown Buenos Aires to collect cardboard and paper from trash piles, which they could trade in for about 2 pesos (4 cents) per kilo. Other families were simply looking for scraps in the garbage cans of restaurants. Tomás Eloy Martínez, a prominent novelist, related that, one Saturday night, he saw

at least ten or twelve families waiting for the pizzerias or MacDonald's on Calle Corrientes or Avenida Rivadavia...to close their shutters and put out their garbage, so that these people could eat the refuse. There were kids from 3 to 11 years of age, with their fathers and mothers, whom nobody would ever have imagined before as being in such miserable circumstances.[17]

THREE-SIDED STALEMATE

A three-sided stalemate between the federal government and the provinces, on the one hand, and the federal government and foreign lenders on the other, made the crisis intractable. In the past, Argentina had been able to avoid painful cuts in government spending by borrowing from abroad. Now neither European nor American investors were willing to lend any more money unless the IMF certified that the Argentines were actually making progress in bringing their budget deficits under control—which the IMF was not willing to do. Since the end of the Proceso, it had loaned a total of some $30.6 billion to bolster the newly recovered democracy, but now its patience was at an end. Despite Duhalde's pleas that great hardship would result from sharp spending cutbacks, there would be no more aid until the government closed its fiscal deficit. Both the U.S. government and the European Union backed the IMF in its newfound intransigence. The Bush administration insisted on "drastic reforms," while the European press kept up a barrage of critical articles about Argentina that emphasized its xenophobia, fascist past, corruption, drug trafficking, and demagoguery. Duhalde didn't help matters by losing his temper at one point and threatening to nationalize all foreign property and seal off Argentina from the world economy.

Just as Duhalde was unable to force foreign lenders to give money to Argentina, so there was no way that he could force provincial governors to exercise fiscal discipline. All throughout 2002 and the first quarter of 2003, the federal government and the provinces engaged in periodic, and ultimately futile, negotiations over revenue sharing. The federal government wanted the provinces to limit their spending, raise their taxes, close their budget deficits, and stop printing "bonds" or scrip. Its threats to hold up payments to the provinces were never really credible, however, given the realities of intra-party politics and the need for congressional cooperation. Nor were the "concessions" that the provincial governments might make now and then really credible. Once the federal government resumed payments, the provinces always went back to their old spending ways. For example, in February 2002 the provincial governors signed an agreement not to issue any more scrip, in return for the federal government's commitment to buy up the scrip already in circulation. By April, however, the IMF noted that the provinces were back to printing new "bonds" for the purposes of paying their creditors and employees. But when it demanded that Duhalde put a stop to it, he refused, saying that he did not wish to provoke new conflicts. In March of the following year, he again agreed to have the federal government buy up the worthless provincial bonds. In fairness to the provinces, they saw no reason to tighten their economic belts when the federal authorities were failing to do the same. Duhalde had promised the IMF that he would trim back the federal bureaucracy by abolishing several ministries and secretariats. Not only did he fail to do so, but he actually increased the size of the bureaucracy by about 25 percent. Nevertheless, the Argentines felt slighted when they learned, in June, that while they would receive no aid from the IMF, the more cooperative Brazilians were awarded a $10 million loan.

MENEM REDUX

An alarming sign of the public's growing desperation was the breakdown in law and order, as seen in the increase in the crime rate and the rise of the *piquetero* movement. The newspapers were filled with stories of burglary, robbery, and kidnapping. At the same time, organized street violence began escalating, promoted by so-called "popular assemblies." These were formed by various extreme-left groups who proposed to replace mere "representative democracy" (the courts, Congress, parties, governments at all levels) with "direct democracy." They called for a big, open, sovereign, popular convention that would write a whole new constitution, outside the control of the current elites. Their "shock troops" were the *piqueteros,* the "pickets" recruited from the "combative" unions, the unemployed, and various "militants" who previously had blocked streets and highways.[18] As the demonstrations became more violent, Duhalde warned the *piqueteros:* "We respect the right to protest, but not to prevent the free movement of those who want to go to work. We won't allow that." Nevertheless, the disturbances escalated until finally, on 26 June, Duhalde ordered the police to use whatever force was necessary to suppress them. Bloody clashes over the next few days left forty *piqueteros* dead and the protest movement despondent because there had been no popular outrage against police repression. As one "popular assembly" militant confessed: "That part of society which, for simplicity's sake we can call 'the common man,' is the part that said 'enough.' Not because of any ideological conviction but because...we went too fast and shortened the time needed for the majority to form the necessary consciousness." Other disillusioned militants agreed that the protest movement had suffered from excessive euphoria, elitist "vanguardism," and the delusion that the "popular assemblies" represented the "immense majority" of the population.

Duhalde, for his part, concluded that elections should be moved forward from December to April 2003, so that Argentina could have a government of indisputable legitimacy. Duhalde could not himself be a candidate for the presidency, but ex-President Carlos Menem immediately threw his hat into the ring. Having sat out a term, he was now eligible to run.

Since stepping down in 1999, Menem had undergone a series of judicial investigations and had endured house arrest in connection with the old scandal about illegal arms sales to Croatia and Ecuador. Close associates such as Emir Yoma, Antonio Erman González, and General Martín Balza also had suffered "preventative imprisonment" under the De la Rua government. Many observers thought that Menem and the others were being treated unfairly because Federal Judge Jorge Urso gave them no time to present a defense in court. Others attributed the judge's zeal to prompting by Domingo Cavallo, who had just entered the De la Rua cabinet and was perceived as taking revenge on Menem and his former officials. President De la Rua, however, had no desire to prosecute the case, whether or not Menem was guilty. For him, an unfettered Menem was certain to divide the Justicialist Party. Thus, he offered to pardon Menem, but Menem refused the offer, preferring to fight the charges up through the courts. In the end, the Supreme Court cleared the ex-president and all of the other accused "for lack of sufficient evidence." The fact that all of the justices were Menem appointees must surely have favored the outcome. Ironically, after Duhalde took office, Domingo Cavallo was sentenced to "preventative imprisonment" for a few months at the National Gendarmerie base in Buenos Aires for *his* alleged involvement in the arms sales, as well as for the "misappropriation of funds" while in office. Eventually, he too would be released for "lack of evidence."

Once he was cleared of criminal charges, Menem began plotting his comeback. He denied that his policies were responsible for Argentina's economic problems and reminded his audiences of the high levels of growth without inflation that the country had enjoyed under him. The big mistake, he insisted, was the freezing of bank deposits. On the other hand, he praised De la Rua and Cavallo for sticking to the Convertibility Plan. He also made it clear that he would challenge Duhalde for control of the PJ and soon began contacting provincial governors to line up support. Although he was unable to prevent Duhalde from assuming the presidency, he kept up a constant barrage of criticism. The ending of convertibility was "unfortunate," he said, and would only lead Argentina back to stagflation. Rather than devaluing the peso, Argentina should abandon it and use only dollars as legal tender. "Dollarization" would eliminate the black market in currency and also the provincial governments' practice of issuing scrip. It would protect those who had borrowed in dollars against having their debt burdens rise to unsustainable levels and would allow the unfreezing of bank deposits. Not everyone accepted those arguments. Nationalists replied that dollarization would be a surrender of sovereign control over the country's currency, while agro-exporters noted that, so long as the dollar remained strong, their products would be uncompetitive.

Early polls showed that Menem might easily capture the PJ's nomination, but Duhalde began working to prevent that. First came the personal attacks. A retired Iranian intelligence officer testified before a federal judge that Menem had accepted a $10 million bribe from Teheran to impede the investigation of the 18 July 1994 bombing of the Israeli-Argentine Mutual Association (AMIA). Indeed, he went on, Menem had many secret overseas bank accounts, one of which, in Switzerland, had $600,000 on deposit.[19] Second, Duhalde got a PJ convention to adopt a "list system" by which each Peronist presidential hopeful would run separately, instead of having a primary election to choose a single nominee. Menem challenged this in court, but despite a ruling in his favor, he was unable to halt the process. Third, Duhalde sought other Peronist hopefuls to challenge Menem. His first choices were Governor Carlos Reutemann of Santa Fe and Governor José Manuel De la Sota of Córdoba, but neither of them wanted to get into a bruising match against Menem. Then two other men finally stepped forward: Governor Adolfo Rodríguez Saá of San Luis and Governor Néstor Kirchner of Santa Cruz.

Although a majority of the PJ's executive committee was for Menem, Kirchner had Duhalde's backing and vowed to put a definitive end to Menem's career. He had strong credentials, having served as mayor of Río Gallegos and as provincial governor. In both those posts, he had earned a reputation for careful financial management. As governor he had balanced the budget by eliminating tax exemptions for the oil industry and trimming unnecessary spending, while preserving social programs. He also attracted new investment and so was able to reduce unemployment. As a former political prisoner under the Proceso, he had been forceful in punishing people who were guilty of human rights violations, and now he criticized Menem for pardoning the Proceso's junta leaders. He also opposed Menem's neo-liberal reforms and promised to make government more active in the economy.

Meanwhile, the Radicals were in disarray, with many of their prominent figures splitting off to form independent parties. Ricardo López Murphy had his Federal Movement for Regenerating Growth, which reflected his orthodox liberal views; and the anti-corruption idol, Elisa Carrió, still headed her Alternative for a Republic of Equals. That left Senator Leopoldo Moreau to carry the UCR's tattered banner into the elections. The left was represented by Alfredo Bravo, a former liberation theology Catholic who now ran on the Socialist ticket; and Patricia Walsh, of The United Left, a deputy closely involved with the "popular assemblies."

The 27 April election gave Menem a first place finish, with just over 24 percent of the vote. Kirchner was a close second, with 22 percent. After them came López Murphy, with 16 percent, and Rodríguez Saá and Carrió with 14 percent apiece. Moreau's 2.3 percent was the UCR's worst showing ever in a presidential race. The two leftist candidates split about 3 percent of the total vote, and the remaining votes were spoiled ballots. Thus, Menem and Kirchner would face each other in the second round of voting, scheduled for 8 May.

An analysis of the voting patterns showed Menem to be strongest in small towns, and among lower-class traditional Peronist voters of the interior. He did poorly in Buenos Aires Province, because Duhalde threw his support to Kirchner. In Buenos Aires City, he ran fourth, behind López Murphy, Kirchner, and Carrió. Those three candidates were the chief beneficiaries of the old 1999 Alliance breakup.[20] In the days that followed, polls and news stories indicated that supporters of López Murphy and Carrió were going to vote for Kirchner in the runoff. As this trend became more certain, Menem, who had predicted that he would win the second ballot easily, now saw Kirchner garnering between 60 and 70 percent of the vote. Rather than suffer such a humiliating defeat, he withdrew from the race and conceded the victory to his opponent. Kirchner was sworn in as president on 25 May.

Chapter Eleven

The Illusions of Progress

Néstor Carlos Kirchner had been a dedicated man of the Peronist left ever since his law school days at the University of La Plata. While in law school, he met and married Cristina Fernández, a law student and Peronist like himself. After graduating, in 1975, they moved to his native province, Santa Cruz, and set up a practice in Río Gallegos. The next year the Peronist government of María Estela ("Isabel") Perón was ousted by a military coup. Although apparently he never joined the Montoneros, Kirchner had been a militant in the Peronist Youth, and his acquaintances among the guerrillas earned him the Proceso's attention. He was arrested and imprisoned, only to re-emerge in 1982 as the military began to enter its final days in power following the disastrous Falkland Islands War. He and Cristina threw themselves into politics, she as a Peronist provincial deputy, and he first as the head of the provincial Social Security Fund and later as mayor of Río Gallegos.[1]

Kirchner quickly built a reputation as an incorruptible public servant. As head of the Social Security Fund, he had fought his nominal leader, Peronist governor Arturo Puricelli, when the latter tried to raid the pension funds for political purposes. Puricelli fired him, but Kirchner's popularity rose as a result. His law practice prospered, and his growing network of young reformers in the local *Partido Justicialista* gained him a broad political base. Elected mayor in 1987, he moved to the Governor's Palace in 1991, when the incumbent Ricardo de Val was impeached for corruption, leading to a special election to fill the vacancy. Kirchner won with 61 percent of the vote. On taking office, he worked hard to put the province's finances in order, not only balancing the budget but actually achieving a small surplus. He succeeded by eliminating unnecessary expenditures and getting the oil companies to pay royalties to the province.

These were the early Menem years, but Kirchner was not swept along by the apparent success of neo-liberalism. He was critical of economic policies that he considered speculative and harmful to national interests. He also expressed strong dissent from Menem's pardons of the Proceso's junta leaders, and placed himself firmly on the side of the human rights organizations that were protesting. He did not, however, criticize Menem's pardons of the top Montoneros, or show any sympathy for victims of the terrorist left. At the same time, Kirchner was not a traditional populist in the Peronist mode, for he was equally opposed to the corrupt labor union bureaucracy that constituted the PJ's urban base. Elected as a convention delegate to rewrite the Constitution in 1994, Kirchner helped to pave the way for Menem's immediate re-election. He could hardly have done less, since he had only recently succeeded in getting Santa Cruz's constitution changed to permit his own re-election.

Still, he opposed Menem's bid for a third term in 1998, even though the Santa Cruz constitution had been changed in that same year to allow Kirchner an indefinite number of re-elections. He backed Duhalde for the presidency, and although Duhalde lost to De la Rua in 1999, Kirchner won a third gubernatorial term. By this time Kirchner controlled a provincial political machine that was seemingly unbeatable. A full provincial treasury enabled him to subsidize many public works that provided full employment and enriched a large number of local business interests. His control of the local PJ apparatus, whose wheels were well oiled with patronage, gave him a free hand with local judicial and government agency appointments. Most of those went to friends and relatives. Since local newspapers got a significant portion of their revenues from advertising by government agencies, there was seldom any opposition in the press.

THE KIRCHNER COALITION

As president, Kirchner applied to national problems the same formula he had used while governing Santa Cruz. Economic reactivation was a prerequisite for building a personal political machine that would be hegemonic. There already were a few signs of an economic turnaround during the last months of Duhalde's administration, mainly because Argentina had stopped paying its foreign creditors and was using the money to "pump-prime" the economy through public works. Still, the foreign debt, which stood at $178 billion, was a stumbling block to sustained growth. Fresh investment capital was not available, and what little economic improvement there was stemmed from a few sectors, such as construction, where some of the country's former idle capacity was back at work. Nonetheless, about one-fifth of the labor force was still unemployed, and just under half of the population lived below the poverty line.

Although Kirchner strongly rejected Menem's free market ideas, when it came to political tactics, he followed the time-honored practice of trying to anticipate and remove any institutional obstacles to his policies. As with Menem, Kirchner first targeted the Supreme Court and the lower courts. Ignoring the warning of the

World Association of Jurists that he was precipitating "a grave institutional crisis," soon after taking office he got the Peronist majority in Congress to impeach two Supreme Court justices, Eduardo Moliné O'Connor and Adolfo Vázquez. Moliné O'Connor was replaced as chief justice by Enrique Petracchi, who had been chief justice back in 1989, before Menem shunted him aside. Vázquez was replaced by Eugenio Zaffaroni, a friend of Kirchner's and a believer that the criminal justice system was "a mechanism for social oppression." In due time, the other justices were pressured into retiring, leaving Kirchner with a pliable Supreme Court. Other federal judges were suspended too, as was the chief federal prosecutor, Carlos Sáenz.[2]

Kirchner followed the same clientelistic practices he had used as governor. For example, he appointed his sister, Alicia, to his cabinet as minister of Social Development. He insisted on complete loyalty and obedience from those around him and would tolerate no dissent either from within the government or from the PJ. When Vice President Daniel Scioli publicly disagreed with the judicial purges and the reopening of the "Dirty War" trials, he was ostracized within the administration, and his friends were removed from their government jobs. Scioli also had disagreed with Kirchner's decision to raise business taxes, as had ex-President Duhalde. Duhalde and Kirchner would also clash over the perennial issue of revenue sharing between the federal government and the provinces. Kirchner wanted to keep more money at the federal level, to give himself a stronger hand in directing the economic recovery program; Duhalde, on the other hand, backed the demands of Buenos Aires Province's governor, Felipe Solá, who was demanding $1.6 billion more than he had received the previous year. Kirchner turned on his former ally and told him to "stop pontificating." The breach between the two was destined to widen in 2005, when Cristina Fernández de Kirchner ran successfully against Hilda "Chiche" Duhalde to represent Buenos Aires in the Federal Senate.[3] Christina's victory was an important step toward undermining Duhalde within the PJ, and also toward her succeeding her husband as president when his term expired in 2007.

Kirchner also sought to solidify his appeal to the left. Human rights groups, such as Hebe de Bonafini's "Madres de la Plaza," applauded his repeal of the amnesty and pardons granted by Alfonsín and Menem to the Proceso's leaders. His newly appointed judges also protected foreign left wing terrorists who had taken refuge in Argentina. At Bonafini's prompting, the Supreme Court rejected Spain's request for the extradition of an ETA guerrilla accused of a car bombing attack. Another federal judge rejected Chile's request for the extradition of a terrorist accused of assassinating a prominent conservative senator.

Kirchner also tried to incorporate the *piqueteros* into his political coalition. The *piquetero* movement was an increasingly potent force, although it was split into various groups: the *Movimiento de Trabajadores Desocupados* (Unemployed Workers' Movement) led by Aníbal Verón, the *Movimiento Independiente de Jubilados y Desocupados* (Independent Movement of Retirees and the Unemployed) led by Raúl Castells, and the *Federación Tierra y Vivienda* (Land and Housing Federation) led by Luis D'Elia. Often working together, but sometimes alone, they blocked the highways between towns, took over the streets in Buenos Aires, and held massive rallies in the Plaza de Mayo and Plaza del Congreso. They occupied government offices, demanding satisfaction, and trashed the premises of foreign businesses like the Sheraton Hotel, McDonald's fast-food outlets, Citibank, Shell Oil, and Repsol.[4]

Not surprisingly, remnants of the old terrorist left infiltrated the *piqueteros:* survivors of the "Dirty War"such as the *Corriente Clasista y Combativa,* a Maoist splinter from the traditional Communist Party, and a coalition of small, Trotskyite groups called the *Bloque Piquetero.* Nevertheless, the *piqueteros'* main strength came from their ties to organized labor and the *Partido Justicialista.* Most of the people who made up the *piquetero* movement were young men drawn from the *Central de Trabajadores Argentinos* (CTA), a radical labor group that had pulled out of the official CGT. Another important component was the *Movimiento de Trabajadores Argentinos,* a radical faction inside the CGT that was led by the transportation workers' boss, Hugo Moyano. The labor union leaders had always recruited lots of bully-boys to battle strikebreakers, cops, and factional rivals. Those young toughs were often involved in criminal activities as well, like extortion or drug dealing; and they were also useful as bodyguards for the union leaders and Peronist party ward bosses.

The relationship of unemployed *piqueteros* to organized labor was based on more than just the sympathy of those with jobs for those without them. Orthodox Marxists might even expect a degree of antagonism between the two groups, since the unemployed masses would constitute an "industrial reserve army" exercising a downward pull on wages. In this case, however, the unions wanted to restrict the supply of labor in order to maintain high wages. Rather than seeking ways to preserve or increase jobs, they preferred the government to provide generous benefits and subsidies to the unemployed. From the unions' perspective, both groups would benefit by that approach.[5]

As Peronism was divided between Kirchner and Duhalde, each with his own network of lieutenants and sub-lieutenants, so the *piquetero* organizations were courted by both sides. In this contest, Kirchner, with the federal government's greater patronage resources, had the upper hand. He made it clear that he would not use the police to suppress the *piqueteros'* violent attacks on business, and ordered his officials to treat protesters with respect when they invaded government offices. The Ministry of Labor provided them with generous unemployment benefits and food subsidies to their families. Luis D'Elia, one of their prominent leaders, became Kirchner's undersecretary for Land and Housing. His followers were known as *piqueteros-K* and became weapons Kirchner could use to intimidate opponents, as he did in March 2005 to force Shell Oil to rescind a recent price increase. Minutes after Kirchner called for a boycott of Shell in a televised speech, D'Elia's *piqueteros* occupied more than thirty Shell gas stations.[6]

Organized labor also looked to the Kirchner government to restore the workers' buying power, which had deteriorated sharply after the peso was devalued in 2002. During 2003 the economy began to rebound, thanks to the government's decision to spend on public works rather than on debt repayments. As a result, some wages went up, but those gains were confined chiefly to certain export industries and the construction sector. Public sector workers had received no raises since 2001. The foreign-owned private utilities, whose rates had been frozen for the past three years, also were resisting wage increases, despite a series of strikes. Although the economy was growing again and unemployment was decreasing slightly, the working classes' buying power in 2005 was, on the whole, still not back up to its 2001 level. As a Peronist, Kirchner was concerned to improve the living conditions of this important component of his political base, but he also had to worry about large government-mandated wage increases fueling inflation, which now was starting to reappear. Nor did he want to abort the glimmerings of a business recovery. His solution was the time-honored Peronist one of calling labor and business leaders together to sign a "social compact" that would allow modest wage increases that would not be passed on to consumers in the form of price increases. Given the economy's underlying infirmities, such an approach satisfied neither the workers nor the employers, but Kirchner was ready to be confrontational, if necessary.

THE DEBT "HAIRCUT"

At the time Kirchner assumed office, Argentina's public debt to foreign creditors stood at around $178 billion, with approximately $16 billion in interest payments coming due in 2003. The newly elected president warned, "We will not pay if that means an increasing number of Argentines will have to go without education, health care, housing, or decent jobs." A default was no idle threat, coming from Argentina. The country had defaulted on its debts many times since achieving its independence: in 1828, 1890, 1982, 1989, and most recently at the end of 2001. Indeed, as early as October 2001, a meeting in New York between the IMF's managing director, Horst Köhler, and senior executives from the world's most powerful financial institutions, including Citigroup, J.P. Morgan, AIG, and Credit Suisse/First Boston, concluded that Argentina was going to collapse and that nothing could be done to save it. A default was inevitable, and the best that the creditors could do would be to approve a restructuring under which they would voluntarily accept less than the face value of their claims. "This was a remarkable moment," Paul Blustein observes. "The major creditors of a country were effectively saying that the government should pay them less than they were owed, on involuntary terms." They would take a "haircut" so that their institutions could still go on mobilizing financing for other emerging markets.[7] As we have seen earlier, however, these big international bankers had previously sold most of those bonds to brokers and pension fund managers in Italy, Germany, Japan, and Spain; and they, in turn, had sold them to small, private investors. It would mainly be the "little guy" who got the "haircut."

During his electoral campaign, Kirchner had promised to unilaterally reduce payments on the foreign debt. On the advice of Roberto Lavagna, his economics minister whom he carried over from the Duhalde administration, he negotiated with the IMF, World Bank, and Inter-American Development Bank to reschedule Argentina's debts. Even so, the international organizations would not furnish him with new loans until Argentina resumed paying its other creditors. Without their imprimatur, there was little hope of aid from private foreign banks or of direct foreign investment. Conversely, to resume payments on an impossible debt would drain the government's budget and plunge the country back into the downward spiral in which the debt mounted as new loans were contracted, at worse terms, to cover those loans currently coming due. Moreover, the economy would shrink, because the government would be unable to stimulate it.

Late in November 2004, Kirchner finally decided to cut the Gordian knot. Speaking on behalf of the president, Lavagna offered to exchange some $140 billion of old bonds held by private creditors for new ones. The new bonds would have the same face value but would be worth only about 30 cents on the dollar in the open market. They would not mature until 2038 and would pay only 1.33 percent annual interest. (Argentine bondholders would get a 3.31 percent interest rate, but would have to wait 40 years to cash in.) Lavagna made it clear that this was a one-time-only, take-it-or-leave-it offer. To discourage creditors from going to court, he announced in advance that if some creditor won a better settlement through the courts, Argentina would pay the same amount to those bondholders who had agreed not to sue, thus saving the latter the costs and risks of a court case while reaping the same benefits. This "free rider" option would presumably discourage any litigation.[8]

Lavagna said that he hoped to get at least two-thirds of the bondholders to accept his terms, after which Argentina would start negotiating with the IMF and World Bank for new loans. As it turned out, almost three-fourths caved in and agreed to the swap. The Global Committee of Argentine Bondholders had been trying for the past three years to get courts in the Group of Seven industrialized countries to embargo Argentina's assets to force it to pay up, but its efforts had proven futile. Most of the bondholders were "small fry" and scattered geographically, making it difficult for them to coordinate any strategy. Having received no support from their own governments or the IMF, many of them had given up hope of ever collecting anything. Some had already sold their bonds at heavy discounts to large institutions, which immediately exchanged them in Argentina for peso-denominated debt, speculating that the recent economic recovery would cause a rise in the peso's value. Other small foreign creditors, most of them pensioners, were so desperate for cash that they were willing to accept even 30 cents on the dollar. The 25 percent of bondholders who refused Argentina's offer were threatening to appeal to the World Bank's arbitration tribunal; but there was no guarantee that the World Bank would accept jurisdiction or, even if it did, that Argentina would obey its decision if it were unfavorable.

In the end, Argentina won its challenge, but at a price. Its restructured private foreign debt was now $35 billion, not including the $25 billion still in the hands of "holdouts," whose bonds the Argentine government now refused to honor. It still owed money to the IMF and to sovereign governments in the Paris Club. Without IMF approval, there was little prospect that international lenders would accept any more Argentine bonds. Indeed, even if they had been willing to take them, there was almost no hope that they would be able to pass them on to other investors. Argentina was now widely perceived as capricious and unreliable. In response, the Kirchner administration turned more nationalistic.

TOWARD A CLOSED ECONOMY

From the "haircut" to the end of Kirchner's term, in 2007, the Argentine economy grew by an average of more than 8 percent a year, fueled in large part by government spending. There were other factors as well—the *peso's* devaluation, which made Argentina's exports cheaper, and rising world prices for agricultural products—but the biggest impact came from money spent on public works, which otherwise would have gone to paying down the foreign debt. Not surprisingly, growth occurred unevenly across the economy. The biggest gains were in construction, followed by tourism, since the devalued peso made Argentina a cheap place to visit.

Economic growth enabled Kirchner to reward his political followers and allies. The construction boom, a sizeable expansion in government jobs, and increased revenue sharing with the provinces cut the unemployment rate from over 20 percent to about half of that. Even at 10 percent, unemployment was still high, and there still were *cartoneros* picking through trash piles at night, but the government could afford to provide a monthly subsidy of about $50 to the 2.5 million families listed as below the poverty line. That came to a monthly outlay of around $125 million a month, for which the recipients were required by the Peronist political apparatus to show up at demonstrations or to help the *piqueteros*.[9] The government also granted large wage increases to its employees and encouraged business to do the same.

Economic growth also allowed Kirchner to pay off Argentina's $9.8 billion debt to the IMF. Lavagna had been negotiating with the IMF for fresh loans, but the agency demanded revisions in the government's economic strategy. Heavy spending without sufficient investment from the private sector would lead to inflation, it argued. Lavagna agreed and began to prepare an economic package that would get the IMF's approval, only to find himself overruled by Kirchner. Not only did an austerity plan run counter to the president's intentions, but he had become increasingly impatient with his economics minister. Lavagna seemed too independent-minded for Kirchner's governing style; moreover, Kirchner suspected that the economics minister was a secret supporter of Duhalde. Thus, Lavagna was forced to resign on 28 November 2005, after which Kirchner announced his intention to liquidate all of Argentina's remaining debt to the IMF. That was done on 3 January 2006, in a single cash payment. Kirchner told a press conference that Argentina was now "burying an ignominious past of eternal, infinite indebtedness." In the street outside, government supporters released hundreds of balloons with the words "Ciao, IMF" on them.

Dismissing the IMF was popular with Argentines, but the IMF was right in saying that without sufficient investment from the private sector, the government's economic program was unsustainable and would lead the country back to stagflation. Although domestic investment almost doubled, from 11 percent of GDP to 21 percent between 2002 and 2006, it was concentrated in construction and non-durable consumer goods. By contrast, foreign direct investment was only a fraction of what it had been in the 1990s. In Menem's day, Argentina had captured around 15 percent of all new foreign investment coming into Latin America; under Kirchner it was only about 3 percent. Compared to its neighbors, Brazil and Chile, Argentina was falling behind in attracting foreign capital. From the end of 2003 to 2006, it received just over $10 billion, while Brazil got over $49 billion and Chile brought in almost $24 billion.[10]

Some foreign companies were leaving the country, including Suez, a French water treatment firm; EDF, a French electric power transmission company; France Telecom; and a British power company, National Grid, to name just a few prominent examples. Over thirty foreign-owned utility and energy companies had sued the Argentine government for some $17 billion in breach-of-contract claims before the World Bank's Center for the Settlement of Investment Disputes. In their original contracts, signed during the Menem era, they had been promised that their profits would be based on the one-to-one dollar/peso exchange rate; but during the 2002 financial crisis, they were forced to collect their fees in devalued pesos, and their rates were frozen. The companies argued that those measures made their contracts worthless and amounted to expropriation. Kirchner warned that he would defy the center if it ruled against him and threatened to nationalize those foreign-owned utilities that failed to make improvements in their production methods as called for in their contracts. Aguas Argentinas, which Suez owned, was one of the first to be taken over. That was followed by Trenes Metropolitano, the commuter train company serving Buenos Aires; Francisco Macri's "Correo Argentino," and by Thales Spectrum, a French company that builds and operates radio towers. France Telecom avoided nationalization by selling out to a local private conglomerate, the Wertheim Group. Shell and Exxon also came under attack when they tried to raise their prices.

Kirchner was unmoved by the utilities' complaints that the rate freeze, combined with the sudden reappearance of inflation, was squeezing them financially. Caught in a bind, the utility companies shelved plans for expanding output, so the supply of gas and electricity soon lagged behind demand. Brown-outs became more frequent, which discouraged investment in energy-intensive industries like steel, aluminum, and petrochemicals. Kirchner fought back by creating a new state oil company, Enarsa (*Energía Argentina, Sociedad Anónima*) in 2004, in which the federal government would have a 53 percent controlling interest. Another 12 percent would be reserved for the provinces, while the remaining 35 percent would be offered to private investors on the Buenos Aires BOLSA.

Enarsa would have exclusive rights to explore and develop oil and gas reserves in Argentine waters. It also intervened in the electric power industry by forcing Brazil's Petrobras to surrender its 50 percent stake in Transener, the country's largest company generating and transmitting electricity. Acting in concert with the Federal Energy Secretariat, Enarsa was intended to bypass the recalcitrant private companies and furnish the domestic market with adequate gas, oil, and electricity. To make certain that local needs were supplied, Kirchner restricted the export of oil and gas. He also supported the Oil Workers and Power & Light Workers unions when they demanded big wage increases from the energy companies. The workers had suffered heavy losses in their real wages during the 1990s, he argued, and now were "just trying to provide their families with a better life." The companies only sought "greater profits than they deserve," he added, "But they have to understand that Argentina's growth has to benefit all classes."[11]

Kirchner knew that his populist strategy carried the danger of inflation, but he preferred to keep this a secret. When the National Institute of Census and Statistics (INDEC) reported that inflation doubled between 2004 and 2005, from 6.1 percent to 12.3 percent, he blamed the price increases on irresponsible businessmen and replaced the offending director of INDEC's economic statistics. Guillermo Moreno, who managed the government's price controls, would thereafter censor INDEC's published figures on the economy, even though private economists no longer took them seriously.[12] For Kirchner, price controls were the weapon of choice for holding down inflation. In addition to rate freezes on utilities, gas, and oil, he frequently called business executives to the Casa Rosada to pressure them into reversing price increases.

It also was necessary to impose controls on exports, such as petroleum and food, to ensure a sufficient supply for the domestic market. Although exports were an important ingredient in the economy's recovery, facilitated by the peso's devaluation, their volume was starting to create domestic shortages and drive up prices. Therefore, in March 2006 Kirchner imposed a 180-day ban on beef exports, since beef has always been a traditional mainstay of the Argentine diet. Relations between the ranchers and the government had been frosty ever since Kirchner first took office. The ranchers and farmers had protested the high export taxes ("retentions") that Duhalde, and now Kirchner, had placed on their goods. As usual, Kirchner seemed to welcome a confrontation. Since taxes on agricultural exports were a major source of government revenue, he refused either to abolish or lower them. Moreover, unlike all of his predecessors, he never attended the *Sociedad Rural Argentina*'s Annual Fair in Palermo Park. (He once sent his agricultural secretary, Javier De Urquizar, in his place; but after hearing a blistering anti-administration speech by the SRA's president, De Urquizar walked out.) The SRA and other agricultural pressure groups responded to the beef export ban by threatening a nationwide strike and organizing public demonstrations against the government. Not until May, however, did the government gradually relax the restrictions, and then it punished the agricultural sector by again raising export taxes on their products.

Kirchner found an outside ally in his fight against foreign companies and Argentina's traditional landowning elite: Hugo Chávez, the radical populist president of Venezuela. After liquidating Argentina's debt to the IMF, Kirchner made a trip (his third) to Venezuela, this time to seek help in replenishing his Central Bank's depleted exchange reserves. The Venezuelan government already had purchased some $950 million of Argentine government bonds, but Kirchner asked Chávez to buy another $300 million and offered to use his influence to get Venezuela admitted as a full partner into MERCOSUR. Chávez, anxious to extend his influence throughout the continent, proved to be even more generous than Kirchner had dared to hope and acquired a total of $2.5 billion of Argentina's IOUs. Chávez also proposed that Enarsa join with the Venezuelan State Oil Company, PdVSA, in exploring and developing oil reserves in the Orinoco River valley, as well as in Argentina's offshore and land-based areas. The joint stock company also would plan to construct a network of oil and gas pipelines that would spread throughout South America. Given Argentina's financial straits, it would be the junior partner in this venture, with 40 percent of the stock to Venezuela's 60 percent. The two governments also agreed, in December 2005, to set up an investment fund, to be known as the Fund for the South. Its purpose was to free South America from dependence on the United States and the IMF, with Venezuela putting up most of the $1 billion in cash as backing for the "bonds of the south" that were issued the following year. Finally, as Kirchner's term wound down in 2007, Chávez bought another $1 billion of Argentine government bonds to boost the Argentine Central Bank's exchange reserves.[13]

THE CONTRADICTIONS OF A CLOSED ECONOMY

Throughout its history, *Justicialismo,* as set forth by Perón, propounded three basic ideas: national sovereignty, economic independence, and social justice. For Perón, those were the "Three Banners" (*Tres Banderas*) that inspired his movement. Kirchner proved to be a faithful practitioner of Peronism. Price controls, trade restrictions, income redistribution, debt repudiation, hostility toward foreign investment, and government spending to stimulate the economy and create jobs: all of those had been characteristic of the original Perón regime and had been restored as official practice when Perón returned to power after years of exile. Menem, though a Peronist, had turned his back on that tradition and embraced the free market. For Kirchner, not only was Menem a traitor to Peronism, but his free market policies were proven failures that had brought disaster to Argentina. Now it was necessary to recover national sovereignty and economic independence by reducing foreign influence, and it was equally important to promote social justice by using the government to raise the living standards of the poor and limit the power of economic elites.

As usual, Argentina's businessmen were divided in their attitudes toward this revival of Peronist populism, depending on how government policies affected their part of the economy. The Argentine Chamber of Construction (*Cámara*

Argentina de Construcción) was on excellent terms with the Kirchner government because its contractors benefitted greatly from public works spending. Two of its members, Tecnit and the Roggio Group, had powerful influence inside the industrialists' umbrella organization, the *Unión Industrial Argentina*, and constituted the backbone of the UIA protectionist wing, the *Movimiento Industrial Nacional* (MIN).[14] The textile industry, which had constantly fought the Convertibility Plan and which had complained of foreign competition under Menem, also belonged to the MIN faction and supported Kirchner. Retail merchants also tended to support the government as economic growth brought back prosperous times. The stores were filled with shoppers, movie theaters were packed, and more people were going out to restaurants. It almost seemed that Argentina had returned to its pre-World War I "golden age."[15]

Even so, there were many sectors in Argentina's capitalist system that opposed Kirchner. The energy sector, largely under foreign control, was chafing under price controls, labor union pressure, and threats from the government. Lack of new investment meant that bottlenecks and shortages were looming in the near future. The rural sector was another hotbed of anti-Kirchner feelings because of export restrictions and high export taxes. Taxes were often used in a punitive manner, as when Kirchner raised taxes on cheese and milk in July 2005 after dairy producers violated government price guidelines. He threatened to do the same to beef, poultry, and wheat producers after their sectoral associations recommended price increases. Those kinds of actions tended to make the rural sector close ranks against the government: small producers as well as large, renters as well as private owners and cooperatives. Moreover, the rural sector's anger affected factional politics inside the UIA, since a sizeable segment of the liberal MIA wing represented agro-industry. Agro-industrialists, who processed farm products, accounted for around 32 percent of Argentina's exports, according to INDEC; when added to the direct export of basic farm goods (approximately 22 percent), those two sectors provided for more than half of Argentina's source of foreign exchange.

Since 1997 MIN and MIA had agreed to rotate the UIA's presidency between them every two years, rather than split the organization. Nevertheless, Argentina's mounting economic problems created constant tension among the industrialists. Claudio Sebastiani, the owner of a tee shirt factory, took over the presidency in 1997. Although he belonged to the nationalistic MIN faction, he also was a Menem supporter, so his election was seen as a compromise, especially since MIA won 7 of the 12 seats on the UIA's executive committee. Sebastiani was also a PJ deputy, however, and as a *menemista* he not only voted for the "flexibilization" of Argentina's labor laws but was even caught trying to bribe other congressmen to support the government's bill. That got him removed as the UIA's president. MIN then placed Eduardo Casullo, a Technit executive, in the top UIA spot, but MIA's majority on the executive committee soon forced Casullo's resignation and replaced him with Alberto Álvarez Gaiani, a sausage manufacturer. He was the head of COPAL (*Coordinadora de la Producción Alimentico*), the pressure group representing Argentina's food and beverage industries. MIA's triumph was short-lived, however, because COPAL itself split over whether Álvarez Gaiani should be president of both it and the UIA. Foreign companies like Cargill and Coca-Cola perceived that Technit had placed several of its men in key posts within the De la Rua government's Economics Ministry, which meant that now MIN would have more influence. Under pressure from them, Álvarez Gaiani gave up the UIA presidency in favor of Osvaldo Rial, who took over in April 1999. Rial, the owner of a small plant that produced ventilating systems for factories, was considered to be a spokesman for the PYMEs, but he was also a front man for MIN politicians representing big industry, like Technit's Sergio Einaudi and Ignacio De Mendiguren, a textile and clothing manufacturer, both of whom were longtime critics of the Convertibility Plan.

MIN's position strengthened within the UIA as the economic crisis worsened and public opinion finally turned against the free market. At the May 2001 UIA convention, the MIN ticket won a majority on the executive committee and made De Mendiguren the new president. In his inaugural address, De Mendiguren attacked free trade, the United States, the IMF, the World Bank, and the Inter-American Development Bank. International finance had succeeded in undermining Argentina's native industries, he claimed. Now it was time to rebuild a national bourgeoisie to counter the influence of foreign capital. The way to do that was to return to the import substitution policies of Peronism, stimulate consumer spending by guaranteeing higher wages, create jobs through public works programs, set price controls on gas and electricity, and provide export subsidies to Argentina's high-cost industries. When the Alliance government finally collapsed and Duhalde became president, De Mendiguren was appointed minister of production. His place as the UIA's president was taken by Héctor Massuh, head of Argentina's second-largest paper company. Over the next five months, De Mendiguren was credited with convincing Duhalde to enact the "hyper-devaluation" of the peso, while at the same time helping to bail out many financially troubled manufacturers. He convinced Duhalde to transfer all their dollar-denominated debts into peso debts at a one-to-one exchange rate—at a time when, on the free market, the peso was trading at three-to-one. His influence ended in May 2002, however, when Roberto Lavagna replaced Remes Lenicov as economics minister and official policy began to favor the bankers.[16] De Mendiguren resigned.

The next UIA elections came in April 2003. Once again, MIA's candidate was Álvarez Gaiani. This time he was opposed by MIN's Guillermo Gotelli, the former president of the Alpargatas textile company. It was the first openly disputed election since the 1997 truce between the two factions, and it was a nasty fight. Gotelli accused Álvarez Gaiani of being a *menemista* and anti-national for selling his family's sausage factory to foreign capital back in the 1990s; but that opened him to the countercharge that he was responsible for leading Alpargatas into bankruptcy (it would soon be bought up by Brazilian capital). Despite powerful backing from Technit, Gotelli lost by a two-to-one margin.

Naturally, the incoming Kirchner government favored MIN over MIA. Its relations with Álvarez Gaiani were strained from the outset. The UIA president demanded that Kirchner suppress the *piqueteros* who were trying to intimidate various businessmen, and he also urged that the government shift its priorities from lavish welfare spending on the poor to credits for private industry so as to create more jobs. That earned him blistering attacks from the left, of course, but no upheaval from within the UIA. As Kirchner's economic strategy became clearer, opinion inside the UIA shifted more strongly to the MIA position. One indicator was a greater tendency for Argentine capitalists to park their capital abroad. Claudio Katz, an economist, estimated that in 1994 about $58 billion was held in overseas accounts by Argentines; but by 2005 that had almost doubled to at least $107 billion.[17] Argentine capitalists, surveying the country's small, static population and the transportation costs resulting from its distance from the major centers of commerce, were pessimistic about future possibilities. In any case, Kirchner's verbal abuse of businessmen, and his propensity to browbeat them into accepting price controls, allowed Álvarez Gaiani to pick a close friend, Héctor Méndez, a plastics manufacturer, as his successor in 2005.

Still, Argentine businessmen were cautious about opposing the government, so in May 2007 the UIA elected MIN's Juan Carlos Lascurain, a manufacturer of boilers and head of the metallurgical sector, as its new president. He was a compromise between the two factions, criticizing price controls and urging the revival of a National Development Bank, but also calling for more cooperation with the government. Kirchner responded by inviting Lascurain and the UIA's other executive officers to the Casa Rosada. It was the first time that he had met with the UIA since his election. The honeymoon was not to last, however. At the end of May 2007, just a few days after the Casa Rosada meeting, a severe Antarctic cold front swept through Argentina, bringing the festering energy situation to a dramatic climax.

The polar air sent temperatures plummeting across the country and caused home and shop owners to turn up their heaters. The sudden increase in the consumption of electricity and natural gas brought on a collapse in the electrical power grid and shortages in the supply of gas to the cities. Parts of Buenos Aires were blacked out; factories shut down and sent their employees home. Filling stations ran out of gas, which disrupted bus and taxicab services. To meet the crisis, Kirchner ordered a two-day suspension of natural gas exports to Chile. In an official statement, he said that the fuel shortages were the result of Argentina's rapid economy recovery, and thus a sign of progress. He also blamed the De la Rua government for failing to make the necessary investments in energy production back in 2001.

Businessmen were not mollified. Factories and stores had been experiencing energy shortages for some time, but owners had been afraid to express their concerns publicly because of government threats to retaliate against criticism. For example, the UIA and the Association of Argentine Entrepreneurs (AEA) had scheduled a public conference in early October 2006, to be held at the downtown

Sheraton Hotel; but they were forced to cancel it when Kirchner sent his under-secretary for planning coordination, Roberto Baratta, with orders to drop the idea. The UIA and AEA then proposed a meeting between them and the Planning Coordination Secretariat to discuss ways of conserving energy, such as cancelling nighttime sports events, reducing the lighting on public buildings and monuments, or shutting off the lights in shop windows at night. Kirchner turned down that proposal too, out of fear that any publicity from such a meeting would give ammunition to his opponents. An exasperated Héctor Méndez, then the UIA's president, then demanded that Kirchner guarantee energy to the factories by restricting the homeowners' supply. Kirchner ignored him.[18]

No sooner had the country recovered from the May cold snap than another hit, in mid-June, forcing more emergency measures on the government. Kirchner, ever mindful of the voters, gave priority to residential energy needs and suspended gas and electricity services to industrial and commercial enterprises. He also suspended exports of natural gas to Chile and Paraguay so as to supply the domestic market. Those export controls were supposed to remain in effect until 2011. Even with gas rationing, the country's electric power generators had to look for substitutes for natural gas, such as diesel and fuel oil; but those were in short supply as well. The UIA reported that some 5,000 of its member companies were forced to either limit their hours of operation or shut down altogether for lack of fuel. On 16 June taxi drivers held a mass demonstration around the downtown obelisk to protest their inability to find gas for their cars. Again, the government denied that there was a serious crisis. The "temporary" shortage, explained Christian Folger, the energy undersecretary, was due to very high rates of economic growth, which meant that "industries and people consume more energy." He did not explain, however, why energy production hadn't kept up with increased demand. Orthodox economists blamed the price controls that had been in place since 2002, but the Energy Secretariat insisted that those controls would remain in effect.

On 9 July (Independence Day) Argentina suffered another freezing blast, with snow blanketing the country and piling up in Buenos Aires' streets for the first time since 1918. Alberto Fernández, Kirchner's chief of cabinet, asked factories and shops to close, in order to save energy for home heating. He denied that the government was considering price increases on gas and electricity to dampen down consumption and insisted that fuel scarcity was a continent-wide problem, not just Argentina's problem. The real villains were the foreign-owned utility companies, which had failed to make the necessary investments to increase production.

The next day the Energy Secretariat ordered filling stations in Greater Buenos Aires to limit sales of gas. They complied, as did their counterparts in Córdoba and Mendoza, by restricting sales to only 25 liters (about 6.5 gallons) per vehicle. There were long lines of taxis, trucks, and delivery vans, and all had to present their licenses and registration as commercial vehicles. Private vehicles were not eligible. By nightfall many of the service stations had run out of gas and closed. All across the country, provincial and municipal governments shortened their working hours, turned off street lights, and ordered merchants to darken their shop windows and street signs. Movie houses closed down, the mountain resort town of Bariloche was completely darkened, and in Buenos Aires wealthy neighborhoods like the Barrio Norte suffered equally with poorer ones like Florencio Varela or La Matanza. In La Matanza protestors took to the streets as *piqueteros*, cutting off Route 3 into the city.

Out in the countryside, the Argentine Agrarian Federation (FAA), which represents tenant farmers and has traditionally been part of Peronism's base, warned that energy shortages would have a serious impact on farm production that would lead to food shortages and rising prices. Some agro-businesses, such as flour millers, dairies, and meatpackers, were curtailing their hours of operation, which in turn meant that supermarkets were soon out of bread, milk, and meat.

As the crisis worsened, Kirchner turned to Guillermo Moreno, the secretary for domestic commerce, whose job was to administer price controls. Moreno was used to browbeating producers and retailers into compliance, and his approach to the energy shortage was to order the filling stations to cut their prices by half. Most of the stations shut down instead, and at the few that remained open, there were lines of trucks and taxis stretching for blocks. Meanwhile, Moreno levied fines against Transener and Edesur, two private electricity transmission companies, for failing to maintain quality service. Gas shipments to Chile and Paraguay, which had been partially restored in late June, were once again cut off.

At Moreno's urging, Kirchner summoned the local CEOs of Repsol, Petrobras, and Exxon to the Casa Rosada on 12 July, and got the oil companies to agree to restrict the production of natural gas and instead increase the output of gas oil and fuel oil at the same prices that they were currently charging for natural gas. The companies would lose money, but they feared that the government would take them over if they refused: Moreno recently had gotten Kirchner to intervene Metrogas, a company that operated the gas pipeline to Chile, and appoint its new manager. To soften the blow for them, Julio De Vido promised that the Planning Ministry would pay them subsidies of $310 million a month for the next three months, just enough to get the government through the October general elections.[19]

FROM NÉSTOR TO CRISTINA, WITH LOVE

Although he was eligible for an immediate second term, Néstor Kirchner stepped aside in 2007 in favor of his wife, Cristina. His decision puzzled many commentators. Despite the energy shortages, rising inflation, a recent scandal involving a Swedish construction company that was building a gas pipeline from Bolivia, frosty relations with most of the country's businessmen, and the worrisome decline in new investment, Kirchner was still a popular leader who could count on an easy re-election. The economy had been booming along for the past four years at an annual growth rate of over 8 percent, and while there was still a lot of unemployment and poverty in the country, their levels had been much reduced. The most plausible explanation for his action was that if Cristina won in 2007, as she was expected to do, he would then be able to have his second term starting in 2011. Then, when it came to be her turn again, he would not be a "lame duck" because the two of them were a political tag team.

Cristina Fernández de Kirchner, the child of a wealthy La Plata family, was perhaps not as popular as her husband, but she had good political credentials. She had served in the Santa Cruz Provincial Legislature from 1989 to 1995, represented the province in the Federal Senate from 1995 to 1997, in the Federal Chamber of Deputies from 1997 to 2001, and again in the Senate from 2001 to 2005. In 2005 she ran against Hilda "Chiche" Duhalde to represent Buenos Aires Province in the Senate, and won by a handy margin. Like many other politically ambitious Argentine women, she modeled herself after Eva Perón, including the expensive designer clothes.

Cristina's running mate was Julio Cobos, a former member of the UCR who headed a breakaway faction called "Radicales-K" (for Kirchner). Polls had Cristina as the odds-on favorite to win the 28 October elections, and the results confirmed their accuracy. In a fourteen-candidate race, she won just under 45 percent of the vote; almost twice that of the runner-up, Elisa Carrió, the indefatigable anti-corruption candidate, who got 23 percent. Roberto Lavagna, the ex-economics minister, ran third with 17 percent. Eleven other candidates split the remaining 15 percent.

Most of Cristina's ministerial appointments were holdovers from her husband's cabinet, and her policies also followed the same populist/nationalist path. Hugo Chávez still was a valued ally; indeed, a Venezuelan courier had been stopped at the Buenos Aires airport on 4 August 2007 with $800,000 in his suitcase as a Chávez contribution to her campaign. Guido Alejandro Antonini Wilson, a naturalized American citizen of Venezuelan background, had brought the money in a private airplane belonging to Enarsa. A resident of Miami, he was arrested and sent to the United States to face criminal charges as an unregistered agent of a foreign government. Subsequently, five other Venezuelans were arrested in Miami for trying to influence witnesses in the case. Elisa Carrió and other opposition party congressmen seized on the incident to accuse the government of corruption, but the Kirchners and Chávez brushed aside their charges as an American plot to discredit Argentine-Venezuela cooperation.

The new government faced a difficult economic situation, despite high growth rates. After the foreign debt "haircut," foreign lenders avoided Argentina. The country's credit was so bad that money could be had only at ruinous interest rates and only on short terms. Furthermore, the Kirchners' belligerent attitude toward the foreign-owned energy companies discouraged most direct investment. Nor could much credit be obtained inside the country. No Argentine bank would make long-term loans. Indeed, banks were short of deposits, because most people parked their money abroad. Those people who did deposit money, for business convenience, seldom did so for more than 180 days. Even the government's ability to pump-prime the economy was limited because almost half of that economy was "underground," to avoid taxes and regulations. In brief, Argentina was suffering a severe credit shortage that was finally manifesting itself in rising inflation. No one could be sure exactly what the level of inflation was: INDEC's statistics were no longer believable because the government began "cooking" them back in 2005. As of early March 2008, however, estimates ranged between 25 and 35 percent.

Four years of heavy government spending and large wage increases had driven up demand, but supply was no longer able to match it. The initial high growth rates were due to the government's economic stimulus that had put industry's previously idle capacity back to work. In addition, the devalued peso, together with a large world demand for agricultural goods, caused a boom in Argentina's exports. To keep the economy growing without inflation, however, would require new investment to increase the country's productive capacity. But private investment was not forthcoming, and that was the chief bottleneck threatening the Kirchners' closed system.

Chapter Twelve

Defiance

The Treaty of Asunción, which established MERCOSUR, expressly forbade taxes on exports inside the free trade zone. That suited the neo-liberal ethos of the Menem administration, and satisfied the farmers and ranchers who provided an important share of Argentina's exports. It denied the Argentine government a traditionally large source of revenue, however. So, after the 2001 crash, interim-President Duhalde issued an executive decree reimposing a 10 percent tax on agricultural exports in order to close a daunting budgetary gap. Before Duhalde left office, he had doubled those taxes (euphemistically called "retentions") to 20 percent; and for soybeans, the rate was 24 percent. (The price of soybeans was rising sharply on the world market.)

Néstor Kirchner's economic stimulus strategy required even more revenue, so "retentions" were increased several more times. Their rates varied according to commodity, but by 2008, soybeans were being taxed at 35 percent, wheat at 28, corn at 25, and sunflower seeds at 10. In addition to raising more revenue, retentions were supposed to help in the fight against inflation. To keep down the cost of living, Kirchner had put price controls on "basic foodstuffs" like meat, milk, and bread and also had banned exports of beef and wheat back in 2006, hoping to ensure a bountiful supply for the domestic market. The farmers and ranchers had thwarted him, however, by producing soybeans and sunflower seeds for export instead. The switch was profitable for them because world market prices were at record highs for those crops, but on the domestic market meat and flour remained in short supply.

Therefore, when Cristina Fernández de Kirchner took over the presidency, she raised taxes on agricultural exports three times within her first six months in office. The top rate, which eventually reached 44 percent, was levied on soybeans. Moreover, the "retentions" were adjustable, meaning that they would automatically increase if prices continued going up; they could reach as high as 58.5 percent. World prices for soybeans and sunflower seeds, she noted, had resulted in "windfall profits." It was only fair that farmers should share their wealth with Argentina's poorer classes, who were still struggling to get out of poverty. Besides, the farmers should be producing food for their fellow-Argentines and helping to keep down prices at the grocery store. The retentions would help to correct their selfish behavior.

For the farmers, however, the "retentions" were confiscatory. Inflation had increased the prices they had to pay for seeds, fertilizers, pesticides, farm labor, and land rents. That was the government's fault, they argued. Its uncontrolled spending had raised their production costs. Now such a heavy tax would wipe out their profits and drive many of them out of business.

According to *Clarín*, simple arithmetic proved the farmers' case. Taking the soybean crop as an example, a single hectare of farmland would produce an average of 2.85 tons of soya, which, at current world prices, would fetch $1,314. At the time of *Clarín*'s article, the retention rate on soybean exports was 40.5 percent, so the government would claim $532 and leave the farmer with $782. From that $782 the farmer would have to repay himself for the initial costs of producing his crop and shipping it, which averaged $551 a hectare. His profit would then be reduced to only $231. From that he would have to deduct the fee for his export license ($25) and his income taxes, whose rate was 35 percent. He then would be left with $134 in net profits, if he were the owner of the land he worked. But if he rented his farmland, as an estimated 55 percent of all farmers did, he would have to deduct that rent from his profits too. In that case, he would probably make no profit at all, and might even incur a loss.[1]

Small farmers were especially hurt by the export taxes, and they also had other serious grievances that the government seemed to overlook. They were gradually being driven to extinction by the rise of "sowing pools"—large agricultural investors who already had acquired about half of all the farmland. Unlike the old-fashioned agricultural oligarchy, these were modern businessmen who used capital-intensive methods in their production. They leased their land to tenant farmers; provided them with seeds, fertilizers, machinery, and credit; and determined which crops they would grow—usually insisting that they diversify in order to reduce the risks of climate and price changes. The "sowing pools" had arisen in the 1990s, when investors, many of them foreign, had bought up tens of thousands of acres in response to high world prices for grain crops. By doing so, they drove up land prices and rural rents, thus accelerating the gradual decline in the number of independent farmers that had been going on since the 1960s. Just since 2002, approximately 100,000 small farmers had sold out and become either tenants or truck drivers carrying the produce to market.[2] The apparent lack of concern about this upheaval in the farm sector by Peronist governments under Menem, Duhalde, or Kirchner was a sore point for the FAA, which traditionally was part of the PJ coalition.

On 11 March 2008 the farmers' rage finally boiled over. The 10,000 or so largest *estancieros* in the *Sociedad Rural Argentina* (SRA), the 100,000-strong *Confederaciones Rurales Argentinas* (CRA) representing middle-sized ranchers and farmers, the 100,000 or so tenant farmers and small owners in the *Federación Agraria Argentina* (FAA), and the cooperative societies in the *Confederación Intercooperativa Agropecuaria* (CONINAGRO) announced a general strike and brought out their tractors to block the highways. The fighting mood was most intense in Argentina's secondary farm belt—the fertile regions bordering the Pampa, which had been settled later, often in planned immigrant communities. Unlike the Pampa, where large *estancias* prevailed, those regions were typified by small and medium farmers, the great majority of whom (possibly 70 percent) rented their land. Alfredo De Angeli, the head of Entre Ríos' branch of the FAA, was typical. He farmed about 2,250 acres (900 hectares) of rented land near Gualeguaychú, where his family had lived for over 100 years.

Although the city of Buenos Aires experienced serious food shortages by the last week of March, the government stood its ground. The rural organizations were attempting "extortion," Ms. Kirchner said, and she would not allow it. She warned that if the strike continued, she would ask the Justice Ministry to declare it illegal. The government's political base rallied behind her. Hugo Moyano, head of the transport workers union and now the CGT's general secretary, protested the farmers' blocking of the highways, preventing truck drivers from delivering food. Ironically, Luis D'Elia, the *piquetero* leader, also expressed indignation about those tactics and threatened to send his men out to the countryside to break the blockade. In the city of Buenos Aires, the SRA's president, Luciano Miguens, was jostled by D'Elia's men outside of the *estanciero* organization's headquarters.

This confrontation pitted Argentina's most important economic groups against a popular Peronist government. Apart from natural resources like oil and gas, the country's ability to earn foreign exchange was almost entirely dependent on its exports of agricultural products and agro-industrial byproducts. In addition, the annual revenue from "retentions" was necessary to keep the Kirchners' populist strategy operating. Raising the "retentions" was projected to increase those revenues from $5 billion in 2007 to $10 billion in 2008. So long as each side remained united, there was little room for compromise. Argentina's farmers as a whole were modern and efficient capitalists, unlike most domestic industrialists, whose inability to compete in open markets made them dependent on state protection. Argentine industrialists could be bullied, but not its agriculturalists. On the other hand, the farmers were a political minority, and the Peronists controlled the state.

Thus, the confrontation between the rural sector and "Kirchnerism" became a struggle to win over public opinion while maintaining unity on one's own side. Could the farmers remain solid in their opposition to the government, or would the government succeed in dividing them? Would the loss of revenue and rising prices because of food shortages upset the populist economic strategy and force the government to back down? Or would they cause the government to bring down the full force of the state on the strikers? If that happened, what would be the reaction of the industrialists and merchants, who were being hurt by the strike but who also shared the farmers' concern for private property and profits? Would the use of force against large masses of citizens bring the military back into politics in its former role as the ultimate referee? The stakes were high.

TACTICAL MANEUVERS

To divide the striking farmers, on 31 March the government offered to reduce the "retentions" on small farmers back to pre-March levels. Ms. Kirchner then followed this up, on 2 April, by holding a pro-government rally at which she gave a tough speech to the 20,000 supporters who packed the Plaza de Mayo. On the following day the four rural organizations announced that they would temporarily lift the strike. The truce would last for thirty days, to see whether the government would agree to lower export taxes, but if by the beginning of May there was no agreement, they would resume the fight.

The truce created tensions on both sides. Among the rural groups, CONINAGRO, whose cooperatives were the most dependent on government support, was more willing than the others to compromise. Its small farmers were tempted by the government's offer to treat them more leniently on taxes. The SRA also expressed a greater willingness to "dialogue" with the government. Many of its members were not just *estancieros:* they also had investments in the financial, commercial, and industrial sectors. With their diverse interests and their large overseas accounts, they could afford to compromise. The CRA and FAA represented small and medium-sized producers whose entire capital was in their farms, and therefore they were more combative.

On the government's side, the struggle split the Justicialist Party. Out in Argentina's farm districts, the *Federación Agraria Argentina* was one of the traditional mainstays of PJ provincial machines. Now, as one of the more militant participants in the strike, it was causing some Peronist politicians to distance themselves from the Kirchners and demand that the government negotiate a settlement. Carlos Reutemann, Santa Fe's former governor and now a federal senator, was seen on television driving around the province on a motorcycle and encouraging the strikers. Santa Fe's current governor, Hermes Binner, a Socialist, invited the strike leaders to the governor's palace and expressed his support for them. So did Juan Schiaretti, the popular Peronist governor of Córdoba. Governor Sergio Urribarri, of Entre Ríos, where strikers were especially militant, wobbled. At first he encouraged them, but then he backed away under pressure from the Casa Rosada. The same was true of Governors Juan Manuel Urtubey, of Salta, and Oscar Jorge, of La Pampa. Urtubey wouldn't meet with the strike leaders, but allowed his lieutenant governor to do so in his place. Jorge, like Urribarri, said he would meet with the strikers but then cancelled the meeting. By contrast, the Peronist boss of Entre Ríos, former governor Jorge Busti, now president of the Federal Chamber of Deputies, came out strongly for the rural organizations. So did Salta's former governor, Juan Carlos Romero, who now represented the province in the Federal Senate. Jorge Capitanich, the governor of Chaco Province, and Daniel Scioli, Néstor Kirchner's former vice president and now governor of Buenos Aires Province, supported the administration; but former governor and ex-president Eduardo Duhalde urged the Kirchners to compromise.

The opposition party leaders seized upon the strike as an opportunity to castigate the government. Raúl Alfonsín, Elisa Carrió, Roberto Lavagna, and Mauricio Macri (Francisco Macri's son and currently mayor of Buenos Aires City) blamed the Kirchners for prolonging a crisis that was becoming a burden on the urban population. At one point there appeared to be signs of a breakthrough, when Cristina dismissed her economics minister, Martín Lousteau, and replaced him the next day with Carlos Fernández, the Treasury secretary. Lousteau had been the author of Resolution 125, the controversial decree establishing the sliding scale of export taxes. The rural organizations interpreted his dismissal as a signal that the government was ready to compromise, so they sent representatives to the new minister's inauguration. Elisa Carrió and other opposition leaders thought differently. They pointed out that Lousteau had been one of Cristina's few new additions to a cabinet largely carried over from her husband's administration, and that Fernández was another holdover and a notable supporter of Néstor Kirchner's hardline position toward the IMF. For them, the appointment signaled that the former president was really running the government. A long meeting on 6 May between the leaders of the four rural organizations and Alberto Fernández, Cristina's chief of cabinet, seemed to confirm this pessimistic view. The government made it clear that it would not compromise. The strike was renewed on 7 May.

Mixed signals came from the Casa Rosada when, on 14 May, Néstor Kirchner assumed the presidency of the Justicialist Party, thus tightening the Kirchners' grip on political power. Instead of giving a speech at his inauguration, however, the ex-president turned the microphone over to Cristina, who then made an appeal to the rural groups for a "dialogue." However, she made it clear that the government would offer no concessions. When a meeting finally was scheduled for 22 May, Cristina absented herself to prepare for a big official event to be held in Salta on 25 May to celebrate Argentina's revolt against Spain. The meeting, held in the Casa Rosada, lasted only an hour and a half, and consisted mainly of the chief of cabinet, the interior minister, and the economics minister berating the rural organizations' leaders for scheduling a competing event in Rosario for 25 May. After the meeting broke up, the farm leaders angrily announced that they had been duped, while the government's spokesman, Interior Minister Florencio Randazzio, accused them of wanting to impose their minority views on a democratically elected government.

THE STRUGGLE FOR PUBLIC OPINION

The parallel events on 25 May gave a rough idea of the two sides' popular appeal. Some 200,000 people converged on Rosario to show support for the farmers and gather around the Plaza del Monumento a la Bandera ("the Flag

Monument Plaza"). Members of the four rural organizations came in caravans of cars, trucks, and buses from all parts of the interior. Also present were representatives of the opposition parties, such as Mauricio Macri and Elisa Carrió, and dissident Peronists like Governor Alberto Rodríguez Saá of San Luis. Even groups from the far left, like Raúl Castells' *piqueteros,* the Revolutionary Communist Party (PCR), and the Corriente Clasista y Combativa showed up to lend their support. Despite the latter's presence, the mood was peaceful and festive. Most of the crowd was made up of families. Each of the national leaders of the four rural organizations made a speech, calling on the government to hold a serious dialogue. De Angeli, the FAA's leader in Entre Ríos, gave the harshest address, warning the government that the strike and roadblocks would resume in two days if negotiations were not resumed. He chided the president: "You could have headed this rally yourself, señora, if only you had signed an agreement with us." The most quoted line of the day, however, was from Eduardo Buzzi's speech. "The Kirchners are an obstacle to growth," asserted the FAA's national president.

The government's official Independence Day celebration in Salta was a more somber affair. After a Te Deum Mass at the cathedral, Cristina Fernández de Kirchner briefly addressed a crowd estimated at no more than 50,000, calling upon all groups, including the farmers, to come together for the good of the country. The president was accompanied by her cabinet ministers, several pro-administration provincial governors, the CGT's general secretary Hugo Moyano, and Luis D'Elia and his *piqueteros.* The UIA and the Chamber of Commerce absented themselves from both rallies, to avoid taking sides.

Néstor Kirchner stayed in Buenos Aires to prepare a more aggressive strategy for ending the strike. On the day after the two rallies, he met with Cristina and Alberto Fernández at the presidential residence in Olivos, to discuss ways to heighten the pressure on the rural organizations and increase support for the government in light of recent unfavorable polls. There were signs that the economy was suffering. One economist estimated that the strike had so far caused losses amounting to around $1 billion. The trucking industry was badly hurt, with more than 160,000 vehicles idled for lack of cargo. The agricultural machinery industry reported a $70 million loss because of cancelled orders since the beginning of the strike. The drop in exports averaged about $300 million a week, leaving the country's port facilities, stockyards, and packinghouses without work to do. The Bolsa de Cereales in Rosario, the chief clearinghouse for soybeans and corn, had no business; nor did the Bolsa de Cereales in Bahía Blanca, where most of Argentina's wheat was marketed. Without exports to tax, the government was estimated to have forfeited as much as $1.3 billion in revenue. Fearing another economic collapse, people were exchanging pesos for dollars, causing an approximately $1.7 billion drop in the Central Bank's exchange reserves as it desperately sold dollars to prevent a free fall in the value of the national currency. The bankers' association (ADEBA) and the UIA, which previously had preferred to remain on the sidelines in the struggle, now favored a compromise with the farmers as soon as possible. Editorialists in the country's two major newspapers, *La Nación* and *Clarín,* urged the two sides to end the strike for the good of the country, noting that a prolonged cutoff of exports would damage Argentina's already poor image abroad, forcing its current customers to view it as an unreliable source of food. *Clarín,* especially, called on the government to take the initial step toward compromise, since it had started the dispute by raising the "retentions." Even the Catholic Church had begun to insert itself into the dispute, as Bishop Jorge Casaretto noted publicly that more people were falling into poverty and criticized the government for forcing INDEC to manipulate its poverty and inflation statistics.

Bishop Casaretto had a valid point: no one trusted official statistics. Although the government announced that the inflation rate was only 9 percent, private economists (and, unofficially, INDEC's own staff) estimated it at closer to 25 percent and rising. Meanwhile, commercial activity was contracting. Then, at the end of May, a bitter cold front swept across Argentina, bringing on another energy crisis. The temperatures were the lowest ever recorded in Buenos Aires for the month of May. Once again the supply of gas to Chile was cut off so as to meet the shortages at home. Factories and schools closed, to save fuel for home heating. The trouble was caused partly by striking oil workers in Santa Cruz Province, who were complaining that their wages were not keeping up with the cost of living. The oil companies blamed the government's price controls for their inability to meet the union's demands.

These troubles put a strain on the Kirchners' labor union supporters. As retail sales fell and employees were laid off, Armando Cavalieri, head of the Commercial Employees Federation, began calling for a change in the CGT's leadership. For him, Hugo Moyano was too supportive of the Kirchners' authoritarian approach, which was eroding labor's real wages through inflation. Although INDEC was holding back figures on the distribution of national income for 2007, a private economic research company estimated that the workers' share had fallen. The Metallurgical Workers' Union (UOM) agreed with Cavalieri, as did the Health & Sanitation Workers Union. Both were large components of the CGT.

Faced with such rumblings, Néstor Kirchner took steps to firm up support by calling Peronist governors and congressmen to the Casa Rosada. Those who showed up and professed their loyalty were "patriots"; dissidents were accused of favoring reactionary, elitist interests. To step up the pressure on the striking farmers, Kirchner had recourse to the two chief weapons that all governments possess: taxes and the courts. In Buenos Aires Province, the loyalist government of Daniel Scioli sent out dunning notices to 79,500 farmers, reminding them that they had missed their quarterly tax payments, amounting to a total of 200 million pesos. Unless they paid up quickly, there would be fines, indictments, and judgments against their property. A few days earlier, eight protestors were arrested and jailed in San Pedro, Buenos Aires, for blocking a highway. Among them were the president of the San Pedro branch of the SRA and his son. Also arrested were two women representing opposition parties. The prisoners were held for twelve hours in the neighboring town of San Nicolás. Federal judge Juan Murray, who issued the arrest order, was a former member of FREPASO who had become a *Kirchnerista*. On orders from the Justice Ministry, Judge Murray also sent out summons to Eduardo Buzzi, Mario Llambías, Luciano Miguens, Fernando Gioino, and Mario Barbieri (the mayor of San Pedro), accusing them of ordering the highway blockade and threatening them with two years in prison.

To add to the tension, the truck haulers' *Confederación Argentina del Transporte Automotor de Cargas* (CATAC) launched its own strike on 3 June and began blocking the highways, demanding that the farmers and the government negotiate a quick end to their stalemate. CATAC's 160,000 members were heavily dependent on hauling grain and foodstuffs. Furthermore, most of their business was squeezed into two short periods coinciding with the grain harvests: from the end of March to the end of July, and during December and January. A majority of them were owners, as well as drivers, of their vehicles. Quite a few owned from two to five trucks, and hired drivers for them. Now many of the truckers were in a financial bind because, in anticipation of the harvest, they had traded in their ancient vehicles (the average age of a CATAC truck was eighteen) and brought new ones on the installment plan. Unless grain started moving to market soon, the industry faced bankruptcy.[3]

The strike was creating great damage to Argentina's economy as a whole, especially in the interior provinces. In the small and medium-sized provincial towns, where relatives, friends, and neighbors transcended occupational categories, most people blamed the deteriorating situation on the Casa Rosada's intransigence. Thus, in Córdoba, Santa Fe, Entre Ríos, and Buenos Aires provinces, industrial, commercial, and service workers and employers joined the farmers at public rallies in front of the town halls. The governors of Santa Fe and Córdoba reaffirmed their support for the strikers, while Senator Carlos Reutemann publicly urged Cristina Kirchner to end the three-month-old strike "in a minute" by repealing the "retentions." Otherwise, he said, the situation would get much worse in his province. Within weeks, factories would start closing down or working shorter hours, which would mean more unemployment. "The episode in San Pedro didn't frighten people," Eduardo Buzzi told the press. "To the contrary, there's a stronger urge to protest." Néstor Roulet, the CRA's vice president agreed. "After what happened in San Pedro there's an even greater number of people at the rallies. Everyone's anxious to find a solution to the conflict." He was right, in every sense. Although the rural organizations were estimated to have enough grain stored in elevators and enough strike funds to hold out at least another four months, their leaders were beginning to display signs of exhaustion. The farmers had foregone an estimated $2 billion in export earnings, and there were serious concerns that major customers like China would try to find more dependable sources of food grains and meat. Serious food shortages loomed for the cities, with supermarkets complaining that they would soon be out of meat, fruit, vegetables, and dairy products. Would the television networks show pictures of farmers dumping food and milk into ditches while people in the cities, including children, went hungry? How much longer would the industrialists and merchants sympathize with them if their business losses brought them to the verge of bankruptcy? Already the press was carrying more stories about violent clashes between striking farmers and striking truckers. What if increasingly angry farmers and truckers really lost control, with television cameras recording the bloodshed?

Cardinal Bergoglio, the head of the Catholic Church in Argentina, made a strong plea to both sides to negotiate a compromise. Although he denied that the Church wished to mediate, he especially called on Cristina to "act with grandeur" and "make a statesmanlike gesture" to the farmers. Speaking through Justice Minister Aníbal Fernández, the government responded indignantly, saying that the cardinal had shown "a lack of respect" for the president. By contrast, the four rural organizations seized on the cardinal's plea to make a "statesmanlike gesture" of their own. "Eighty-five percent of the country wants a compromise," Eduardo Buzzi told *Clarín*. "The bishops are right: to go on would be suicide." The farm leaders announced that, as of midnight on Sunday, 8 June, they would lift the strike. They also met with Argentina's Public Defender, Eduardo Mondino, and asked him to mediate between them and the government. This did not please many of the FAA and CRA rank and file, but in most parts of the interior they grudgingly agreed to obey their leaders' orders to lift the highway roadblocks.

The Kirchners felt triumphant. They had outlasted the striking farmers, who, according to Néstor, were the very *golpistas* (conspirators) responsible for the fall of Perón in 1955 and Isabel in 1976! This anti-national minority was now exhausted and waving the white flag! No, there would be no meeting with the Public Defender. Now the people's enemies would be brought to their knees and forced to ask the government for forgiveness!

Even the FAA, one of the main pillars of provincial Peronism, was slated for punishment. The government would take away from the FAA the right to issue licenses to farmers allowing them to ship their grain to market. From now on the National Office of Agricultural Regulation (*Oficina Nacional de Control Agropecuaria,* or *ONCCA*), currently headed by a Kirchner crony from Santa Cruz, would take over that function. It would cost the FAA's treasury an estimated 80 million pesos a year, leaving the organization financially weakened. That brought many of the rural picketers back on to the highways. The Kirchners' snide dismissal of Cardinal Bergoglio's plea for dialogue and their refusal to meet with the Public Defender were also tactical mistakes in the contest for public support. Polls showed widespread public gloom about Argentina's economic future, as did the continuing flight from the peso to the dollar. Private economists were predicting that inflation could reach 30 percent by the end of the year, and many people feared it would go higher. Retail sales were down, as consumers began hoarding dollars. The slowly contracting economy fueled fears of massive layoffs in the near future, which would dramatically end the "economic miracle" of the past five years.

Local and provincial governments had suffered revenue losses, partly because of the commercial recession and also because the federal government had been unable to collect export taxes. Although it claimed to have raised 24 billion pesos in revenue from other tax sources, it did not have enough to satisfy the provinces' dependence on federal aid. There were too many other demands on the government's budget, such as the public works program that was pledged to spend around $14 billion to stimulate the economy and provide full employment, and the $12 billion the government paid in subsidies to the private utilities companies to compensate them for price controls.

Without money from "co-participation," however, municipal governments throughout the interior were caught in a painful squeeze between rising costs due to inflation and falling tax revenues. Key provinces like Córdoba, Santa Fe, and Entre Ríos, where many local mayors and even some governors were farmers, had all but abandoned the Kirchners. With midterm legislative elections scheduled for October 2009, many of their politicians were planning to run on independent tickets. In Santa Fe, Miguel Saredi, a Peronist dissident and former Duhalde supporter, already had founded a new party called Pampa Sur that was collaborating closely with Governor Hermes Binner, an independent Socialist. Saredi was an activist in the provincial branch of the *Confedración Rural Argentina* and was urging Mario Llambías, the CRA leader, to run for national office on the Pampa Sur ticket. Similarly, FAA leaders like Eduardo Buzzi and Alfredo de Angeli were expressing interest in running for office as representatives of a new "agrarian party" distinct from Pampa Sur, which they perceived as too conservative. Divided as they were politically, the farmers still had little chance of bringing down the PJ unless they forged alliances with other opposition groups. Consequently, Mauricio Macri, Elisa Carrió, and other established opposition figures were eager to present themselves as sympathetic listeners at the rural organizations' rallies.

Pro-Kirchner governors like Sergio Urribari (Entre Ríos), Jorge Capitanich (Chaco), and Daniel Scioli (Buenos Aires) were placed in an uncomfortable position with regard to this grassroots turbulence. Capitanich found himself rotten-egged at one his appearances. Urribari's chances of re-election appeared dim. Scioli found his base torn geographically, between the blue-collar unions of the Greater Buenos Aires industrial suburbs and the farming districts in the west, where CARBAP, the CRA's Buenos Aires branch, was especially powerful. Without generous revenue sharing by the federal government, he was in danger of losing control of his province.

Apparently aware that they were losing the public relations battle, on 9 June the Kirchners summoned their Congressional supporters, governors, labor union representatives, and leading industrialists and merchants to a meeting at the Casa Rosada, where President Cristina Fernández de Kirchner would make an important announcement. Before an assembly of approximately 1,000 people, she proclaimed a Program of Social Redistribution. All revenue collected by the federal government from "retentions" on agricultural exports would, after it exceeded the

35 percent rate, be turned over to the Ministries of Health, Economy, and Planning to be distributed to the provinces and municipalities. In her executive decree (#31,423), published the following day in the *Boletín Oficial,* the amount of revenue to be available for co-participation was estimated at $800 million for the remainder of 2008, and at $1.3 billion for 2009. Of this, 60 percent would be earmarked to build public hospitals, 20 percent for low-cost housing, and the remaining 20 percent for building or repairing country roads.[4]

The announcement was greeted with cheers by the Kirchners' supporters. On the other hand, the business leaders were quiet, both during and after the ceremony. Only Cristiano Ratazzi, the president of Fiat Argentina, would agree to be interviewed by the press, and his remarks were ambivalent. "No one can be against the wish to have more hospitals, rural roads, and housing for poor people," he said, "but how you go about financing these things is a little more open to discussion." He added that he would prefer to fund such projects out of a tax on incomes, rather than by taxing exports, which would discourage production. None of the rural organizations were represented at the Casa Rosada, but later in the day the SRA's leader, Luciano Miguens, opined that the Kirchners' Program of Social Redistribution was a belated afterthought: a last attempt to gain public support for their confiscation of the farmers' earnings.

On the same day as the assembly at the Casa Rosada, Liliana Heiland, a federal administrative court judge, declared the new system of "adjustable retentions" unconstitutional. Her decision was in response to a lawsuit brought against the Economics Ministry by Santiago Llorente, a soybean farmer, who charged that the graduated retentions were an unconstitutional violation of his rights "to work, trade, and practice a legitimate occupation," as guaranteed by the Argentine Constitution. Llorente's plea also rested upon a September 2006 decision by an administrative court, that since Article One of the Treaty of Asunción ruled out taxes on exports within MERCOSUR, the export tax could not be constitutionally imposed either by law or executive decree. The government's appeal of that ruling was now before the Supreme Court. In Llorente's case, Judge Heiland upheld his plea on the grounds that only Congress could levy or modify taxes, whereas the retentions policy was the result of an executive decree. The government immediately announced that it would appeal that decision too. Simultaneously, however, Governor Alberto Rodríguez Saá of San Luis Province asked the Supreme Court of the Nation, under its original jurisdiction as arbiter of disputes between provincial and federal authorities, to declare the retentions policy unconstitutional on the grounds that it adversely affected the revenues that provinces would otherwise have received through the Law of Co-Participation. The court agreed to take the case, but warned that deliberations might take at least a year. Supreme Court Justice Carmen Argibay gave the Kirchner government 60 days to file a brief.

In the meantime, the truckers were still out on strike, and few goods were reaching the markets. For example, on 10 June, a Tuesday, only 23 truckloads of grain reached the port of Rosario, as compared to 4,529 on the same day a year ago. Although the SRA's *estancieros* and the cooperatives belonging to CONI-NAGRO were hopefully awaiting a call to dialogue from the Casa Rosada, the leaders of the two largest rural organizations, the CRA and the FAA, admitted that their members were deeply disgruntled and ready to resume the strike. Many of them were lining the highways and occasionally clashing with the striking truckers. They were angry and desperate, Buzzi said, because the government "had decreed their extermination." De Angeli gave the government two more days to show a willingness to negotiate before his followers ended their truce. He and Buzzi were meeting with anti-Kirchner *piqueteros,* militants from the Revolutionary Communist Party, and representatives from CARBAP, the most aggressive component of the CRA, in the event that a violent confrontation with the truckers became necessary. A meeting between President Cristina Kirchner and Santa Fe's governor, Hermes Binner, at the Casa Rosada on 10 June, to discuss the rural situation, only underlined the government's intransigence.

A few days later, on 13 June, the government made another show of force. The National Gendarmerie (National Guard) was ordered to clear Route 14, outside of Gualeguaychú, Entre Ríos, where farmers and truckers had thrown up a roadblock. The order came from Federal Judge Guillermo Quadrini, who in turn had been contacted by the Justice Ministry. On arriving at the roadblock, the guardsmen's ranking officer ordered the picketers to disperse. When the farmers and truckers refused, the guardsmen advanced and a melee ensued. Alfredo De Angeli, the province's FAA leader, and eighteen other men were seized and carried away in a van, with reporters and cameramen recording the incident. As the arrested men were being driven to jail, more protesters arrived at the scene, outnumbering the remaining guardsmen and retaking possession of the highway. Although the Gendarmerie turned fire hoses on them, they drove a harvester onto the road, completely blocking it, and finally forced the guardsmen to leave by pelting them with showers of rocks and burning tires. Not long afterward, they marched on Gualeguaychú, and, with their numbers further increased to about 2,500 by sympathetic town-dwellers, they surrounded the Gendarmerie's headquarters, demanding the prisoners' release. Nervous phone calls went back and forth between Judge Quadrini and the guardsmen as the crowd became more threatening. Finally, after seven hours, De Angeli and the other arrested men were set free. As they emerged from the building, they were greeted as heroes. To the approving roars of his supporters, De Angeli hoisted himself to the bed of a pickup truck and made a speech, assuring the listeners that the fight would continue.

As the farm crisis threatened to explode once more, another energy shortage arose, partly due to the truckers' strike. In Greater Buenos Aires, Santa Fe Province, Córdoba, and Chaco, service stations were running short of gas. Public transport companies, which were cutting back on the number of buses being used and laying off drivers, blamed Shell Oil, their main provider. Shell, they said in their complaints to the Planning Ministry, was delivering only about one-third of its normal daily provision of gas to the stations. Shell admitted to *La Nación* that its refineries were not operating at full capacity, but it blamed Repsol-YPF for failing to provide the crude oil for them to refine. Repsol, in turn, blamed the truckers' highway blockades for its failure to deliver the crude.

New statistics issued by INDEC, showing a low inflation rate and gains in real wages, only prompted the press to issue stories about widespread skepticism throughout the public, and to report radically different estimates by private economists. The BOLSA reacted to the government's sunny news with sharply plunging stocks and deeply discounted government bonds. Foreign banks like Barclay's and J.P. Morgan issued pessimistic estimates about Argentina's economic future. Rising inflation, energy shortages, and a lack of private investment would produce a "hard landing," they predicted, despite the government's "creative accounting" practices. Most puzzling of all, for foreign observers, was Argentina's failure to take advantage of high world prices for agricultural commodities and oil. As Santa Fe's Governor Binner observed after his meeting with the president, "There's no hope for the country unless we consider the farmers. With the farmers, we have a great opportunity for growth, but we'll have none if we go against the farmers." He was right: although the agricultural sector accounted for only 10 percent of the GNP, it provided about half of Argentina's exports, was the single most important source of the nation's income, provided the raw materials for many industries and purchased inputs from still others, and employed 4 million people, or a third of the economically active population. It was an essential part of the economy.

On the evening of 16 June, anti-government demonstrations erupted all over the country, with mass marches of people beating with spoons on pots and pans (*cacerolazos*): in Córdoba, Santa Fe, Entre Ríos, La Pampa, Salta, La Rioja, Mendoza, Chaco, San Juan, Santiago del Estero, and even Santa Cruz. In Buenos Aires Province they marched in the capital, La Plata, as well as in Mar del Plata and Bahía Blanca. The biggest assemblies were in the city of Buenos Aires, and not just in the Barrio Norte but in more modest wards like Caballito and Flores. Protesters gathered outside the presidential residence in Olivos and in huge numbers around the Obelisk in the city's center. They avoided the Plaza de Mayo, however, on learning that Luis D'Elia's *piqueteros* were waiting for them with clubs and knives.

The Kirchners were caught by surprise—but were not intimidated. They quickly called for a pro-government rally in two days, in which D'Elia's men and Hugo Moyano's CGT would provide the turnout, and summoned the PJ governors and mayors in the Greater Buenos Aires industrial suburbs to appear on the balcony with them. Cristina's speech at the 18 June rally was a harsh attack on the rural leaders, whom she characterized as "four people whom nobody ever voted for." They were throwbacks to the old oligarchy of reactionaries and coup-mongers. Their *cacerolazos* and highway roadblocks were not the democratic way to settle things. But, since they had questioned the constitutionality of Resolution 125, she would trump them by sending it to Congress to be ratified as a law. Then there would be no doubt about whether the farm groups had to obey.

As the crowd roared its approval, the Kirchners went back inside the Casa Rosada, confident of victory.

THE CONGRESSIONAL STRUGGLE

Cristina and Néstor Kirchner had reason to feel confident that they could get their bill through Congress easily. Their Peronist faction, known as the *Frente para la Victoria (FpV)* had 118 votes out of the 129 needed for a majority of the Chamber of Deputies. With the addition of the *Radicales-K,* the UCR mavericks that Vice President Julio Cobos led, and a few other Peronists, they would command a substantial majority. In the Senate, the FpV by itself had 42 of 72 votes, more than enough to pass the bill. Agustín Rossi, an FpV deputy from Santa Fe, and Miguel Pichetto, leader of the FpV's senatorial bloc, were charged with steering the project through quickly and without amendments.

From the very beginning, however, there was wobbling in the FpV ranks. Many of the deputies and senators were from farming districts, and quite a few were farm owners themselves. Caught between their pledges of loyalty to the Kirchners, who provided them with patronage, and the interests of their neighbors and constituents, they looked for a middle ground between the government's insistence on an unmodified bill and the opposition's demand that the retentions be abolished completely. The news of this softening in the FpV's ranks provoked intense lobbying from all sides. Cabinet ministers, provincial governors, local mayors, congressional block leaders and committee chairman, farm leaders, and agrobusiness leaders met with wavering deputies. As PJ president, Néstor Kirchner summoned the FpV deputies to his office and exhorted them to stand firm. At the same time, however, De Angeli and the other farm leaders were making inroads into the Radicales-K block and among Peronists who were personally opposed to the Kirchners. One reason for their success was Cristina's precipitous plunge in the polls, from a high of 56 percent approval at the beginning of the year to just under 20 percent at the present. The polling firm Poliarquia attributed this to more than just the battle with the farmers. Rising living costs were stoking fears of another bout of hyper-inflation like that of 1989, and consumer confidence was very low. The Kirchners' belligerent governing style—their seeming contempt for opponents and institutions—also made them unpopular, especially with the middle classes. There was a growing perception, too, that President Cristina was just a puppet for her husband.

Sensing that their position might be weakening, the Kirchners suggested that they might be willing to modify their original bill by reducing retentions for small farmers, and even invited the rural leaders to a meeting at the Casa Rosada on 23 June. It would be the first time the two sides met since April. It turned out to be a one-sided meeting, however. Cristina did most of the talking during the 90 minutes they were together, accusing the four rural organizations of violating the public interest, insisting that her bill must be approved without amendments, and calling on the farm leaders to show their patriotism by supporting her new project of a "Bi-Centennial Social Contract" for 2010. The rural leaders came away from the talks angry and insulted. They had been prepared to accept a roll-back of the retentions to their pre–11 March levels; now they called for their complete abolition.

As the focus of the battle returned to the Chamber of Deputies, the Kirchners mobilized their *piqueteros* to erect tents in the Plaza del Congreso to keep up round-the-clock agitation in favor of their bill. However, as it became clear that the bill could not go through without amendments, they agreed that it could be modified to allow tax rebates for the smallest producers. Making a virtue out of necessity, they sought to drive a deeper wedge between the large and small farmers by transferring $1 billion to the National Office of Agricultural Regulation (ONCCA), which would also reimburse farmers who had to sell to the domestic market under price controls that were far below world market prices. On 4 July the Chamber finally voted, and after 19 hours of heated debate, the government won, by 129 votes to 122, with 2 abstentions. The FpV got 111 of its 118 members to vote for it, picked up 4 Radicales-K out of 10, and got the support of 14 other deputies. Modifying the bill to compensate the small producers had been necessary to achieve victory, but even there the Kirchners had diluted their concession: the compensations would terminate after 31 October.

The rural leaders were not as chagrined as might have been expected. They pointed to the closeness of the vote and expressed satisfaction that Congress had displayed its independence by forcing the executive branch to make concessions. Surprisingly, too, there had been defections from both the FpV and the Radicales-K blocks. "The first half of the game is over," Buzzi said. "We'll play the second half in the Senate." Luciano Miguens was less optimistic about their chances in the Senate, where Miguel Pichetto, on orders from the Kirchners, had forced the resignation of Roberto Urquía as chairman of the Budget Committee and as a member of the Agricultural Committee. Although he was officially part of the FpV, Urquía was from Córdoba and known to be close to Governor Schiaretti. He also was the owner of an edible oils factory and had been heard to voice objections to the government's retentions. Clearly, the Kirchners were taking no chances, although they were supposed to have at least 34 certain votes out of the 37 needed for a majority. The opposition had only 26 sure votes, and 12 senators were undecided.

Most of the "undecideds" were Peronists, and some were from the FpV block. They might vote with the government, but they were bothered by the 31 October cutoff for compensations to the small farmers. Many of them also suspected that those compensations would never be paid anyway, since the government's growing financial problems had recently forced it to suspend its subsidies to the energy and transportation sectors. Nevertheless, the government refused to accept any further amendments to its bill. It argued that the 31 October deadline was simply to give small farmers enough time to shift their production from export crops to food crops for the domestic market.

The Senate began its deliberations on Monday, 7 July, by inviting political leaders, farmers' representatives, businessmen, and economists, to testify before the Budget and Agriculture committees. The hearings were suspended on Wednesday, 9 July, for Independence Day celebrations, but resumed the next day. As of Friday the government's bill was still unmodified. A final vote was scheduled for Wednesday, 16 July.

Although the Kirchners claimed to have more than enough committed votes, there was more muttering among supposedly loyalist senators. Carlos Reutemann had introduced a counterproposal that reduced, rather than eliminated, the retentions, and did away with the 31 October deadline. It did not satisfy the intransigents who wanted no retentions at all, but it established a middle position that other Peronists could accept. The farmers' groups endorsed it as the only viable alternative to the government's bill. What is more, they decided to impress the wavering senators by mobilizing their supporters for a huge march on Buenos Aires, scheduled for Tuesday afternoon, 15 July. The rally would be held around the Spanish Monument in Palermo, just outside the fairgrounds where the SRA's big annual Rural Fair was to open nine days later.

Always ready for a confrontation, Néstor Kirchner met the farmers' challenge by announcing that the government would hold a counter-rally on the same day, at the same hour. He called on Hugo Moyano, Luis D'Elia, and the mayors of Buenos Aires' industrial suburbs to prepare their followers to assemble in the Plaza del Congreso. He also instructed the Peronist mayors of the industrial suburbs that lay along the rural organizations' likely routes into the city to obstruct their march.

Despite such preparations, caravans of rural protesters swarmed into Buenos Aires all through Sunday, Monday, and Tuesday morning. On Tuesday afternoon they marched up the Avenida Libertador in a massive display of popular support and were joined by sympathetic residents of the capital. Estimates of the crowd's size ranged from 200,000 to 300,000. Kirchner's rally was sizeable too: an estimated 95,000 supporters demonstrated before the Congress Building. But just as with the 25 May parallel rallies, the farmers drew many more people, and the participants' enthusiasm was more genuine. All four leaders of the rural organizations spoke to the crowd at the Spanish Monument, as did Luis Barrionuevo, the Restaurant Workers Union chief who had just led a revolt against Hugo Moyano and formed a rival CGT. But the wildest cheering broke out when Alfredo De Angeli stepped to the microphone and made a short, aggressive speech.

Down at the Plaza del Congreso, Moyano, Daniel Scioli, and Governor Sergio Uribarri of Entre Ríos warmed up the crowd until Néstor Kirchner arrived. Cristina was not scheduled to address the rally, but her husband spoke for half an hour, reminding the audience of how he and she had stood up to Argentina's foreign creditors, lowered unemployment, reignited the economy, and built homes and hospitals. Now the rural "oligarchs"—the same people who had always schemed against popular government and supported military rule—were at it again, trying to "destabilize" the country and "enrich themselves at the people's expense." He ended his speech with the crowd cheering loudly, but he had worked himself up into such a passion that he suddenly had a fainting spell and had to be taken in a hurry to the presidential residence. There he received medical attention and soon recovered. As he was being taken to the car, Jorge Capitanich told the crowd: "There are two models in Argentina. One is that of the agro-exporters, which excludes the rest of society. The other, led by our Madam President, offers inclusion and jobs. Whoever votes tomorrow against her bill votes for unemployment and exclusion."

At 10:30 in the morning, on Wednesday, 16 July, the Senate opened up the floor for debate. Each senator was allotted ten minutes to speak, but it soon was clear that this rule was unenforceable. The stakes were high, and so were emotions. Many senators, especially those in the FpV, were cross-pressured. With Vice President Julio Cobos presiding, the speeches went on well past noon, then through the afternoon, then into the evening, and on into the late evening. Finally, just before midnight, the bill was submitted to a vote. The result was a tie: 36 for, 36 against. Unless there was a shift of at least one vote, Cobos would have to vote to break the tie—a prospect he dreaded. For some time he had urged the Kirchners to compromise with the farmers and even had tried to act as a mediator. Personally, he was opposed to the bill in its present form, but he did not want to face the Kirchners' famous wrath if he voted with the opposition. So, he urged the senators to continue debating and retired to his office, where he was seen holding his head in his hands.

Some votes did change. Ramón Saadi, a scion of Catamarca's ruling Peronist clan, had been an outspoken opponent of the Kirchners, but now he changed his vote and backed the bill. Out at Palermo, where farm leaders were getting cell phone reports on the debate's progress, there was shock and dismay. But, just as the government's supporters were about to celebrate, Emilio Rached, from Santiago del Estero and one of Cobos' Radical-K bloc, switched to the opposition side, restoring the tie. At 2:30 in the morning the UCR leader, Ernesto Sanz, demanded that Cobos return to Senate floor and put an end to the excruciating tension. But Cobos remained in his office until just before 4 a.m. Miguel Pichetto, the FpV floor leader, rose to remind him that he was faced with "an historical responsibility." Cobos nodded glumly, and then, with a pallid face and quaking voice, he began a rambling speech that lasted nearly forty minutes. At the end he said simply: "History will judge me. I don't know how. And forgive me if I'm wrong. My vote is not positive."

The news was relayed quickly to the farmers camping out in Palermo Park. They poured into the streets to celebrate, singing the national anthem. In the Plaza del Congreso, where the *piqueteros* had for hours been beating their *bombo* drums, the news provoked a shower of curses, rocks, and bottles aimed at Congress. The *piqueteros* would have stormed the building but for the rapid deployment of the Federal Police to stop them. The angry demonstrators then began chanting "We're going to kill the traitors!" Eventually they calmed down a little, sang the national anthem, and departed. As he left the building, an angry

Pichetto told reporters that Cobos ought to resign after his "betrayal." "History will judge him badly," Pichetto said. "This was a government bill and he is part of the government." Cobos said he would not resign, however, and denied that he had betrayed anyone. "I'm not a Peronist," he said, "and I have a right to a divergent opinion."

THE AFTERMATH

Later that morning, Néstor Kirchner told reporters that Cristina might resign the presidency. If he was hoping to provoke a popular demonstration of support, his ploy failed. Instead, *Kirchnerista* "ultras" like Luis D' Elia and Hugo Moyano expressed strong opposition to the idea, and that afternoon Cristina herself announced that she intended to remain in office. Overruled for once, Néstor left town and took refuge in Santa Cruz for a few days.

The rural organizations called for the government to repeal Resolution 125 and open up a "dialogue" with the farmers about retentions and other important issues, such as the "sowing pools." The Constitution prevented the government from resubmitting its bill during the current year; and if it chose to do so the following year it would require a two-thirds majority in the Chamber. Alternatively, it might submit a new bill to Congress. Also, there was still the possibility that the government might seek to get its retentions approved through the courts.

Thus, the leaders cautioned their members to be moderate in their celebrations of victory, and Buzzi told the FAA locals they should send only "the most minimal" amount of produce to market until it was clear that the government was willing to act in good faith.

On Friday morning Cristina cancelled Resolution 125 and issued a new executive decree restoring retentions to their pre–11 March levels. She was forced to do so, she said, by a "violent lockout" and a stalemate in Congress that had put selfish private interests ahead of the general welfare. She would not eliminate retentions altogether, because it still was necessary to provide revenue for public works and encourage food production for the domestic market. She also left open the possibility of a return to a sliding scale of export taxes in the future. That afternoon she hosted a reception for some 150 FpV senators and deputies at the presidential residence, to thank them for their support. Néstor had never entertained his congressional followers that way, and his absence made the occasion all the more relaxing. Cristina circulated among the guests, smiling and making them feel at home. The closeness of the votes showed that the government still had plenty of support, she told them, and now that the retentions issue was out of the way, it was time to move on to other important matters. Some of the guests raised the question whether Cobos ought to remain in the government. Cristina avoided her husband's angry rhetoric about the vice president being a "traitor." She was "disappointed" in him, since he had pledged to be a loyal member of the governing team when they were running for office, but she made no allusions to any intention to force his resignation.

Nevertheless, during the week that followed, six of Cobos' followers were dismissed from the Planning Ministry. The agriculture secretary, Javier de Urquiza resigned, to be replaced by a *Kirchnerista* agronomist, Carlos Cheppi; and the chief of cabinet, Alberto Fernández also left the government. His replacement was another longtime Kirchner friend, Sergio Massa, the mayor of Tigre, a Greater Buenos Aires suburb.

Although Luciano Miguens and Eduardo Buzzi hailed the cancellation of Resolution 125, a closer reading of the decree's text in the *Boletín Oficial* raised new worries. The actual wording used the term "limit" (*limitar*), not "repeal" (*abrogar*) regarding Resolution 125's legal status. They also noted that the president continued to claim the right to establish retention levels without regard to Congress. The inauguration of the annual Rural Fair, on Wednesday, 23 July, provided another warning about the possibility of a renewed battle because, for the first time in history, not a single representative of the government was present at the opening ceremonies—although the president, the economics minister, and the new secretary of agriculture had been invited. Also missing were exhibits from some of the provinces governed by fervid *Kirchneristas:* Chaco, Formosa, Jujuy, and Santa Cruz. Buenos Aires Governor Scioli authorized an exhibit, but it was very scaled-down in comparison with previous years. And although Mayor Mauricio Macri from Buenos Aires City was there to show his support, the city's Central Market, under Guillermo Moreno's jurisdiction, failed to erect a booth.

On the other hand, there were over 600 other exhibits. It also was the first time in history that the Rural Fair's sponsor, the SRA, shared the balcony with the CRA, FAA, and CONINAGRO, in an impressive display of unity. Large crowds circulated through the tents and exhibits, watched the judging of the prize horses and cattle, sampled the wines and steaks, and had a festive time. As always, it was a big event.

For a brief time, the Rural Fair might distract people's attention from the economy's serious problems—inflation, energy shortages, falling retail sales, lack of investment, and capital flight—but a time of reckoning was getting near. The Kirchners had counted on greatly increased revenues from agricultural exports to fuel their populist economy. Now those would be forfeited. Moreover, Argentina might lose many important customers who would seek more reliable sources of food supplies. During the farm strike it was estimated that idle ships waiting in Buenos Aires' harbor for their cargos had cost the shipping industry around $60,000 a day. The long-term consequences of the farmers' strike promised to be extremely painful.

The Kirchners could take some comfort from the fact that midterm elections, scheduled for October 2009, were more than a year away. There was time to mend fences and recover their lost majority. As Cristina and her supporters kept reminding one another, the votes in Congress had been close. Their defeat had been a narrow thing, not a rout. Even so, the farmers' strike had badly eroded their formerly dominant position and had inflicted some deep wounds on the Justicialist Party. Out in the interior, powerful provincial Peronists like Schiaretti, De la Sota, Reutemann, Romero, Busti, and Solá had sided with the farmers, especially those in the traditionally Peronist FAA. In the Greater Buenos Aires industrial suburbs ex-president Eduardo Duhalde was working in tandem with the dissident labor leader Luis Barrionuevo to detach some of the mayors from the Kirchner coalition. Duhalde also was in close touch with former presidents Adolfo Rodríguez Saá and Ramón Puerta. Francisco Narváez, a rich Buenos Aires businessman and currently a federal deputy, was another dissident Peronist with presidential ambitions.

Surveying this scene, the old veteran Peronist *político,* Antonio Cafiero remarked that "In more than seventy years of political life, I'm seeing unprecedented times. They [the dissident Peronists] still don't have a definite leader, but they are a group of important Peronist figures." He was right: the dissident Peronists had not yet coalesced around a single leader; nor had they reached out to non-Peronists, like the Radicals. The latter were beginning to unite their various factions. Through the efforts of ex-president Alfonsín, the UCR's "grand old man," faction leaders like Julio Cobos and Elisa Carrió were exploring the possibility of returning to the main party. Even so, there was little likelihood that they would join with the Peronist dissidents to form an anti-Kirchner electoral front. Therefore, the Kirchners still had the possibility of avoiding defeat in October 2009 if they could keep their enemies divided and avoid a severe economic crisis.

Consumer confidence was at a five-year low, however, dragged down by fears of a return to hyper-inflation. As in the 1980s, the populist economy was trapped in bottlenecks of its own making. Public spending had increased at the rate of about 40 percent annually over the past two years. In addition to pump-priming the economy, the government was committed to paying subsidies to industries being squeezed by its price controls: gas, electricity, subways, airlines, commuter railways, and basic foodstuffs like milk, meat, bread, and pasta. Those subsidies cost about $30 billion a year and were the primary cause for the rise in government spending. They did nothing to increase the output of goods and services, however. The energy sector was a prime example of stagnant production. The CEOs of big companies like Shell and Exxon were under court orders to invest in expansion, as called for in their contracts; but they replied that government subsidies were insufficient to offset the losses caused by price controls. They refused to risk more money in their factories, preferring instead to import natural gas and diesel fuel for the local markets.

Prudent citizens were parking their money outside the country. Official estimates placed the total amount at $144.3 billion, but that didn't take into account the illegal, undeclared sums that might easily double that figure. An estimated $8.5 billion left the country just between the beginning of the farmers' strike in mid-March and the end of June. Some economists believed that the amount of Argentine capital being held abroad was about equivalent to the country's official gross national product. That might have been offset by foreign investment, but little money was coming in from outside. The situation of the privatized industries was a warning to those who might have been direct investors. A week after the Senate rejected the retentions bill, Aerolíneas Argentinas was renationalized after months of skirting bankruptcy. The Argentine government refused to compensate Marsans, the Spanish owners, alleging that the company's debts were equal to its total worth.

In the past, the Argentine government had managed to survive economic crises by issuing bonds to raise ready cash. Now there was no market for them. Hugo Chávez, Venezuela's "strongman," had previously been willing to buy them, at double-digit interest rates, but the precipitous fall in world oil prices during the latter half of 2008 forced him to tighten his own belt. Though unable to borrow, Argentina still owed money to the Paris Club and to old bondholders who had refused to accept Néstor Kirchner's "haircut." Some $2 billion of Argentine government bonds were scheduled to mature in 2008, and another $5 billion would come due the following year. In addition, some $6.5 billion in interest was owed in 2008, and that would rise to $14.6 billion in 2009.

Desperate for cash to keep the Paris Club at bay and to continue stimulating the economy, Cristina Kirchner sent a bill to Congress on 21 October that would nationalize the deposits in Argentina's AFJP (Administración de Fondos de Jubilaciones y Pensiones), the private pension scheme set up by Menem in the 1990s. At stake were some $30 billion in assets, spread over ten different investment funds. The move was rationalized originally as a way to save pensioners' savings, which were suffering from the worldwide financial crisis that struck in late September. The final bill, approved by the Senate on 21 November, would transfer all the funds to the government's Social Security Administration (ANSES). The chief administrator of ANSES, Amado Boudou, affirmed that the money would then be used "for long-term investments" by the state "to sustain the Argentine economy during the times were are living in."[5]

FACING THE FUTURE: THE THREE ARGENTINAS

Manuel Mora y Araujo, a social scientist and pollster, published a paper in 2003 titled *La Argentina: Una víctima de sí misma* ("Argentina: A Victim of Itself") that presaged this stalemate.[6] He divided the economically active population into three more or less numerically equal parts, according to their ability to compete in a modern open economy. At the top were the "very competitive" sectors, which he estimated at around 36 percent of the whole. These were people with the skills to participate successfully in a free market system, among whom the farmers, being efficient, were the largest segment. They wanted limited government and viewed politicians with suspicion. They had done better under Menem than under Duhalde—and, by extension, the Kirchners. The better-educated young professionals among them would leave Argentina if it failed to modernize, while the older ones who had money would send it abroad. Though it was the most economically dynamic segment of the society, it lacked a unified leadership and felt itself to be politically unrepresented.

Below this group were the "less competitive," about 30 percent of the adult population. They tended to have less education and fewer skills than the top group. For them, the 1990s were a disaster. They had done passably well in pre-Menem Argentina, having been protected by strong labor unions and/or civil service rules, but were devastated by privatizations and free trade. Many of them lost their jobs and became either unemployed or poorly paid, insecure *cuentapropistas*. Even those who managed to hang on and survive felt menaced by globalization. This group as a whole had become politically radicalized and combative. It wanted the protection of a strong anti-capitalist, anti-foreign Peronist state.

The "uncompetitive" 34 percent that constituted the bottom segment was subdivided into the usual uneducated, unskilled "stragglers" (*rezagados*), and the "new poor" of former middle-class people who now found themselves impoverished. Both were bitterly anti-capitalist and inclined toward Peronism, but unlike the "less competitive," they were more sensitive to inflation, because they were less able to protect themselves from its consequences.

The traditional Peronist coalition was an alliance between the "less competitive" middle group and the "stragglers" in the bottom third. The old corporatist system, with its protectionism, subsidies, full employment, and "social pacts," aimed at preserving a modest prosperity for everyone. It favored distribution over growth. The Kirchner political base was now the traditional Peronist coalition, plus the "new poor," but minus the tenant farmers of the FAA. It was still the largest political coalition in Argentina, but its weakness lay in the fact that the bottom third of the population produced practically nothing, and the middle third produced less than it consumed. Also, holding it together required moderate but non-inflationary growth, whereas populist economics usually produces inflation.

For politicians, concerns about survival in the short term trump considerations of economic rationality. Peronists, especially, are bored by economic arguments. Although the upper third of Argentina generates the wealth that the rest depends on, it is only a minority at the polls. Ever since the Perón Era, this group has been politically isolated, except for periods of military rule, or when a Peronist maverick like Menem might forge a temporary alliance between the upper and lower thirds of the population. Alternatively, the Alliance attempted to base itself on the upper and middle segments, but as in Menem's case, the coalition was inherently unstable. Indeed, in a shrinking economy, all possible combinations seem fraught with contradictions. The Kirchners' populist coalition also appears to be approaching its time of crisis, including perhaps another default on the nation's debts. Argentina seems stuck in a three-cornered political standoff, while its capitalist economy continues its agonizing downward course.

Notes

PREFACE

1. The term "reversal of development" is taken from the title of Carlos Waisman's excellent study, *Reversal of Development in Argentina* (Princeton, NJ: Princeton University Press, 1987).

2. *The Crisis of Argentine Capitalism* (Chapel Hill: The University of North Carolina Press, 1990).

3. *Guerrillas and Generals: The "Dirty War" in Argentina* (Westport, CT: Praeger Publishers, 2002).

4. Quoted from *The Review of the River Plate,* 30 September 1971, 571.

CHAPTER 1

1. W. H. Koebel, *Argentina, Past and Present* (London: Adam & Charles Black, 2nd ed., 1914), 43–61.

2. Domingo F. Sarmiento, *Life in the Argentine Republic in the Days of the Tyrants; or, Civilization versus Barbarism* (New York: Collier Books, 1961), 82–84.

3. Gabriela Cerruti, *El Jefe: Vida y obra de Carlos Saúl Menem* (Buenos Aires: Editorial Planeta, 1993), 15–17.

4. Alfredo Leuco and José Antonio Díaz, *El heredero de Perón: Menem entre Dios y Diablo* (Buenos Aires: Editorial Planeta, 1988), 69–70.

5. Cerruti, *El Jefe,* 19–20.

6. Cerruti, *El Jefe,* 22–24.

7. Cerruti, *El Jefe,* 26–28.

8. María Matilde Ollier, *El fenómino insurreccional y la cultura política (1969–1973)* (Buenos Aires: Centro Editor de América Latina, 1986), 117–119; María José Moyano, *Argentina's Lost Patrol: Armed Struggle, 1969–1979* (New Haven: Yale University Press, 1995), 27, 36, 53; Guillermo O'Donnell, *Bureaucratic Authoritarianism: Argentina,*

1966–1973, in Comparative Perspective (Berkeley: University of California Press, 1988), 296–300.

9. Cerruti, *El Jefe,* 41–47.

10. Cerruti, *El Jefe,* 61–67.

11. José Antonio Borello, *Bulones, patillas y lugares: Cambios en la industria, el interior y las grandes ciudades de la Argentina contemporánea* (Buenos Aires: Centro de Estudios Urbanos y Regionales, 1992), 46–48, 55; Díaz and Leuco, *El heredero,* 179–180; Paul Blustein, *And the Money Kept Rolling In (and Out): Wall Street, the IMF, and the Bankruptcy of Argentina* (New York: Public Affairs, 2005), 22; James W. McGuire, "Strikes in Argentina: Data Sources and Recent Trends," *Latin American Research Review,* vol. 31, no. 3 (1996), 140; *Somos,* 20 December 1989, 7.

12. Cerruti, *El Jefe,* 194–203; Díaz and Leuco, *El heredero,* 179–185.

13. Andrew MacAdam, *Cafiero, el renovador* (Buenos Aires: Ediciones Corregidor, 1996), 113–151; Díaz and Leuco, *El heredero,* 38–40; Cerruti, *El Jefe,* 156–60, 186–199.

14. Cerruti, *El Jefe,* 207–252.

15. Rubén Lo Vuolo and Alberto Barbeito, *La nueva oscuridad de la política social* (Buenos Aires: Miño y Dávila, Editores, 1998; Carlos Waisman, "The Legitimation of Democracy Under Adverse Conditions: The Case of Argentina," in Mónica Peralta Ramos and Carlos Waisman, eds., *From Military Rule to Liberal Democracy in Argentina* (Boulder: Westview Press, 1987), 97; Gary W. Wynia, *Argentina: Illusions and Realities* (New York: Homes & Meier, 1986), 145, 176–178; William Smith, "Democracy, Distributional Conflicts and Macroeconomic Policymaking in Argentina, 1983–1989," *Journal of Inter-American Studies and World Affairs,* vol. 32, no. 2 (Summer, 1990), 1–42; Roberto Bouzas, "¿Más allá de la estabilización y la reforma? Un ensayo sobre la economía argentina a comienzos de los '90," *Desarrollo Económico,* vol. 33, no. 129 (1993), 3–11; Juan Pablo Gerchunoff and Juan Carlos Torre, "La política de liberalización económica en la administración de Menem," *Desarrollo Económico,* vol. 36, no. 143 (October–December 1996), 735; *Somos,* 8 July 1987, 49; 22 July 1987, 52; *Buenos Aires Herald,* 5 July 1987, 2.

16. James Nielson, *El fin de la quimera* (Buenos Aires: Editorial Emecé, 1991), 59–61; Ignacio Massun, *Menem: Cirugía sin anestesia* (Buenos Aires: Editorial Métodos, 1999), 48, 79–80; *Somos,* 14 June 1989, 40–41.

CHAPTER 2

1. Horacio Verbitsky, *Robo para la corona: Los frutos prohibidos del árbol de la corrupción* (Buenos Aires: Editorial Planeta, 1991), 31–32; Cerruti, *El Jefe,* 258–259, 262–266, 273–275.

2. Vicente Palermo and Marcos Novaro, *Política y poder en el gobierno de Menem* (Buenos Aires: Grupo Editor Norma, 1996), 38, 46–47.

3. Marcelo Diamond, "Overcoming Argentina's Stop-And-Go Cycles," in Jonathan Hartlyn and Samuel Morley, eds., *Latin American Political Economy: Financial Crisis and Political Change* (Boulder: Westview Press, 1986), 129–30; Manuel Mora y Araujo, *Argentina—una víctima de sí misma: Débil gobernabilidad y bajo consenso social* (Buenos Aires: Ediciones La Crujía, 2003), 10–11.

4. Enrique Silberstein, *Los ministros de economia* (Buenos Aires: Ediciones La Campana, 1982), 23–25.

5. Marcelo Cavarozzi, "La agenda progresista en la Argentina y la política: ¿Solución o disolución?" *Política y Gestión.* No.2 (November 2001), 11, 19.

6. *Review of the River Plate,* 8 October1984, p.114.

7. *Somos,* 5 August 1987, 53.

8. *Mercado,* 30 July 1987, 42, 48–49; *Somos,* 20 May 1987, 56–57; 5 August 1987, 54; *La Nación,* 3 August 1987, 8.

9. *Mercado,* 30 April 1987, 44, 46; *Somos,* 27 May 1987, 60–61; 3 June 1987, 62–63; *Expreso,* 22 May 1987, 55.

10. Susan and Peter Calvert, *Argentina: Political Culture and Instability* (Pittsburgh: University of Pittsburgh Press, 1989), 204, based on articles appearing in *The Buenos Aires Herald* on 17 August 1986, p. 3, and 31 August 1986, p. 2; *Mercado,* 28 February 1985, 18; *Review of the River Plate,* 31 August 1983, 195; 13 June 1984, 510–511; 13 March 1985, 204; 11 July 1986, 14–15.

11. *Mercado,* 28 February 1985, 24, 26; *Somos,* 29 April 1987, 54–58; *Review of the River Plate,* 13 March 1985, 204.

12. William Smith, "Democracy, Distributional Conflicts and Macroeconomic Policy-making in Argentina, 1983–1989," *Journal of Inter-American Studies and World Affairs,* vol. 32, no. 2 (Summer 1990), 12–14, 17–18, 25–28; Palermo and Novaro, *Política y poder,* 71–88.

13. *Somos,* 8 July 1987, 49; 22 July 1987, 52; 6 January 1988, 44; 13 January 1988, 43; 20 January 1988, 43; 10 February 1988, 43; 25 May 1988, 4–8; 8 June 1988, 20–21; 28 June 1989, 41; *Buenos Aires Herald,* 5 July 1987, 2.

14. Roberto Bouzas, "¿Más allá de la estabilización y la reforma? Un ensayo sobre la economía argentina a comienzos de los 90", *Desarrollo Económico,* vol. 33, no. 129 (1993), 3, 6; Díaz, Rodolfo, *¿Prosperidad o ilusión? Las reformas de los 90 en la Argentina* (Buenos Aires: Editorial Ábaco, 2002), 34; Pablo Gerchunoff and Juan Carlos Torre, "La política de liberalización económica en la administración de Menem," *Desarrollo Económico,* vol. 36, no. 143 (October–December 1996), 735; Rubén M. Lo Vuolo and Alberto C. Barbeito, *La nueva oscuridad de la política social: del estado populista al neoconservador* (Buenos Aires: Miño y Dávila, Editores, 1998), 63; *Somos,* 21 September 1988, 45; 16 November 1988, 18–19; 8 March 1989, 42.

15. Ignacio Massun, *Menem: cirugía sin anestesia* (Buenos Aires: Editorial Métodos, 1999), 79–80; James Nielson, *El fin de la quimera* (Buenos Aires: Editorial Emecé, 1991), 59–61.

16. Lo Vuolo and Barbeito, *La nueva oscuridad,* 51: n.23.

17. Carlos H. Acuña, Mario R. Dos Santos, David García Delgado, and Laura Golbert, "Relación estado-empresarios y políticas concertadas de ingresos: el caso argentino," Dos Santos, García Delgado, and Golbert, eds., *Política económica y actores sociales: La concentración de ingresos y empleo* (Santiago de Chile: PRELAC, 1988), 203, 211; Alejandro Gaggero and Andrés Wainer, "Burgesía nacional–crisis de la convertibilidad: El rol de la UIA y su estrategia para el tipo de cambio," *Realidad Económica* (29 August 2006), 2, http://www.iade.org.ar; Andrés Malamud, "Grupos de interés y consolidación de la democracia en Argentina," *América Latina Hoy* (28 August 2001), 173–189; *Mercado,* 30 April 1987, 43–44; *Somos,* 18 April 1990, 46–47.

18. For this, and other capsule histories of Argentine conglomerates, I have consulted chiefly Luis Majul, *Los dueños de la Argentina: La cara oculta de los negocios* (Buenos Aires: Editorial Sudamericana, vol. 1, 1992 and vol. 2, 1994). Also, Daniel Azpiazu, Eduardo M. Basualdo and Miguel Khavisse, *El nuevo poder económico en la Argentina de los años 80* (Buenos Aires: Editorial Legasa, 1986); Roberto Bisang and Martina Chidiak, *Apertura económica, reestructuración productiva y medio ambiente: La siderúrgia*

argentina en los 90 (July 1995), http://www.fund-cenit.org/ar; Andrés López and Martina Chidiak, *Reestructuración productiva y gestión ambiental en la pteroquímica argentina* (July 1995), http://www.fund-cenit.org/ar.

19. For a history of Bunge & Born, see Raúl Green and Catherine Laurent, *El poder de Bunge y Born* (Buenos Aires: Editorial Legasa, 1988). Also, Majul, *Los dueños,* vol.1, 249–292.

20. Majul, *Los dueños,* vol. 1, 250; Green and Laurent, *El poder,* 11.

21. Verbitsky, *Robo,* 31–32; Cerruti, *El Jefe,* 275.

CHAPTER 3

1. Rubén Lo Vuolo and Alberto Barbeito, *La nueva oscuridad de la política social* (Buenos Aires: Miño y Dávila, Editores, 1998), 210–211; Delia Ferreira Rubio and Matteo Goretti, "Cuando el presidente gobierna solo: Menem y los decretos de necesidad y urgencia hasta la reforma constitucional (julio 1989–agosto 1994)," *Desarrollo Económico,* vol. 36, no. 141 (April–June 1996), 444, 451, 454.

2. Strictly speaking, Congress' decision to increase the size of the Supreme Court was illegal because the vote was taken on a day when the Chamber of Deputies lacked a quorum. See Christopher Larkins, "The Judiciary and Delegative Democracy in Argentina," *Comparative Politics,* vol. 30, no. 4 (July 1998), 428. Also, Andrés Gil Domínguez, "El poder judicial desde 1973 hasta nuestras días," *Todo Es Historia* (May 2002), 13–14; Jorge Juan Ramos Mejía, "The Supreme Court and Democracy," *Review of the River Plate* (11 October 1989), 243; Horacio Verbitsky, *Robo para la Corona* (Buenos Aires; Editorial Planeta, 1991), 43, 67, 71, 73–75, 92, 94–97; Fernando Horacio Molinas, *Delitos de "cuello blanco" en la Argentina* (Buenos Aires: Ediciones Depalma, 1989), 59–72, 81–82.

3. Pablo Gerchunoff and Juan Carlos Torre, "La política de liberalización económica en la administración de Menem," *Desarrollo Económico,* vol. 36, no. 143 (October–December 1996), 740, 755–756; Mariana Llanos, "Understanding Presidential Power in Argentina: A Study of Privatization in the 1990s," *Journal of Latin American Studies,* vol. 33, no. 1 (February 2001), 76–77.

4. Ana Margheritis, *Ajuste y reforma en Argentina (1989–1995): La economía política de las privatizaciones* (Buenos Aires: Nuevohacer, Grupo Editor Latinoamericano, 1999), 161, 165, 175–177, 180, 301–302; Luigi Manzetti, "The Political Economy of Privatization Through Divestiture in Lesser Developed Countries, *Comparative Politics,* vol. 25, no. 4 (July 1993), 445–446; Daniel Chudnovsky, Andrés López, and Fernando Porta, "Más allá del flujo de caja. El boom de la inversión extranjera directa en la Argentina," *Desarrollo Económico,* vol. 35, no. 137 (April–June 1995), 40; Alejandra Herrera, "The Privatization of the Argentine Telephone System, *CEPAL Review,* no. 47 (August 1992), 149, 153–155, 160.

5. Artemio Luis Melo, *El primer gobierno de Menem: Análisis de los procesos de cambio político* (Rosario: Editorial de la Universidad Nacional de Rosario, 2001), 33.

6. Margheritis, *Ajuste,* 44–46, 100–102, 142–145; Eduardo Sguiglia, *Los grandes grupos industriales en la Argentina actual: Estado y sociedad* (Buenos Aires: Centro Editor de América Latina, 1988), 67–72, 78–81; Gabriel Yoguel, "El ajuste empresarial frente a la apertura: la heterogeneidad de las respuestas de las PYMEs," *Desarrollo Económico,* vol. 38, número especial (Autumn 1998), 177, 179, 182: n. 5, 183, 188: n. 20, 189: n. 23; Leonardo Bleger and Guillermo Rozenwurcel, "Financiamiento a las PYMEs y cambio

estructural en la Argentina: Un estudio sobre fallas de mercado y problemas de informa-ción," *Desarrollo Económico,* vol. 40, no. 157 (April–June 2000), 52. PYMEs were defined as firms having fewer than fifty salaried employees, although the great majority were "mom and pop" microbusinesses that had no staff other than the owner himself and perhaps a few unpaid family members.

7. Margheritis, *Ajuste,* 301–337; Chudnovsky, López, and Porta, "Más allá," 39; Judith Teichman, *The Politics of Freeing Markets in Latin America* (Chapel Hill: University of North Carolina Press, 2001), 124.

8. Vicente Palermo and Marcos Novaro, *Política y poder en el gobierno de Menem* (Buenos Aires: Grupo Editora Norma, 1996), 156–157; Gabriel Cerruti, *El octavo círculo: Crónica y entretelones del poder menemista* (Buenos Aires: Editorial Planeta, 1991), 107; *International Currency Review,* vol. 20, no. 3 (February–March 1990), 162–164.

9. *Somos,* 30 August 1989, 40–41; 18 October 1989, 4–8.

10. Melo, *Primero gobierno,* 45; Cerruti, *Octavo círculo,* 107; *Somos,* 16 August 1989.

11. *Somos,* 14 February 1990, 8–9; Domingo Cavallo, *El peso de la verdad* (Buenos Aires: Editorial Planeta, 1997), 58.

12. *Somos,* 21 February 1990, 9–10, 12.

13. "Intervention" is both a legal and political term in Argentina and is permitted under the Constitution, in the case of a province, and by the Law of Professional Associations in the case of a private group. It allows the federal executive to take action in a crisis by removing the officers of a province or a private organization, and substituting government-appointed officials, or "interventors," for them, with the aim of "reforming" the practices of the affected institution.

14. Consejo Técnico de Inversiones, *La economía argentina/The Argentine Economy,* (Buenos Aires, 1984–1993); Teichman, *Freeing Markets,* 162–166; Danilo Martuccelli and Maristella Svampa, *La plaza vacía: los transformaciones del peronismo* (Buenos Aires: Editorial Losada, 1997), 211–213; Sebastián Etchemendy and Vicente Palermo, "Conflicto y concentración. Gobierno, Congreso y organizaciones de interés en la reforma laboral del primer gobierno de Menem (1989–1995)," *Desarrollo Económico,* vol. 37, no. 148 (January–March, 1998), 561–567; Palermo and Novaro, *Política y poder,* 344–350; Carlos Acuña, "Politics and Economics in the Argentina of the Nineties (Or, Why the Future No Longer Is What It Used To Be")," in William C. Smith, Carlos H. Acuña and Eduardo Gamarra, eds., *Democracy, Markets, and Structural Reform in Latin America* (New Brunswick: Transaction Publishers, 1993), 63–64, 67; Rodolfo Díaz, *¿Prosperidad o ilusión? Las reformas de los 90 en la Argentina* (Buenos Aires: Editorial Ábaco, 2002), 175, 177, 188–195; Sylvina Walger, *Pizza con champán: Crónica de la fiesta menemista* (Buenos Aires: Editorial Planeta, 1994), 128–130, 136.

15. Pamela K. Starr, "Government Coalitions and the Viability of Currency Boards: Argentina Under the Cavallo Plan," *Journal of Inter-American Studies and World Affairs,* vol. 39, no. 2 (Summer 1997), 91.

16. *International Currency Review,* vol. 20, no. 3 (February–March 1990), 165.

17. *Somos,* 10 January 1990, 5–14; 17 January 1990, 4–10; *International Currency Review,* vol. 20, no. 4 (April–August 1990), 158, 162; *Review of the River Plate,* 31 January 1990, 42.

18. Cerruti, *El Jefe,* 288; *Somos,* 5 July 1989, 3.

19. On Colonel Seineldín and the last *carapintada* revolt, a useful summary of events can be found in Paul H. Lewis, *Guerrillas and Generals: The "Dirty War" in Argentina* (Westport, CT: Praeger Publishers, 2002), 232–235.

20. Cerruti, *El Jefe,* 341–344; *Somos,* 16 May 1990, 4–7; *Review of the River Plate,* 30 November 1990, 344.

21. Beto Casella and Dario Villarruel (with Néstor Esposito), *La mano en la lata: Diccionario de la corrupción argentina* (Buenos Aires: Editorial Grijalbo, 2000), 19, 29, 69–71; Marcelo Zlotogwiazda, *La mafia del oro* (Buenos Aires: Editorial Planeta, 1997, 48–49; Fernando Horacio Molinas, *Delitos de "cuello blanco" en la Argentina* (Buenos Aires: Ediciones Depalma, 1989), 43–44; Carlos S. Nino, *Un país al margin de la ley: Estudio de la anomía como componente del subdesarrollo argentino* (Buenos Aires: Emecé Editores, 1992), 25; *Somos,* 16 March 1988, 4–8.

22. Adrián Guissarri, *La Argentina informal: Realidad de la vida económica* (Buenos Aires: Emecé Editores, 1989), 15, 31–42, 46–48, 53–54, 58, 67–78, 105–106, 109, 134, 166, 168, 177, 187–188; Nino, *Un país,* 91–97.

23. Max Weber, *The Protestant Ethic and the Spirit of Capitalism* (New York: Charles Scribner's Sons, 1958), see especially chapter 2, "The Spirit of Capitalism," 47–78.

24. *The Economist,* 26 November 1994, 16; *Somos,* 14 October 1991, 7; *Review of the River Plate,* 31 January 1995, 17; Walger, *Pizza con champan,* 130.

25. Cerruti, *El Jefe,* 319–321.

26. Casella and Villarruel, *Mano,* 81–82; Melo, *Primer gobierno,* 86.

27. Verbitsky, *Robo,* 11–15; Cerruti, *El Jefe,* 360–363; Cerruti, *Octavo círculo,* 235, 243–247, 254; Melo, *Primer gobierno,* 95–96.

28. James W. McGuire, "Strikes in Argentina: Data Sources and Recent Trends," *Latin American Research Review,* vol. 31, no. 3 (1996), 138; William C. Smith, "State, Market and Neoliberalism in Post-Transition Argentina: The Menem Experiment," *Journal of Inter-American Studies and World Affairs,* vol. 33, no. 4 (Winter, 1991), 61; Ignacio Massun, *Menem: Cirugía sin anestesia* (Buenos Aires: Editorial Métodos, 1999), 57–68, 185–189; Rafael Olarra Jiménez and Luis García Martínez, *El derrumbe argentino: De la convertibilidad al "corralito,"* (Buenos Aires: Editorial Planeta, 2002), 48–52; Melo, *Primer gobierno,* 85; Pablo Gerchunoff and Juan Carlos Torre, "Argentina: La política de liberalización económica bajo un gobierno de base popular," in Gerchunoff and Torre, eds., *El cambio del papel del Estado en América Latina* (Mexico City: Siglo Veintiuno, Editores, 1997), 168; *Somos,* 20 June 1990, 4–8; 29 August 1990, 16.

CHAPTER 4

1. Paul Blustein, *And the Money Kept Rolling In (and Out): Wall Street, the IMF, and the Bankrupting of Argentina* (New York: Public Affairs, 2005), 13, 118–119; Rubén Lo Vuolo and Alberto Barbeito, *La nueva oscuridad de la política social: Del estado populista al neoconservador* (Buenos Aires: Miño y Dávila, Editores, 1998), 54; Ana Margheritis, *Ajuste y reforma en Argentina (1989–1995): La economía política de las privatizaciones* (Buenos Aires: Nuevohacer, Grupo Editor Latinoamericano, 1999), 107–109; Ignacio Massun, *Menem: Cirugía sin anestesia* (Buenos Aires: Editorial Métodos, 1999), 70.

2. Guillermo Cherashny, *Menem, Yabrán, Cavallo: Final abierto* (Buenos Aires: Editorial Solaris, 1997), 130, 134.

3. Artemio Luis Melo, *El primer gobierno de Menem,* 105–109, 128, 138: n. 100, 177–179; Pamela Starr, "Government Coalitions," 91–93; Ana Margheritis, *Ajuste,* 55–56; Palermo and Novaro, *Política y poder,* 288–290, 302–311; *Latin America Regional Report: Southern Cone,* 12 September 1991, 2; Olarra Jiménez and García Martínez, *El*

derrumbe argentino, 59–63; Acuña, "Politics and Economics in the Argentina of the Nineties," 45–48.

4. Melo, *Primer gobierno,* 120.

5. Olarra Jiménez and García Martínez, *El derrumbe,* 70; Pablo Gerchunoff and Guillermo Canovas, "Privatizaciones en un contexto de emergencia económica," *Desarrollo Económico,* vol. 34, no. 136 (1995), 500–502; *Somos,* 11 January 1989, 4–8; 18 January 1989, 4–8; *Review of the River Plate,* 13 March 1991, 130.

6. Magheritis, *Ajuste,* 197, 200–204, 210, 216, 225; Olarra Jiménez and García Martínez, *El derrumbe,* 70.

7. Massun, *Menem: Cirugía,* 71.

8. Domingo Cavallo, *El peso de la verdad* (Buenos Aires: Editorial Planeta, 1997), 136–140; *Somos,* 31 May 1993, 16–18.

9. Luigi Manzetti, "The Political Economy of MERCOSUR," *Journal of Inter-American Studies and World Affairs,* vol. 35, no. 4 (Winter 1993–1994), 105, 113.

10. Eduardo M. Basualdo, *Concentración y centralización del capital en la Argentina durante la década del noventa* (Quilmes: Universidad Nacional de Quilmes, 2000), 241.

11. Basualdo, *Concentración,* 242–243; Gerchunoff and Canovas, "Privatizaciones," 487–488, 491–492; Daniel Chudnovsky, Andrés López, and Fernando Porta, "Mas allá del flujo de caja," 39.

12. Gerchunoff and Canovas, "Privatizaciones," 485, 488–492, 496.

13. Chudnovsky, López, and Porta, "Más allá," 47–49; "Hoover's Profile: Telefónica," 4; Margheritis, *Ajuste,* 187, 223; Andrés López and Martina Chidiak, *Reestructuración productiva y gestión ambiental en la petroquímica argentina,* (July 1995), 2, 33–38, http://www.fund-cenit.org.ar; Luigi Manzetti, "The Political Economy of Privatization Through Divestiture in Lesser Developed Countries,"*Comparative Politics,* vol. 25, no. 4 (July 1993), 446–448.

14. Guillermo Rosenwurcel and Leonardo Bleger, "El sistema bancario argentino en los noventa: de la profundización financiera a la crisis sistémica" *Desarrollo Económico,* vol. 37, no. 146 (July–September 1997), 165: Table 1; Margheritis, *Ajuste,* 155: n. 68; Cerruti, *Octavo círculo,* 230.

15. Cerruti, *Octavo círculo,* 211.

16. Margheritis, *Ajuste,* 157–234; "Hoover's Profile: Telefónica de Argentina, S.A.," *Answers.com* http://www.answers.com/topic/telefónica de argentina, 1–6; Olarra Jiménez and García Martínez, *El derrumbe,* 70; Hernán López Echagüe, *La política está en otra parte* (Buenos Aires: Grupo Editorial Norma, 2002), 95–194.

17. Luis Beccaria and Aida Quintar, "Reconversión productiva y mercado de trabajo: Reflexiones a partir de la experiencia de Somisa," *Desarrollo Económico,* vol. 35, no. 139 (October–December 1995), 403–405; Melo, *Primer gobierno,* 118–119.

18. Cavallo, *Peso,* 231. Statistics on public employment are from *El Cronista Comercial,* 2 December 1986, as cited in *Review of the River Plate,* 10 December 1986, 533; and Argentine Republic, Instituto Nacional de Estadística y Censos, *Censo '91: Censo Nacional de Población y Vivienda, 1991,* 73.

19. Martuccelli and Svampa, *Plaza vacia.,* 279–301; M. Victoria Murillo, "La adaptación del sindicalismo argentino a las reformas de mercado en la primera presidencia de Menem," *Desarrollo Económico,* vol. 37, no. 147 (October–December 1997), 436; Estela Grassi, Susana Hintze, and María Rosa Neufeld, *Políticas sociales, crisis, y ajuste estructural* (Buenos Aires: Espacio Editorial, 1994), 164; Peter Ranis, *Class, Democracy and Labor in Contemporary Argentina* (New Brunswick, NJ: Transaction Publishers,

1995). Ranis' estimate of CTERA membership, out of some 600,000 primary and secondary school teachers, makes it one of the weakest unions in terms of the percentage of members unionized (p. 86).

20. James McGuire, "Strikes in Argentina," 138–139.

21. Sebastián Etchemendy, "Constructing Reform Coalitions: The Politics of Compensations in Argentina's Economic Liberalization," *Latin American Political Sociology,* vol. 43, no. 3 (Fall 2001), 6–8; Rodolfo Díaz, *¿Prosperidad o ilusión?,* 260–263; Nancy R. Powers, "The Politics of Poverty in Argentina in the 1990s," *Journal of Inter-American Studies and World Affairs,* vol. 37, no. 4 (Winter 1995), 99.

22. Gerchunoff and Torre, "La política," 758; Argentine Republic, Banco Central, Secretaría de Programación, cited in Reed College, "Economics 201: Case of the Day, Inflation in Argentina," http://academic.reed.edu/economics/course, 201–206; Carola Pessino, "La anatomía del desempleo," *Desarrollo Económico,* vol. 36, número especial (Summer 1996), 224, 227–231, 235, 241–242, 253–254; Lo Vuolo and Barbeito, *La nueva oscuridad,* 758.

CHAPTER 5

1. Casella and Villarruel, *Mano en la lata,* 60, 143–144; Cerruti, *Octavo círculo,* 133–134; Walger, *Pizza con champán,* 128–130; Melo, *Primer gobierno,* 150–151; Cavallo, *Peso de la verdad,* 254–256; *Review of the River Plate,* 30 November 1990, 318; 31 January 1992, 34; 16 March 1994, 105; 30 March 1994, 131; 29 July 1994, 34; 31 January 1995, 17; 28 February 1995, 66; 15 June 1995, 252; 30 June 1995, 266, 268; *Somos,* 30 December 1991, 4–9; 6 January 1992, 4–7, 10–13; 4 January 1993, 4–5; 10 May 1993, 4–8.

2. For Spinoza Melo's account of this trip, see his interview with Susana Viau: "Menem le prometió un reactor a los sirios," *Página 12,* 3 October 1999, 11. See also, Alain Labrousse and Laurent Laniel, eds., *The World Geopolitics of Drugs, 1998–1999* (Norwell, MA: Kluwer Academic Publishers, 2002), 194–195.

3. Matthew Brunwasser, "Monzer Al Kassar, The Prince of Marbella: Arms to All Sides," *Frontline/World,* http://www.pbs.org/frontlineworld/stories/sierraleone/alkassar. html.

4. Carlos Escudé and Beatriz Gurevich, "Limits to Governability, Corruption and Transnational Terrorism: The Case of the 1992 and 1994 Attacks in Buenos Aires," *Estudios Interdisciplinarios de América Latina y El Caribe,* vol. 14, no. 2 (July–December, 2003), 3, http://www.tau.ac.il/eial/XIV_2/escude.html.

5. Cerruti, *El Jefe,* 348–351.

6. *Ibid.,* 129–132.

7. For the fullest description of the entire "Yomagate" operation, see Román Lejtman, *Narcogate* (Buenos Aires: Editorial Sudamericana, 1993).

8. "Etchegoyen estaba por hablar cuando murió," *La Nación,* 6 April 1997, http://www.lanacion.com.ar/archivo. As the date of this article shows, the case remained controversial and eventually would be reopened—but without results, since many crucial files were lost.

9. Sylvina Walger, *Pizza con champán,* 135. Walger alleges that it was Antonio who suggested Servini de Cubría to Menem. In an interview with the press, Antonio blamed sinister international influences, social democrats, and Jews for trying to discredit the Yomas, because they were Muslims.

10. Alejandro Margulis, *Junior: Vida y muerte de Carlos Saúl Menem (h)* (Buenos Aires: Editorial Planeta, 1999), 209–211.

11. Lejtman, *Narcogate,* 335–336; *Somos,* 9 March 1992, 19–21; 14 September 1992, 4–11; "La historia secreta: El escándalo Servini de Cubría," (14 June 1993), 31 pp.

12. The two principal sources for this section are: Daniel Santoro, *Venta de armas: Hombres del gobierno* (Buenos Aires: Editorial Planeta, 1998); and Domingo Cavallo, *El peso de la verdad* (Buenos Aires: Editorial Planeta, 1997).

13. Santoro, *Venta,* 91–96.

14. Eduardo Tagliaferro, "Las pistas que llevan a Karim," *Página 12* (1 July 2007), 13, http://www.pagina12.co.ar.

15. Santoro, *Venta,* 133–138, 150–151, 173–176.

16. Santoro, *Venta,* 273–274; Massun, *Menem,* 121.

17. Melo, *Primer gobierno,* 155–156, 160: n114.

18. Massun, *Menem: cirugía sin anestesia,* 115–116

19. Blanca Madani, "New Report Links Syria to 1992 Bombing of Israeli Embassy in Argentina," *Middle East Intelligence Bulletin,* March 2000, 1, http://www.meib.org/articles.

20. Escudé and Gurevich, "Limits to Governability," 4–6, 9–10. The authors also mention that the head of DAIA, the chief lobbying organization for the Argentine Jewish community, received about $350 million to keep his troubled bank from collapse. In 1999, as Menem was leaving office the Banco Mayo finally failed and its owner, Rubén Beraja, was indicted for malfeasance and money laundering.

21. *Ibid.,* 7. For book-length descriptions of how the investigations of the 1992 and 1994 bombings were conducted, it is probably best to start with the most recently published: Roberto Caballero, *AMIA: La verdad imposible* (Buenos Aires: Editorial Sudamericana, 2005). Caballero was a police reporter for *La Prensa.* Silvia Chab's *Entre la crisis y la esperanza: La comunidad judeoargentina tras el atentado a la AMIA* (Buenos Aires: Catálogos, 2001) is useful for describing the factional fights in the Jewish community over how strongly to lobby the Argentine government for a more vigorous investigation. Gabriel Levinas, *La ley bajo los escombros: AMIA: lo que no se hizo* (Buenos Aires: Editorial Sudamericana, 1998) is an extension of a report he made to the U.S. Congress in 1995 about the Argentine government's coverups. Jorge Lanata, *Cortinas de humo* (Buenos Aires: Editorial Planeta, 1994) criticizes judicial and police procedures in investigating the two bombings. Lanata was editor-in-chief of *Página 12.*

22. Larry Rohter, "Iran Blew Up Jewish Center in Argentina, Defector Says," *New York Times,* 22 July 2002, http://query.nytimes.com/gst/fullpage/html.

23. Margulis, *Junior,* 45, 244.

24. *Ibid.,* 209; Lejtman, *Narcogate,* 78, 134.d.

25. Margulis, *Junior,* 35–36, 49–51, 76–78, 92, 282.

26. *Ibid.,* 325–332, 364–366 (for Judge Villafuerte's report); 343–347, 353–363 (for the air force report). One of the witnesses was killed by a car while drunk and crossing the road; the other was killed in a holdup by a carjacker, who was himself killed by police shortly afterward while attempting a robbery.

27. *Somos,* 30 August 1993, 16–17; 6 September 1993, 14–15.

28. Carlos Ares, "Bandas de matones 'ultras' arremeten en los periodistas que critican a Menem," *El País,* 29 August 1993, http://www.elpais.com/articulo/internacional; "El fenómeno 'batatas' vuelve 13 años después: fue un grupo de chocque menemista," *La Nación,* 12 October 2006, 8, http://www.lanacion.com.ar.

29. Omar Lavieri, "The Media in Argentina: Struggling With the Absence of a Democratic Tradition," in Richard R. Cole, ed., *Communication in Latin America: Journalism, Mass Media, and Society* (Wilmington: Scholarly Resources Press, 1996), 183–98; Santoro, *Venta de armas,* 246; *Somos,* 21 September 1992, 12–15; 30 August 1993,

16–17; 6 September 1993, 14–15; 13 September 1993, 10–15; 20 September 1993, 18–20; Marcela Valente, "Media-Argentina: 'Subtle' Means of Censorship," *Inter Press Service News Agency,* 22 January 2008, http://ipsnews.net; "Investigation of Ricardo Gangeme's Assassination Focusing on His Private Life," *IFEX: International Freedom of Expression Exchange,* 19 May 1999, http://www.ifex.org.

30. *Annual Report on Press Freedom in Argentina During 1997* (Buenos Aires: Argentinean Association for the Defense of Independent Journalism, December 1997), http://www.netizen.com.ar/periodistas/reporte_1997e.htm.

CHAPTER 6

1. Article 30 of the Constitution allowed it to be changed, wholly or partially, by a convention summoned by the two houses of Congress by a two-thirds vote. There was no senatorial election in 1993. In the Chamber of Deputies elections, the UCR won in Córdoba, Catamarca, Río Negro, and Santiago del Estero. Provincial parties won in Corrientes and Neuquén.

2. Juan Manuel Abal Medina, "El Partido Frente Grande, análisis de una experiencia inconclusa," *América Latina Hoy,* no. 20 (December 1998), 102–103.

3. Pablo Gerchunoff and Guillermo Canovas, "Privatizaciones en un contexto de emergencia económica," *Desarrollo Económico,* vol. 34, no. 136 (1995), 485; Lo Vuolo and Barbeito, *La nueva oscuridad,* 311; Olarra Jiménez and García Martínez, *El derrumbe argentino,* 62–65.

4. Cavallo, *Peso de la verdad,* 180; Melo, *Primer gobierno,* 152–153, 161: n. 126; *Review of the River Plate,* 27 March 1991, 162–164; Adolfo Canitrot, "Crisis and Transformation of the Argentine State (1978–1992)," in William C. Smith, Carlos H. Acuña, and Eduardo A. Gamarra, eds., *Democracy, Markets, and Structural Reform in Latin America* (New Brunswick, NJ: Transaction Publishers, 1993), 89.

5. Melo, *Primer gobierno,* 152–153, 176–177; *Review of the River Plate,* 29 January 1993, 45; 12 February 1993, 68.

6. Palmero and Novaro, *Política y poder,* 325–328, 416–421; Alfredo F. Calcagno, "Convertibility and the Banking System in Argentina," *CEPAL Review,* no. 61 (April 1997), 88; Olarra Jiménez and García Martínez, *El derrumbe argentino,* 95–96; Gerchunoff and Torre, "La política," 174–177, 190–191, 747, 758; *Business Latin America,* 22 June 1992, 206–207; 27 July 1992, 256–257; 2 November 1992, 377–383; 16 November 1992, 405–406; *Review of the River Plate,* 14 January 1994, 10; 11 February 1994, 50.

7. Argentine Republic, Instituto Nacional de Estadeística y Censos (INDEC), *Censo Económico,* 1994. In 1994 the economy's resurgence temporarily raised the number of manufacturing firms back up to 101,524.

8. *Ibid.*

9. Chudnovsky, López, and Porta, "El boom de la inversión extranjera directa," 48–56.

10. Melo, *Primer gobierno,* 54–57, 84–85, 147–149, 164–167; Carlos S. Nino, *Un país al margen de la ley,* 162–166.

11. Gabriel Negretto, "Constitution-making and Institutional Design: The Transformations of Presidentialism in Argentina, " *Archives of European Sociology,* vol. 40, no. 2 (1999), 215–216, 222–226; Melo, *Primer gobierno,* 185–190, 206: n. 18, 207: n. 20; Catalina Smulovitz, "Reforma y constitución en la Argentina: del consenso negativo al acuerdo," *Revista Uruguaya de Ciencia Política,* no. 8 (1995), 69–83.

12. Isidro Cheresky, "La innovación política: reflexiones a partir de los resultados electorales del 10 de abril de 1994 en Argentina," *Documento de Trabajo, No. 1* (Buenos Aires: Instituto de Investigaciones, Faculdad de Ciencias Sociales, Universidad de Buenos Aires, 1994).

13. United Nations, *Economic Survey of Latin America and the Caribbean, Part 2: Economic Developments by County* (Santiago, Chile: Economic Commission for Latin America, 1994–1995), 131–141; Alfredo F. Calcagno, "Convertibility and the Banking System in Argentina," *CEPAL Review,* no. 61 (April 1997), 68, 73–74; Rafael Rofman, "The Pension System and the Crisis in Argentina: Learning the Lessons," (background paper for the Office of the Chief Economist, Latin America and Caribbean Region, World Bank), 2002, http://info.worldbank.org.

14. The source was Roque Fernández, who eventually replaced Domingo Cavallo as economics minister. He was quoted in the 20 April 2001 edition of *Ámbito Financiero,* and this was cited in Olarra Jiménez and García Martínez, *El derrumbe argentino,* 76, 93.

15. Under the new Constitution, a presidential candidate could win on the first ballot if he had at least 45 percent of the vote and was at least 10 percentage points ahead of his nearest rival. The remaining 10 percent of the votes in the race was scattered among minor parties. For more analysis of the 1995 presidential election, see: Gabriela Delamata, "Las elecciones presidenciales en Argentina: ¿Menemismo o victoria de Menem?" *América Latina Hoy* (Madrid), vol. 2, nos. 11–12 (December 1995), 53–60.

16. Olarra Jiménez and García Martínez, *El derrumbe argentino,* 80–82; Gerchunoff and Torre, "La política de liberalización económica," 174–177, 190–93; Blustein, *And the Money Kept Rolling In (and Out),* 47–52; Palermo and Novaro, *Política y poder,* 446–448; *Review of the River Plate,* 25 February 1994, 82; 31 August 1994, 86–87; 14 October 1994, 174–175, 182–183, 186; 15 December 1994, 316.

17. United Nations, *Economic Survey, Part 2,* 1994–1995, 129–139; Margheritis, *Ajuste y reforma,* 60–61; Rofman, "The Pension System," 12–13.

18. Margheritis, *Ajuste y reforma,* 237–248; Rofman, "The Pension System," 3; U.S. Government, Congressional Budget Office, "The Pension System in Argentina: Social Security Privatization: Experiences Abroad," (Washington DC: January 1999), 4, http://www.cbo.gov.

19. Rofman, "The Pension System," 5–7; Congressional Budget Office, "The Pension Sysem," 3; Massun, *Menem: cirugía sin anestesia,* 78; Argentine Republic, Ministerio de Economía y Producción, "Capital Markets: Table 7.7: Investments of Private Pension Funds as of December 31, 1995," 16, http://www.mecon.gov.ar/report/report.

20. Marc Bou, *El federalismo argentino: aproximación teórica y desempeño institucional,* (Barcelona: Institut Internacional de Governabilitat de Catalunya, 2005), 14.

21. *Ibid.,* 10.

22. Edward Gibson and Ernesto Calvo, "Federalismo y sobrerepresentación: la dimensión territorial de la reforma económica en la Argentina," in Ernesto Calvo and Juan Abal Medina (h), eds., *El federalismo electoral argentino* (Buenos Aires: EUDEBA, 2001), 179–190.

23. Blustein, *And the Money Kept Rolling In,* 22–23, 35; *Somos,* 29 August 1990, 17.

24. *Review of the River Plate,* 31 January 1995, 11, 14; McGuire, "Strikes in Argentina," 143, based on figures from *Clarín,* 20 July 1991, 8; *Somos,* 8 July 1991, 50.

25. Díaz *¿Prosperidad o ilusión?,* 260–262.

26. Sebastián Etchemendy, "Constructing Reform Coalitions: The Politics of Compensations in Argentina's Economic Liberalization," *Latin American Political Sociology,* vol. 43, no. 3 (Fall 2001), 7–8.

27. Gibson and Calvo, *Federalismo,* 194: n. 212; Mónica Panadeiros, "Organización del seguro de salud en la Argentina: análisis y propuesto de reforma," *Desarrollo Económico,* vol. 36, número especial (Summer 1996), 274–275; Lo Vuolo and Barbeito, *La nueva oscuridad,* 164–165.

28. *Somos,* 27 December 1993, 10–13.

29. Pablo Torres, *Votos, chapas y fideos: Clientelismo político y ayuda social* (Buenos Aires: Editorial de la Campana, 2002), 80.

30. Sebastián Saiegh and Mariano Tommasi, "Why is Argentina's Fiscal Federalism so Inefficient? Entering the Labyrinth," *Journal of Applied Economics,* vol. 2, no. 1 (May 1999), 170, 175–179, 182–183, 189; Michael Mussa, *Argentina y el FMI* (Buenos Aires: Editorial Planeta, 2002), 26, 29, 34; Palermo and Novaro, *Política y poder,* 317–318.

31. Torres, *Votos, chapas y fideos,* 48–51, 54, 62, 69–73, 80–83. The term *puntero* originally applied to employees on *estancias* who lived on distant parts of the estate and took care of the cattle. Its application to politics is an example of the Argentine sense of humor.

32. Torres, *Votos, chapas y fideos,* 104–105, 108, 121, 129–130; Steven Levitsky, "An 'Organized Disorganization': Informal Organization and the Persistence of Local Party Structures in Argentine Peronism,"*Journal of Latin American Studies,* vol. 33, no. 1 (February 2001), 29–30, 35–65; Auyero, *Poor People's Politics,* 90–91, 94–97; Daniel P. Míguez, "Democracy, Political Machines, and Participation in the Surroundings of Buenos Aires," *Revista Europea de Estudios Latinoamericanos y el Caribe,* no. 58 (June 1995), 94–98, 104.

33. Palermo and Novaro, *Política y poder,* 436: n. 26, 437–38; Danilo Martuccelli and Maristella Svampa, *La plaza vacía: las transformaciones del peronismo* (Buenos Aires: Editorial Losada, 1997), 381–383.

CHAPTER 7

1. Palermo and Novaro, *Política y poder,* 418–419; Gerchunoff and Torre, "La política," 758; Massun, *Menem: cirugía sin anestesia,* 86.

2. Margheritis, *Ajuste,* 60–61; Palermo and Novaro, *Política y poder,* 449: n. 39. Argentina's private debt in 1995 added up to another $12 billion.

3. Javier Auyero, *La protesta: Retratos de la beligerancia popular en la Argentina democrática* (Buenos Aires: EUDEBA, 2002), 43–51.

4. Guillermo Cherashny, *Menem, Yabrán, Cavallo: final abierto* (Buenos Aires: Editorial Solaris, 1997), 12, 50.

5. Enrique O. Sdrech and Norberto Colominas, *Cabezas: Crimen, mafia y poder* (Buenos Aires: Editorial Atuel, 1997), 78–82, 118, 121–122; Alejandro Vecchi, *El crimen de Cabezas: Radiografía del país mafioso* (Buenos Aires: Editorial Biblos, 2001), 39; Cherashny, *Menem, Yabrán, Cavallo,* 78–79; Ken Warn, "The Rise and Fall of Yabrán—Alfredo Yabrán," *Latin Trade* (August 1998), http://findarticles.com.

6. Domingo Cavallo, *El peso de la verdad* (Buenos Aires: Editorial Planeta, 1997), 96–114.

7. Casella and Villarruel, *Mano en la lata,* 91–92, 190, 195, 197; Cherashny, *Menem, Yabrán, Cavallo,* 188–193, 196–197, 206–207.

8. Cherashny, *Menem, Yabrán, Cavallo,* 219–220.

9. Olarra Jiménez, *El derrumbe argentino,* 95–98.

10. Palermo and Novaro, *Política y poder,* 442: n. 32.

11. *Ibid.*, 23–28; Cavallo, *Peso*, 281.

12. Eduardo M. Basualdo, *Concentración y centralización del capital en la Argentina durante la década del noventa* (Quilmes: Universidad Nacional de Quilmes, 2000), 13, 23–35, 60–66, 248–256.

13. United Nations, Economic Commission for Latin America and the Caribbean, *Principales operaciones de F&A concretadas en la economía argentina entre 1995 y 1999,* www.eclac.org/publicaciones/xml/0/7320/icl/1530e_AI.

14. United Nations, Economic Commission for Latin America and the Caribbean, *Foreign Investment in Latin America and the Caribbean, 1998 Report: Argentina* (press conference: 10 December 1998).

15. Basualdo, *Concentración*, 98, 198–199, 219, 222, 225, 229–231.

16. Silvia Naishtat and Pablo Maas, *El Cazador: La historia secreta de los negocios de Juan Navarro y el Grupo Exxel* (Buenos Aires: Editorial Planeta, 2000), 218–220; Reuters News Service, *Company Profile: Bunge & Born,* 14 May 2007, http://www.stocks. us.reuters.com; Answers.com., "Bunge Brasil, S.A.," http://www.answers.com/topic/ bunge-brasil-sa; "Atanor, S.A.—Company Profile, Information, Business Description, History, Background Information on Atanor, S.A.," *NetIndustries,LLC,* 2007, http://www. referenceforbusiness.com/history2/37/atanor-sa.html.

17. *Clarín,* 31 May 1998, 1–5, http://www.clarin.com/suplementos/economico; "Latin America: Decline of an Argentine Dynasty," *Euromoney* (January 1999), 1–8, http://salsa.babson.edu/pages/articles; Naishtat and Maas, *El Cazador,* 218–223.

18. Claudio Zlotnik, "El Grupo Soldati da su opinión: 'No habrá caída, somos y seremos líderes,'" *Cash: Suplemento Económico de Página 12,* http://www.pagina12.com.ar/ 1998/suple/cash.

19. United Nations, Economic Commission for Latin America and the Caribbean, *El impacto del proceso de fusiones y adquisiciones en la Argentina sobre el mapa de grandes empresas. Factores determinantes y transformaciones en el universo de las grandes empresas de capital local* (Santiago de Chile: 2001), 48, 65–66; "History and Expansion of the Technit Group," *The Technit Group,* 2004, http://www.technitgroup.com.

20. U.N., ECLAC, *El impacto,* 48, 66–67; *Somos,* 20 July 1992, 56–63; "Pérez Companc ya es el número uno en alimentos," *Clarín,* 19 January 1999, http://www.clarin.com.

21. Ana Ale, *La dinastía: Vida, pasión y ocaso de los Macri* (Buenos Aires: Editorial Planeta, 2001), 221–235; U.N., ELAC, *El impacto,* 47, 67–68; Franco Macri, *El futuro es posible: mi experiencia de medio siglo como empresario en la Argentina* (Buenos Aires: Editorial Planeta, 2004), 119–130; Cledis Candelaresi, "Siempre estuve de acuerdo con que no había que pagar," *Página 12,* 7 March 2005, [http://www.pagina12.com]; *Somos,* 28 December 1992, 4–5.

22. U.N., ECLAC, *Principales operaciones de F&A,* anexo II, 85–101; Argentine Embassy, Washington, "American Investments in Argentina," 5, http://emb-eeuu.mrecic. gov.ar/news; Alfredo F. Calcagno, "Convertibility and the Banking System in Argentina," *CEPAL Review,* no. 61 (April 1997), 69, 71–74, 77, 79, 81–83.

23. Nathaniel Nash, "'Deal of the Century': Debt-to-Riches at Citicorp—a Special Report: How an Argentine Bonanza Helped Big Bank and Friends," *New York Times* 19 April 1994, http://query.nytimes.com.

24. *Ibid.*

25. Susana Viau, "El fantasma existe, y es de Raúl Moneta," *Página 12,* 28 February 2001, http://www.pagina12.com.ar; Nicolás García, "El gran socio del Citi," *Mercado Digital,* 2 January 2008, http://www.mercado.com.ar; Francesc Relea, "Los trapos

sucios de la expansión," *El País,* 21 May 2001, http://www.elpais.com/articulo/economia; "Los sucios negocios de Telefónico en Argentina," *Equipo Nizkor* (n.d.), http://www2. nodo50. org/altavoz/timofonica.htm; Peter Hudson, "Argentina's CEI Connects the First Latin American High-Tech Media Empire, but Gets Shocked in the Process," *Latin Trade,* May 1999 [http://209.85.165.104 Find Articles at BNET.com]; "Handley dirigirá los negocios que antes manejaba Moneta," *Clarín,* 23 June 1999, http://www.clarin.com; "World Business Briefing: Americas; Fugitive Sells Stake," *New York Times,* 27 July 1999, http://query.nytimes.com; "Telefonica in $4 billion Argentine Deal," *New York Times,* 4 January 2000, http://query.nytimes.com; Peter Hudson and John Hopewell, "Hicks, Muse and Telefonica Settle Argentine Asset Split, *Variety,* 8 November 1999, http://www.variety.com; Charles Newbery, "Court Tosses Lawsuit vs. Hicks, Muse," *Variety,* 27 October 2003, http://www.variety.com; Juan Ignacio Irigaray, "El juicio político contra la Corte Suprema argentina en marcha," *El Mundo,* 6 February 2002, http://www.elmundo.es.

26. Naishtat and Maas, *El cazador,* 25, 31, 47–48, 58–60, 69–70, 73–77, 85–86.

27. *Ibid.,* 110–111, 116.

28. *Ibid.,* 120, 123–124, 129, 145–146, 148–150, 154–155, 163, 171–178; Argentine Republic, Cámara de Diputados, Comisión Especial Investigadora Sobre Hechos Ilícitos Vinculados con el Lavado de Dinero, *Informe Final Sobre Lavado de Dinero* (Buenos Aires: 2001), Chapter 9: "Exxel Group: Un modelo de inversión y gestión empresarial," 468–498.

CHAPTER 8

1. United Nations, ECLAC, *Economic Survey of Latin America and the Caribbean* (Santiago de Chile: Part 2, 1997–1998), 127–137; International Monetary Fund, *World Economic Outlook, April 2002,* http://www.imf.org, 31; Olarra Jiménez and García Martínez, *El derrumbe argentino,* 67 (based on statistics from the Economics Ministry); Basualdo, *Concentración y centralización,* 241; Alejandro Bonvecchi, "Estrategia de supervivencia y tácticas de disuasión," in Marcos Novaro, *El derrumbe político, en el ocaso de la convertibilidad* (Buenos Aires: Grupo Editorial Norma, 2002), 139.

2. Javier Auyero, *Poor People's Politics: Peronist Survival Networks and the Legacy of Evita* (Durham: Duke University Press, 2001), 31–39; Marta Bekerman, "Reforma comercial y desempleo. Reflexiones para el caso de la economía argentina," *Desarrollo Económico,* vol. 38, número especial (Autumn 1998), 130–132; Carola Pessino, "La anatomía del desempleo," *Desarrollo Económico,* vol. 36, número especial (Summer 1996), 224, 227–229, 231, 235, 241–242, 253–254, 260.

3. Javier Auyero, *La protesta: Retratos de la beligerencia popular en la Argentina democrática* (Buenos Aires: EUDEBA, 2002), 14–20, 65–66; Massun, *Menem: Cirugía sin anestesia,* 201–203.

4. My principal sources on the Cabezas murder are: Antonio Fernández Llorente and Oscar Balmaceda, *El caso Cabezas* (Buenos Aires: Editorial Planeta, 1997); Enrique O. Sdrech and Norberto Colominas, *Cabezas: Crimen, Mafia, y poder* (Buenos Aires: Atuel, 1997); and Alejandro Vecchi, *El crimen de Cabezas* (Buenos Aires: Editorial Biblos, 2001).

5. Auyero, *Poor People's Politics,* 104–115, 123, 127, 140–145, 148, 192–203.

6. Ángel Rodríguez Kauth, "Lectura psicopolítica de los resultados electorales de 1997 en Argentina," *Politeia* (Caracas), no. 22 (1999), 149, 157–59.

7. Adriana Rossi, "Argentina: Internal Insecurity," *Transnational Institute,* December 1997, 7, http://www.tni.o.

8. Massun, *Menem: Cirugía sin anestesia,* 212.

9. Javier Corrales, *Presidents Without Parties: The Politics of Economic Reform in Argentina and Venezuela in the 1990s* (University Park PA: Pennsylvania State University Press, 2002), 214, 216.

10. Carlos Navarro and Robert Sandels, "Argentina: Business Tycoon Alfredo Yabrán Is Apparent Suicide Following Arrest Order for Murder of Journalist," *NotiSur-Latin American Political Affairs,* 22 May 1998, 2–4, http://ssdc.ucsd.edu/news/notisur; *Clarín* 28 May 1998, 1.

11. Blustein, *And the Money Kept Rolling In,* 37, 48, 50, 52–55, 57–58, 79; Corrales, *Presidents,* 216–219; Olarra Jiménez and García Martínez, *El derrumbe,* 112–114; Michael Mussa, *Argentina y el FMI* (Buenos Aires: Editorial Planeta, 2002), 41, 43–51; Guillermo Arisó and Gabriel Jacobo, *El golpe S.A.: La guerra de intereses que estalló en el 2001 y dejó al país en ruinas* (Buenos Aires: Grupo Editorial Norma, 2002), 49; Roque Fernández, "No se cura de palabra," *Ámbito Financiero,* 20 April 2001, cited in Olarra Jiménez and García Martínez, 93.

12. Blustein, *And the Money Kept Rolling In,* 59–60; Bonvecchi, "Estrategia," 139–140.

13. Massun, *Menem: Cirugía sin anestesia,* 219–222.

14. Marcos Novaro, "Los partidos argentinos en los '90: Los desafíos de la competencia, la sucesión y la alternancia," *Estudios Sociales,* vol. 8, no. 15 (2nd semester, 1998), 137, 139–142; Oscar Landi, "El triunfo de la Alianza en la Argentina: Notas de una campaña electoral," *Comunicação Política,* vol. 4, no. 3 (September–December 1997), 13.

CHAPTER 9

1. Gerardo Adrogue and Melchor Armesto, "Aún con vida: Los partidos políticos argentinos en la década del noventa," *Desarrollo Económico,* vol. 40, no. 160 (January–March 2001), 640, 644. Other unpopular groups and institutions that enjoyed high "little or no" public confidence ratings were: labor unions (90 percent "little or no" public confidence), the courts (69 percent), police (68 percent), the military (59 percent), and television news (63 percent). The Catholic Church came off relatively well with a 61 percent "some or much" public confidence rating.

2. For this and other capsule biographies of cabinet ministers, I have consulted, chiefly, Germinal Nogués, *Diccionario biográfico de políticos argentinos* (Buenos Aires: Editorial Planeta, 1989), and Analía Argento and Ana Gerschenson, *Quién es quién en la política argentina* (Buenos Aires: Libros Perfil, 1999). Also, for Terragno, *Somos* (special supplement), 7 September 1992.

3. Javier Tizado, vice president of Technit's steel company, Siderar; and president of its holding company for investments, PROSID, headquartered in the British Virgin Islands, became secretary of state for industry, trade, and investment. Gonzalo Martínez Mosquera, the brother of a top Technit executive, was made undersecretary for industry. Eduardo Casullo, head of Technit's Human Resources Department, was appointed director general of Customs.

4. Blustein, *And the Money Kept Flowing In,* 81; Joaquín Morales Solá, *El sueño eterno: Ascenso y caída de la Alianza* (Buenos Aires: Editorial Planeta, 2001), 26–27,

33–34; Andrés Méndez and Aldo Andrés Romero, "Frente al nuevo gobierno," *Herramienta*, vol. 5, no. 12 (Autumn 2000), 149–152, 155-157.

5. Morales Solá, *El sueño eterno*, 50–51, 65–67, 76, 85.

6. Mariana Llanos and Ana Margheritis, "Why Do Presidents Fail? Political Leadership and the Argentine Crisis (1999–2001)," paper presented at the 44th Annual International Studies Association, Portland, OR (February–March 2003), 18–19, 22–23; Alejandro Bonvecchi, "Estrategia de supervivencia y tácticas de disuasión," in Marcos Novaro, ed., *El derrumbe político en el ocaso de la convertibildad* (Buenos Aires: Grupo Editorial Norma, 2002), 120–121; Morales Solá, *El sueño eterno,* 46, 65, 72.

7. The Senate bribery scandal is covered throughly by Morales Solá in his *El sueño eterno,* 101–158.

8. Llach's reform package aimed at "decentralization, debureaucratization, choice, merit-based compensation for teachers, accountability for school principals, and greater parent involvement." See Sebastian Edwards, "Argentina's De La Rua Flunks Education Reform 101," *The Wall Street Journal,* 20 October 2000, A19.

9. Guillermo Arisó and Gabriel Jacobo, *El Golpe, S.A: La guerra de intereses que estalló en el 2001 y dejó al país en ruinas* (Buenos Aires: Grupo Editorial Norma, 2002), 37–38.

10. Michael Mussa, *Argentina y el FMI* (Buenos Aires: Editorial Planeta, 2002), 44, 49, 53–55, 66, 76, 81.

11. Olarra Jiménez and García Martínez, *El derrumbe,* 123–124; Morales Solá, *El sueño eterno,* 200–202; "Timeline: Argentina's Road to Ruin," *washingtonpost.com: Business Section* 3, August 2003; Julio Godio, *Argentina: En la crisis está la solución* (Buenos Aires: Editorial Biblos, 2002), 48–49; *La Nación,* 7 September 2001, 6; *Lanacion,* 26 December 2000, http://www.lanacion.com.ar.

12. International Monetary Fund, Independent Evaluation Office, *The IMF and Argentina* (Washington: International Monetary Fund, 2004), 46–47; Mussa, *Argentina y el FMI,* 59–60. See also, Morales Solá, *El sueño eterno,* 159–63, 167–168, 178–182, 202; *La Nación,* 15 March 2001, 20 March 2001, 22 March 2001, http://www.lanacion.com.ar.

13. Morales Solá, *El sueño eterno,* 285.

14. Bonavecchi, "Estrategia de supervivencia," 146; Mussa, *Argentina y el FMI,* 63–64.

15. For the full account of the Argentine and Mexican money laundering operations, see Andrés Oppenheimer, *Ojos vendados: Estados Unidos y el negocio de la corrupción en América Latina* (Buenos Aires: Editorial Sudamericana, 2001). Also, U.S. Senate, Permanent Subcommittee on Investigations, *Minority Staff of the Permanent Subcommittee on Investigations Report on Correspondent Banking: A Gateway for Money Laundering* (Washington: 5 February 2001). See especially, "Supplemental Case Histories 8, 9, and 10, 64–111, http://www.senate.gov/~gov-affairs/020501_psi_minority_report.htm.

16. Losanovsky Perel was in charge of Antfactory Latin America's finances and earned a decent salary there. But he lived on a much more luxurious scale and had very large debts. One of his coworkers told police that Losanovsky Perel made frequent flights to the United States, leaving and returning the same day, and that these had no connection to his job at Antfactory. See, "Contactan al FBI para esclarecer el crimen de Perel," *La Prensa Digital,* 9 February 2001, http://www.laprensa.com.ar.

17. Blustein, *And the Money Kept Rolling In,* 7–8, 125, 128–131; Mussa, *Argentina y el FMI,* 67; The International Monetary Fund, *The IMF and Argentina,* 90–94.

18. Blustein, *And the Money Kept Rolling In,* 6–7; Arisó and Jacobo, *El Golpe, S.A.,* 135.

19. Arisó and Jacobo, *El Golpe, S.A.,* 78; Bonavecchi, "Estrategia," 148–149.

20. Blustein, *And the Money Kept Rolling In,* xx–xxi, 136, 171–172, 185; Eduardo Basualdo and Martín Kaufas, *Deuda externa y fuga de capitales en la Argentina* (no date: 2001?), http://www.unsl.edu.ar/librosgratis/gratis/fuga.pdf, 38–47.

21. Embassy and consulate personnel could withdraw any amount; trucking and bus companies could withdraw $500. People traveling overseas were limited to $10,000. Arisó and Jacobo, *El Golpe, S.A.,* 159.

22. Arisó and Jacobo, *El Golpe, S.A.,* 167–168, 192–198; Godio, *En la crisis,* 126; *Buenos Aires Herald,* 21 December 2001, 1–4, http://www.buenosairesherald.com. For a thorough book-length description of the riots by a reputable Argentine journalist, see Jorge Camarassa, *Días de furia* (Buenos Aires: Editorial Sudamericana, 2002).

23. *La Nación,* 20 December 2001, 6, 8–12; 21 December 2001, 4–5, 9–10, 12–13, http://www.lanacion.com.ar.

CHAPTER 10

1. Camarassa, *Dias de furia,* 163; *La Nación,* 19 January 2002, 6; *BBC News,* 8 January 2002, http://news.bbc.co.uk.

2. Based on a report from the National Institute for Statistics and Census (INDEC), reported in *La Naciónline* 2 May 2002, and *Clarín.com* 10 May 2002.

3. Anthony Faiola, "Fleeing a 'Broken' Argentina," *Washington Post Foreign Service,* 13 January 2002, p. A–17, http://www.washingtonpost.com.

4. Godio, *En la crisis,* 55; *La Nación,* 17 January 2002, 9; United Nations, *Economic Survey, 2001–02,* Second Part, 97–105.

5. *The IMF and Argentina,* 57–58; Blustein, *And the Money Kept Rolling In,* 192; *La Nación,* 4 January 2002, 5–6; 6 January 2002, 5–7, 9 (see p. 6 for the full text of the convertibility law); 1 February 2002, 5; 14 February 2002, 6.

6. *La Nación,* 14 April 2002, 12; *Wall Street Journal,* 28 May 2002, A–15.

7. Arisó and Jacobo, *El Golpe S.A.,* 244–245; *Clarín.com,* 29 June 2002, http://www.clarin.com; *La Nación,* 22 January 2002, http://www.lanacion.com/ar.

8. *Clarín.com,* 18 January 2002; *Diario La Prensa: Nota de tapa,* 31 January 2002; *La Nación,* 20 January 2002, 9; 22 February 2002, 10.

9. *La Nación,* 24 January 2002, 6.

10. *Clarín.com,* 4 February 2002; *Diario La Prensa, Nota de Tapa,* 19 February 2002; *La Nación,* 9 February 2002, 9; 21 February 2002, 1, 8; 12 March 2002, 6; *La Nación Line,* 11 April 2002.

11. *Diario La Prensa, Nota de Tapa,* 16 April 2002.

12. *La Nación,* 25 March 2002, 7.

13. *La Nación,* 25 March 2002, 7.

14. *Buenos Aires Herald online,* 11 June 2002; *Wall Street Journal,* 16 July 2002, A–14.

15. World Bank, *Argentina–Crisis and Poverty 2003: A Poverty Assessment,* 24 July 2003, 17, http://wbln0018.wordbank.org/LAC/lacinfoclient.ns.

16. Luis Gurevich, "El derrumbe industrial de la Argentina," *Prensa Obrera,* 25 October 2001, http://www.po.org.arg/po/po726; Julio Magri, "El 'procesista' Pérez Companc," *Prensa Obrera,* 1 August 2002 [*ibid.,* po765]; Joshua Goodman, "Back in Black: Fixing Failed Companies Is the New Game in Town for Argentina's Money Crowd," *Look Smart Find Articles—Finance,* October 2002, http://findarticles.com; "Impsat entrega sus

acciones a los proveedores," *Noticias*, 5 March 2002 (Pescarmona), http://www2. noticias.com; Luis Ceriotto, "Un gigante brasileño compró Loma Negra y tendrá 48% del cemento," *Clarín.com*, 20 April 2005, http://www.clarin.com; Internet Bankruptcy Library, *Troubled Country Reporter: Latin America*, 4 October 2002 (Pérez Companc), vol. 3, no. 197; and 12 April 2006 (Alpargatas), vol. 7, no. 73, http://bankrupt.com/ TCRLA_Public; Hoover's Profile, "Telefónica de Argentina SA," *Answers.com*, http://www.answers.com/topic/telefonica-de-argentina; also, on Telecom, http://www. unfarallon.info/investargentina.asp; "El Grupo Soldati refinancia su deuda con una fuerte rebaja," *Clarín.com*, 10 October 2003, http://www.clarin.com; on Federcámaras, see *La Nación Line*, 30 April 2002; on other troubled companies, see *Clarín.com*, 11 June 2002.

17. Tomás Eloy Martínez, "Fábula de la cigarra y las hormigas," in Joaquín Morales Solá, *Argentina, un país desperdiciado* (Buenos Aires: Editorial Taurus, 2003), 156.

18. On "popular assemblies" see: Oscar Caram, *Que se vaya todo: Asambleas, horizontes y resistencias (Un cruce de voces en el movimiento popular)* (Buenos Aires: Manuel Suárez, editor, 2002); and Aníbal Kohan, *¡A las calles!: Una historia de los movimientos piqueteros y caceroleros de los '90 al 2002* (Buenos Aires: Ediciones Colihue, 2002).

19. Argentine investigators later claimed to have located, and with the cooperation of Swiss authorities frozen, over $10 million in bank deposits belonging to Menem and his friends. In reply, Menem said that Christine Junod, a Swiss judge, had concluded after an investigation, that no accounts had existed in his name while he was president from 1989 to 1999. Menem claimed that he was being persecuted for political reasons. On 16 December 2004 Federal Judge Néstor Oyarbide struck down an arrest warrant for Menem, who was then living in Chile with his new wife Cecilia Bolocco (the former Miss Universe) and their son.

20. *Clarín.com*, 30 April 2003.

CHAPTER 11

1. Fundación CIDOB, "Biografías de Líderes Políticos: Néstor Kirchner," http://www.cidob.org/bios/castellano/lideres.

2. *La Nación,* 18 November 2003, http://www.lanacion.com/ar; *Clarín.com*, 18 November 2003; *Diario La Prensa, Nota de Tapa*, 18 November 2003.

3. "Kirchner v Duhalde: The Big Fight Over Fiscal Reform," *Economist.com, Latin America: Argentina*, 17 June 2004; Mary Anastasia O'Grady, "Don't Count on Argentina to Help Fight Terror," *Wall Street Journal*, 8 July 2005, A11.

4. Kohan, *¡A las calles!*, 13–18, 141–144; Blustein, *And the Money Kept Rolling In*, 206–207; Michael J. Casey, "Kirchner's Next Challenge," *Wall Street Journal*, 31 August 2004, A10.

5. Aldo Fernando Ponce, *Unemployment and Clientelism: The Piqueteros of Argentina* (Munich: Munich Personal RePEc Archive, September 2006), 21–25, 31–32, http://mpra.ub.uni-muenchen.de/23.

6. Monte Reel, "In Buenos Aires, A Friend in Need," *Washington Post Foreign Service*, 11 April 2005, A13, http://washingtonpost.com.

7. Blustein, *And the Money Kept Rolling In*, 159, 162.

8. Economist Intelligence Unit, "Argentina Finance: Emerging From Default," *The EIU Viewswire*, http://viewswire.com; Matt Moffett, "Argentina Squeezes Bondholders," *Wall Street Journal*, 14 January 2005, C1; *Diario La Prensa, Nota de Tapa*, 3 December 2004.

9. Mark Falcoff, "Argentina Has Seen the Past—and It Works (For Now)," *Latin American Outlook*, 22 December 2004, http://www.aei.org.

10. United Nations Conference on Trade and Development (UNCTAD), *World Investment Report, 2006: Country Fact Sheets: Argentina, Brazil, and Chile*, http//www.unctad.org.

11. *Bloomberg.com*, 3 April 2006, 9 April 2006.

12. The Economist, "Cooking the Books," *Country Briefings: Argentina*, 8 February 2007, 1. *La Nación* also reported, on 17 August 2007, that anonymous employees at INDEC said that recently reported statistics on unemployment were also derived by "irregular methods."

13. "Chavez, Kirchner in 'unity' talks," *BBC News*, 22 November 2005, http://news.bbc.co.uk; "Argentina's Enarsa may join PdVSA in upstream activities," *Alexander's Gas and Oil Connections*, 22 November 2005, http://www.gasandoil.com/goc; Jorge Rueda, "Argentina's Kirchner Backs Chavez," *CBS News*, 28 February 2007, http://www.cbsnews.com; "Chavez Touts $500 Million Bond Deal With Argentina," *CNN.com/world*, 8 August 2007, http://edition.cnn.com; Uki Goni, "Argentina Cries Foul Against Chavez," *Time*, 1 August 2007, http://www.time.com; Christopher Swann, "Hugo Chavez Exploits Oil Wealth to Push IMF Aside," *International Herald Tribune*, 1 March 2007, http://www.int.com; "PDVSA and Enarsa firm up Orinoco venture." *Upstreamonline*, 7 March 2008, http://www.upstreamonline.com; "No confían en Enarsa como socia: Creen que no tiene capacidad financiera para trabajar con Pdvasa en el Orinoco," *Lanacion.com*, 16 March 2008, http://www.lanacion.com.ar/economia.

14. Aldo Roggio, head of the Roggio Group, was instrumental in getting Roberto Lavagna fired as economics minister after the latter addressed a CAC convention in November 2005 and accused the contractors of misappropriating some $500 million of World Bank loans. Roggio complained to Kirchner and Julio De Vido, the secretary for infrastructure. A few days later Lavagna was out of the government.

15. "Tucking In to the Good Times," *TheEconomist.com: Country Briefings: Argentina*, 19 December 2006. The Economist reported that Argentina's GDP had grown by 45 percent since March 2002.

16. This survey of the UIA's internal politics draws heavily upon Alejandro Gaggero and Andrés Wainer, "Burguesía nacional—crisis de la convertibilidad: El rol de la UIA y su estrategia para el tipo de cambio," *Realidad Económica* (Buenos Aires: Instituto Argentino para el Desarrollo Económico, 29 August 2006), http://www.iade.org.ar.

17. Claudio Katz, "Qué buguesía hay en Argentina," *La página de Claudio Katz*, 30 June 2005, http://lahaine.org/katz. Lahaine is a organization of Spanish and Latin American revolutionary leftists. INDEC put the level of Argentine capital in overseas accounts at $108 billion in 2004. See "Argentina: Capital Flight at Lowest Level Since Crisis," *Internet Securities, Inc.*, 23 December 2004, http://www.institutionalinvestor.com.

18. "La UIA pide fuertes castigos al uso excesivo de energía," *LaNacion.com*, 20 October 2006, http://www.lanacion.com.ar.

19. "Subsidiarán a petroleras para que den gasoil barato a la industria," *LaNacion.com*, 12 July 2007; "Se extiende a todo el país la nafta subsidiada y sigue cortado el GNC," *LaNacion.com*, 13 July 2007. (GNC stands for compressed natural gas.) Shell wasn't invited because it had defied Kirchner back in 2005 by ignoring his orders and raising its prices. "Una interna que casi terminó a los golpes," *LaNacion.com*, 13 July 2007.

CHAPTER 12

1. Matias Longoni, "Los contratistas son los que más pierden en la pulseada," *Clarín.com*, 2 June 2008. For the description of events concerning the farmers' strike, I have used daily online news stories from *La Nación, Clarín, La Prensa, La Voz del Interior,* and *MERCOPRESS,* March–June, 2008.

2. "Argentina's Soy King Explains Modern Farming and Taxing," *MERCOPRESS,* 9 July 2008. Between 2002 and 2008 the number of truckers carrying produce to market increased from about 300,000 to 700,000.

3. Antonio Rossi, "Quién mueve los hilos en la protesta de los transportistas," *Clarín.com*, 12 June 2008.

4. *Boletín Oficial de La República Argentina: Primera Sección, Legislación y Avisos Oficiales* (Buenos Aires: 10 June 2008).

5. "Boudou afirmó que el dinero de la AFJP se utilizará para sostener la economía," *La Nación*, 21 November 2008, http://lanacion.com/ar.

6. Manuel Mora y Araujo, *Argentina: Una víctima de sí misma. Débil gobernabilidad y bajo consenso social* (Buenos Aires: Instituto Torcuato Di Tella and Ediciones La Crujía, 2003), esp. chapter 2, 27–33.

Selected Bibliography

Ale, Ana. *La dinastía: Vida, pasión y ocaso de los Macri*. Buenos Aires: Editorial Planeta, 2001.

Argentine Republic, Cámara de Diputados, Comisión Especial Investigadora Sobre Hechos Ilícitos Vinculados con el Lavado de Dinero. *Informe Final Sobre Lavado de Dinero*. Buenos Aires, 2001.

Arisó, Guillermo and Gabriel Jacobo. *El golpe S.A.: La guerra de intereses que estalló en el 2001 y dejó al país en ruinas*. Buenos Aires: Grupo Editorial Norma, 2002.

Auyero, Javier. *La protesta: Retratos de la beligerancia popular en la Argentina democrática*. Buenos Aires: Editorial de la Universidad de Buenos Aires, 2002.

————. *Poor People's Politics: Peronist Survival Networks and the Legacy of Evita*. Durham, NC: Duke University Press, 2001.

Basualdo. Eduardo M. *Concentración y centralización del capital en la Argentina durante la década del noventa*. Quilmes: Universidad Nacional de Quilmes, 2000.

Beccaria, Luis and Aida Quintar. "Reconversión productiva y mercado de trabajo: Reflexiones a partir de la experiencia de Somisa," *Desarrollo Económico,* vol. 35, no. 139 (October–December 1995), 401–418.

Bleger, Leonardo and Guillermo Rozenwurcel, "Financiamiento a las PYMEs y cambio estructural en la Argentina: Un estudio sobre fallas de mercado y problemas de información," *Desarrollo Económico,* vol. 40, no. 157 (April–June 2000), 45–72.

Blustein, Paul. *And the Money Kept Rolling In (and Out): Wall Street, the IMF, and the Bankruptcy of Argentina*. New York: Public Affairs, 2005.

Calcagno, Alfredo F. "Convertibility and the Banking System in Argentina," *CEPAL Review,* no. 61 (April 1997), 63–90.

Casella, Beto and Dario Villruel (with Néstor Esposito), *La mano en la lata: Diccionario de la corrupción argentina*. Buenos Aires: Editorial Grijalbo, 2000.

Cavallo, Domingo. *El peso de la verdad*. Buenos Aires: Editorial Planeta, 1997.

Cerruti, Gabriela. *El Jefe: Vida y obra de Carlos Saúl Menem*. Buenos Aires: Editorial Planeta, 1993.

————. *El octavo círculo: Crónica y entretelones del poder menemista.* Buenos Aires: Editorial Planeta, 1991.

Cherashny, Guillermo. *Menem, Yabrán, Cavallo: Final abierto*

Chudnovsky, Daniel, Andrés López and Fernando Porta, "Más allá del flujo de caja. El boom de la inversión extranjera en la Argentina," *Desarrollo Económico,* vol. 35, no. 137 (April–June 1995), 35–62.

Díaz, Rodolfo. *¿Prosperidad o ilusión? Las reformas de los 90 en la Argentina.* Buenos Aires: Editorial Ábaco, 2002.

Fernández Llorente, Antonio and Oscar Balmaceda. *El caso Cabezas.* Buenos Aires: Editorial Planeta, 1997.

Ferreira Rubio, Delia and Matteo Goretti. "Cuando el president gobierna solo: Menem y los decretos de necesidad y urgencia hasta la reforma constitucional (julio 1989–agosto 1994)," *Desarrollo Económico,* vol. 36, no. 141 (April–June 1996), 443–474.

Gerchunoff, Juan Pablo and Guillermo Canovas. "Privatizaciones en un contexto de emergencia económica," *Desarrollo Económico,* vol. 34, no. 136 (1995), 483–512.

Gerchunoff, Juan Pablo and Juan Carlos Torre. "La política de liberalización económica en la administración de Menem," *Desarrollo Económico,* vol. 36, no. 143 (October–December 1996), 733–768.

Green, Raúl and Catherine Laurent. *El poder de Bunge y Born.* Buenos Aires: Editorial Legasa, 1988.

Guissarri, Adrián. *La Argentina informal: Realidad de la vida económica.* Buenos Aires: Emecé Editores, 1989.

International Monetary Fund, Independent Evaluation Office. *The IMF and Argentina.* Washington: International Monetary Fund, 2004.

Larkins, Christopher. "The Judiciary and Delegative Democracy in Argentina," *Comparative Politics,* vol. 30, no. 4 (July 1998), 423–442.

Lejtman, Román. *Narcogate.* Buenos Aires: Editorial Sudamericana, 1993.

Leuco, Alfredo and José Antonio Díaz. *El heredero de Perón: Menem entre Dios y Diablo.* Buenos Aires: Editorial Planeta, 1988.

Levitsky, Steven. "An 'Organized Disorganization': Informal Organization and the Persistence of Local Party Structures in Argentine Peronism," *Journal of Latin American Studies,* vol. 33, no. 1 (February 2001), 29–66.

Llanos, Mariana. "Understanding Presidential Power in Argentina: A Study of Privatization in the 1990s," *Journal of Latin American Studies,* vol. 33, no. 1 (February 2001), 67–99.

Lo Vuolo, Rubén and Alberto Barbeito, *La nueva oscuridad de la política social.* Buenos Aires: Miño y Dávila, Editores, 1998.

Majul, Luis. *Los dueños de la Argentina: La cara oculta de los negocios,* vols. 1 and 2. Buenos Aires: Editorial Sudamericana, 1992, 1994.

Manzetti, Luigi. "The Political Economy of MERCOSUR," *Journal of Inter-American Studies and World Affairs,* vol. 35, no. 4 (Winter 1993–1994), 101–141.

Margheritis, Ana. *Ajuste y reforma en Argentina (1989–1995): La economía política de la privatizaciones.* Buenos Aires: Nuevohacer, Grupo Editor Latinoamericano, 1999.

Margulis, Alejandro. *Junior: Vida y muerte de Carlos Saúl Menem (h).* Buenos Aires: Editorial Planeta, 1999.

Martucelli, Danilo and Maristella Svampa. *La plaza vacía.* Buenos Aires: Editorial Losada, 1997.

Massun, Ignacio. *Menem: Cirugía sin anestesia.* Buenos Aires: Editorial Métodos, 1999.

McGuire, James W. "Strikes in Argentina: Data Sources and Recent Trends," *Latin American Research Review,* vol. 31, no. 3, (1996).

Melo, Artemio Luis. *El primer gobierno de Menem: Análisis de los procesos de cambio político.* Rosario: Editorial de la Universidad Nacional de Rosario, 2001.

Molinos, Fernando Horacio. *Delitos del "cuello blanco" en la Argentina.* Buenos Aires: Ediciones Depalma, 1989.

Mora y Araujo, Manuel. *Argentina: Una víctima de si misma. Débil gobernabilidad y bajo consenso social.* Buenos Aires: Instituto Torcuato Di Tella and Ediciones La Crujía, 2003.

Morales Solá, Joaquín. *El sueño eterno: Ascenso y caída de la Alianza.* Buenos Aires: Editorial Planeta, 2001.

Mussa, Michael. *Argentina y el FMI.* Buenos Aires: Editorial Planeta, 2002.

Naishtat, Silvia and Pablo Maas. *El cazador: La historia secreta de los negocios de Juan Navarro y el Grupo Exxel.* Buenos Aires: Editorial Planeta, 2000.

Nino, Carlos S. *Un país al margin de la ley: Estudio de la anomía como componente del subdesarrollo argentino.* Buenos Aires: Emecé Editores, 1992.

Olarra Jiménez, Rafael and Luis García Martínez. *El derrumbe argentino: De la convertibilidad al "corralito."* Buenos Aires: Editorial Planeta, 2002.

Oppenheimer, Andrés. *Ojos vendados: Estados Unidos y el negocio de la corrupción en América Latina.* Buenos Aires: Editorial Sudamericana, 2001.

Palermo, Vicente and Marcos Novaro. *Política y poder en el gobierno de Menem.* Buenos Aires: Grupo Editor Norma, 1996.

Powers, Nancy R. "The Politics of Poverty in Argentina in the 1990s," *Journal of Inter-American Studies and World Affairs,* vol. 37, no. 4 (Winter 1995), 89–137.

Ranis, Peter. *Class, Democracy and Labor in Contemporary Argentina.* New Brunswick, NJ: Transaction Publishers, 1995.

Rosenwurcel, Guillermo and Leonardo Bleger, "El sistema bancario argentino en los noventa: De la profundización financiera a la crisis sistémica," *Desarrollo Económico,* vol. 37, no. 146 (July–September 1997), 163–194.

Santoro, Daniel. *Venta de armas: Hombres del gobierno.* Buenos Aires: Editorial Planeta, 1998.

Saiegh, Sebastián and Mariano Tommasi. "Why is Argentina's Fiscal Federalism So Inefficient? Entering the Labyrinth," *Journal of Applied Economics,* vol. 2, no. 1 (May 1999), 169–209.

Sdrech, Enrique O. and Norberto Colominas. *Cabezas: Crimen, mafia y poder.* Buenos Aires: Editorial Atuel, 1997.

Smith, William. "Democracy, Distributional Conflicts and Macroeconomic Policymaking in Argentina, 1983–1989," *Journal of Inter-American Studies and World Affairs,* vol. 32, no. 2 (Summer 1990), 1–42.

———. "State, Market and Neoliberalism in Post-Transition Argentina: The Menem Experiment," *Journal of Inter-American Studies and World Affairs,* vol. 33, no. 4 (Winter 1991), 45–82.

Starr, Pamela K. "Government Coalitions and the Viability of Currency Boards: Argentina Under the Cavallo Plan," *Journal of Inter-American Studies and World Affairs,* vol. 39, no. 2 (Summer 1997), 83–133.

Torres, Pablo. *Votos, chapas y fideos: Clientelismo político y ayuda social.* Buenos Aires: Editorial De la Campana, 2002.

United Nations Economic Commission for Latin America and the Caribbean. *El impacto del proceso de fusiones y adquisiciones en la Argentina sobre el mapa de grandes empresas. Factores determinantes y transformaciones en el universo de las grandes empresas de capital local.* Santiago de Chile, 2001.

United States Senate Permanent Subcommittee on Investigations. *Minority Staff of the Permanent Subcommittee on Investigations Report on Correspondent Banking: A Gateway for Money Laundering.* Washington DC, 2001. www.senate.gov/~gov_affairs/psi_finalreport.pdf.

Vecchi, Alejandro. *El crimen de Cabezas: Radiografía del país mafioso.* Buenos Aires: Editorial Biblos, 2001.

Verbitsky, Horacio. *Robo para la corona: Los frutos prohibidos del árbol de la corrupción.* Buenos Aires: Editorial Planeta, 1991.

Walger, Sylvina. *Pizza con champán: Crónica de la fiesta menemista.* Buenos Aires: Editorial Planeta, 1994.

Yoguel, Gabriel. "El ajuste empresarial frente a la apertura: La heterogeneidad de las respuestas de las PYMEs," *Desarrollo Económico,* vol. 38, número especial (Autumn 1998), 177–198.

Index

About the Author

PAUL H. LEWIS is Professor Emeritus of Political Science at Tulane University. He is the author of nine books, including *Authoritarian Regimes in Latin America* (2005), *Guerrillas and Generals: The "Dirty War" in Argentina* (Praeger, 2002), *Latin Fascist Elites: The Mussolini, Franco, and Salazar Regimes* (Praeger, 2002), and *The Crisis of Argentine Capitalism* (1990).